Nine Plays by José Cruz González

BOOK NINETEEN

Louann Atkins Temple Women & Culture Series

Books about women and families, and
their changing role in society.

Nine Plays by José Cruz González

*Magical Realism and Mature Themes
in Theatre for Young Audiences*

Edited by

Coleman A. Jennings

University of Texas Press

Austin

The Louann Atkins Temple Women & Culture Series
is supported by Allison, Doug, Taylor, and Andy Bacon;
Margaret, Lawrence, Will, John, and Annie Temple;
Larry Temple; the Temple-Inland Foundation; and
the National Endowment for the Humanities.

Library of Congress Cataloging-in-Publication Data
González, José Cruz.
    [Plays. Selections]
    Nine plays by José Cruz González : magical realism
and mature themes in theatre for young audiences / edited
by Coleman A. Jennings. — 1st ed.
        p. cm. — (Louann Atkins Temple women & culture series ; bk. 19)
    Includes bibliographical references.
    ISBN 978-0-292-71854-8 (cloth : alk. paper) —
    ISBN 978-0-292-71855-5 (pbk. : alk. paper)
    1. Children's plays. 2. Young adult drama.
I. Jennings, Coleman A., 1933–   II. Title.
    PS3557.O475A6 2008
    812'.54—dc22
                     2008001844

Dedicated to

Lola H. Jennings, my wife, and our family:

Coleman C. Jennings
and wife, Jill A. Jennings,
sons Ethan
and Avery Jennings;

Adrienne E. Jennings
and husband, Jeffrey S. Hewitt, and
children Lola Grace
and Blake Hewitt

Contents

Acknowledgments

Grateful acknowledgment is made to:

Dramatic Publishing, Inc., for permission to reprint *Two Donuts, Salt & Pepper, Old Jake's Skirts, Lily Plants a Garden,* and *The Highest Heaven.*

José Cruz González, for permission to reprint *The Magic Rainforest—An Amazon Journey, Marisol's Christmas,* and *Watermelon Kisses.*

Domnita Dumitrescu, for the Spanish language corrections.

Random House, for permission to reprint *Tomás and the Library Lady.* The script by José Cruz González is based on the underlying work *Tomás and the Library Lady,* by Pat Mora. Text copyright © 1997 by Pat Mora. Published by arrangement with Random House Children's Books, a division of Random House, Inc., New York, New York. All rights reserved.

Northland Publishing, for permission to reprint *Old Jake's Skirts,* based on the book *Old Jake's Skirts* by C. Anne Scott, illustrated by David Slonim, Northland Publishing, Flagstaff, Arizona.

Dutton Publishing, for permission to reprint *Watermelon Kisses.* *Watermelon Kisses* was originally published in *Dude! Stories and Stuff for Boys,* edited by Sandy Asher and David L. Harrison.

Corey Madden, David Saar, J. Richard Smith, and Graham Whitehead, for their contributions to the developmental process of the plays represented in this collection.

Corey Atkins, Bilingual Research and Editorial Assistant, Austin, Texas.

The Houston Endowment, Inc., for support from the Jesse H. Jones Regents Professorship in Fine Arts, Department of Theatre and Dance, the University of Texas at Austin.

Nine Plays by José Cruz González

Introduction

The purpose of this anthology is not only to share nine plays by an extraordinarily talented playwright, but also to document his creative process as evidenced through his collaboration with other theatre artists. José Cruz González's diverse creative practices are made evident in the following biographical sketch of the playwright; Susan Mason's essay, in which she connects his personal outlook and experiences to the development of specific plays; and, finally, comments from his fellow theatre artists about their work with him.

Significant theatre is the result of creative collaboration between playwright, dramaturg, designers, director, and actors. The section titled "Collaborative Creation" is a collection of responses from theatre artists Corey Madden, David Saar, J. Richard Smith, and Graham Whitehead about their experiences in working with González on the development of new scripts for young audiences.

In the section "Considering the Design Process," the progression of González's play development as it affects production and as production affects the script is elucidated by designer J. Richard Smith, who demonstrates his own creative process through his comments and preliminary working sketches of settings for each of the nine plays of the collection.

The plays of magical realism and mature themes presented in this volume are the product of José Cruz González's imagination, playwriting ability, humanity, understanding and appreciation of the child audience, and enthusiastic collaboration with other theatre professionals, as you will learn within this collection.

José Cruz González

Biography

After his birth in Calexico, California, on March 19, 1957, to María de Jesús González and Fidel Rubén Gama González, José Cruz González was raised in Watsonville, on California's central coast. He recalls instances of engaging in dramatic play as a boy: "I remember getting up early in the morning while the stars were still out, and going with my grandfather to help him irrigate the lettuce fields he was tending. I didn't do much, but I sure had a lot of fun playing. Nature was theatre to me even though I didn't know what theatre was at the time. I played with sticks and dirt clods, anything that was available. I made rivers and forts: whole worlds emerged," he says. That legacy of imagination pervades González's work as a prolific and respected playwright, director, professor, administrator, and activist.

When González was just five years old, his father died, and he, his three siblings, and his mother moved in with the children's grandparents. It was at this point that the boy got his first taste of the power of storytelling. "We grew up working with my mom and grandparents in the fields, canneries, and packing sheds in town," González says. To bring some imagination to the challenging realities of farm worker life, his grandfather, José Luciano Farfán, regaled the family with stories and riddles. "I remember my grandfather entertaining us during the long hours in the apple orchards where we worked. He would tell us stories, jokes, and even whistle a tune when he felt inclined," he says. These tales provided the initial spark of imagination that is so prevalent in the playwright's work today.

González saw his first theatrical performance when he was in first grade. "My older brother Marcos was in a play, and his whole body and face were painted green. I had no clue why, but that event opened a strange new world to me. Impossible things are possible." After graduating from Aptos High School in 1975, he began college at the University of California, San Diego (UCSD). "Before then," he says, "I loved to sketch, paint, and shape things with my hands, but I didn't get interested in theatre until I was in college. I took a performance course at the university, because I thought I'd need to brush up my interview skills for graduate school. Little did I know that that performance class would tap that early creative energy I had as a child. I never looked back."

Throughout his college and graduate studies, González's interest was mainly in directing. He earned a B.A. in U.S. History/Chicano Studies from the University of California, San Diego, with a minor in theatre. At UCSD he was introduced to the work of Luís Valdez's *Teatro Campesino.* "I loved how theatre could be immediate and yet instructive," he says. He then earned an M.A. in Theatre from Arizona State University in Tempe, and an M.F.A. in directing from the University of California, Irvine.

A directing grant from the National Endowment for the Arts led González to South Coast Repertory (SCR), in Costa Mesa, California, where his professional career began to change and grow. At SCR he founded one of the nation's premiere venues for the development of Latino playwrights and their work: the renowned Hispanic Playwrights Project (HPP). From its inception in 1986 until González left the company in 1996, González's HPP created opportunities for some of the top Latino talent in the country. As South Coast Repertory's Web site states, the creation of the Hispanic Playwrights Project "prompted the submission of over a thousand manuscripts, of which more than fifty received workshops, and more than half of those went on to full productions at South Coast Repertory and other resident theatres. Participating playwrights have included Luís Alfaro, Cusi Cram, Nilo Cruz, Jorge González, Lisa Loomer, Josefina López, Eduardo Machado, Oliver Mayer, Cherríe Moraga, José Rivera, Edwin Sánchez, Milcha Sánchez-Scott, Luís Santeiro, Bernardo Solano, Octavio Solís, Caridad Svich, and Edit Villarreal."

González's accomplishments as a director include credits at South Coast Repertory; Borderlands Theatre, Tucson, Arizona; Coterie Theatre, Kansas City, Missouri; the Sundance Theatre Institute, Sundance, Utah; Los Angeles Theater Center's Bilingual Foundation for the Arts; and the Edinburgh Festival in Scotland, among others.

Many of González's plays are, of course, written for young audiences. His plays are often produced by youth theatre companies, and he has also begun writing for children's television. He wrote for the Emmy Award–nominated television series *Paz,* a Discovery Kids production for "Ready, Set, Learn!" on the Learning Channel (TLC). Asked what attracts him to writing for youth, he says, "I believe that in the heart and mind of a child everything is possible. Children possess such imagination and spirit despite a grown-up world that sometimes ignores them. They are pure inspiration and should be nurtured and empowered."

Recently González has begun writing more frequently for adult audiences as well. He collaborated with three other playwrights to create *Fast and Loose* as part of the 2005 Humana Festival of New American Plays of Actors Theatre of Louisville, Kentucky. Four questions formed the basis of this "ethical collaboration" play: "If you discover an awful secret, should you tell? Should we base our ethical decisions on principles, or only on consequences? Must we really take the interests of others into consideration? Are there intrinsically right and wrong acts?"

Another play, *Waking Up in Lost Hills*—created with Cornerstone Theater in 2004—is an adaptation of the story of *Rip Van Winkle* that is set in the small rural California community of Lost Hills and based on a collaboration with the town's residents. Victorio Valenzuela, an almond farm worker who has just awakened from a thirty-seven-year sleep, meets a traveler who has just awakened from a car wreck. Together they must rescue themselves, their families, and the town.

In 2006 González received a commission from the Denver Center Theatre for *Sunsets and Margaritas*. His play *September Shoes* premiered at Geva Theatre in 2003, and was produced at the Denver Center Theatre in 2005. *September Shoes* is a play of magical realism in which Cuki, a woman from the border town of Dolores, is preoccupied with shoes while Huilo, the caretaker of the cemetery, is anxiously carving the names of the dead in the legs of a big red chair. Dr. Alberto Cervantes and his wife, Gail, return to the desert town for the funeral of their Chinese-born Aunt Lily, who operates the best Chinese-Mexican restaurant in town. Forced to confront their cultural heritage and past tragedy, the characters learn to forgive, reconnect with their roots and their families, and repair their broken lives.

As a professional playwright González's achievements and affiliations are numerous; his plays have premiered or been produced at:

Denver Center Theatre Company (Denver, Colorado)
Cornerstone Theater (Los Angeles, California)
Childsplay (Tempe, Arizona)
The Kennedy Center (Washington, D.C.)
Actors Theatre of Louisville (Louisville, Kentucky)
Geva Theatre (Rochester, New York)
Cincinnati Playhouse in the Park (Cincinnati, Ohio)
South Coast Repertory (Costa Mesa, California)
Teatro del Pueblo (St. Paul, Minnesota)
Orlando Repertory (Orlando, Florida)
Department of Theatre and Dance, University of Texas at Austin
California Institute of the Arts (Valencia, California)
Northwestern University (Evanston, Illinois)
California State University (Fresno, California)

Among the organizations that have commissioned his work are the Center Theatre Group of the Mark Taper Forum, Disney Theatrical Productions, the Kennedy Center, Denver Center Theatre Company, and Crossroads Theatre.

A measure of González's success is also evident from the many awards and recognitions he has received as playwright, director, and educator:

California State, Los Angeles, President's Distinguished Professor
    Award, 2006
American Alliance for Theatre and Education Award, 2005
Emmy Award nomination for Paz, 2006, 2005
Theatre Communications Group/Pew National Theatre Residency, 2004
Indiana Repertory Bonderman/IUPUI National Youth Playwriting
    Award, 2003, 2001
Kennedy Center/American College Theatre Festival Distinguished
    Educator Award, 2001
West Literary Award for Drama finalist, 2001
Kennedy Center New Visions/New Voices Playwright, 2000, 1996
National Endowment for the Arts Playwright Residency Grant, 1997

Seattle Group Theatre 8th Annual Multi-Cultural Playwrights Festival
   winner, 1991
Theatre Communications Group Artist Observership Program, 1987
Orange County Human Relations Commission Award, 1987
National Endowment for the Arts Directing Fellow, 1985

Since 1989 González has held the position of Professor of Theatre Arts at
California State University, Los Angeles. There he created and now coordi-
nates the John Lion New Plays Festival, which presents the best new scripts
from his playwriting classes. Despite his busy academic schedule, González
continues to diversify his efforts. Asked how he is able to balance his numerous commitments, he says, "I worked in non-profit theatre, and with
raising a young family I had only pockets of time to write. I learned to be
efficient with what little time I had. Once I started teaching at the university
I had chunks of time. It was manna from heaven. As an artist I have been
nourished by the work I have been able to create. When I teach, it is about
nourishing my students."

In addition to his position at California State, Los Angeles, González is
Playwright in Residence at Childsplay in Tempe, Arizona, and an associate
artist with Cornerstone Theater Company in Los Angeles. He has also served
on the board of Theater for Young Audiences/USA (formerly the U.S. center
of ASSITEJ, *Association International du Théâtre pour l'Enfance et la Jeunesse*/Inter-
national Association of Theatre for Children and Young People).

González is married to Cory Marie González, an elementary school
teacher in Santa Ana, California. They have two sons, Casey Cruz González
and Kelsey Miguel González, both college students.

Speaking of his family with appreciation, Gonzáles says: "Over the years,
my wife and sons have been an integral part of my work. Cory has shared
many stories with me, ones that have influenced my writing. For instance,
we love to take walks together in our neighborhood. It's a time to catch up
with each other about our day. Mostly, our discussions center around our
sons and what happened at work. But every now and then, she'll share something that resonates with me. Cory has, for seventeen years, taught at an elementary school that is in a tough neighborhood. And though there's lots of
poverty and heartache, there is also lots of kindness and laughter, too. 'One
day, a student at my school failed to show up,' she said. 'When we called his
home to verify his absence, his mother had assumed he had gone to school.
The police were called and a search began. After about an hour, the little boy
was found walking down a busy street two miles away. When asked what he
was doing, the boy replied that he wasn't happy living in the U.S. He wanted

to go back to Mexico and live with his grandmother. The boy went to a donut shop and had bought two donuts before setting off on his journey home.' After our walk I went to my study and wrote down what she had told me. I asked, 'Is home a place where we hang our hat, or is it a place we carry in our hearts?' Although my *Two Donuts* is very different, there are parallels in Pepito's story, and of course, the title of the play. And as I have watched our sons grow up, I realize how they have influenced my writing—in so many wonderful ways."

Bibliography of Plays

* indicates plays included in this volume.

2006

* *Old Jake's Skirts* (Dramatic Publishing)
  September Shoes (Dramatic Publishing)
  Thaddeus and 'Tila (A Crane and Frog Tale) (Dramatic Publishing)
* *Watermelon Kisses* (In *Dude!: Stories and Stuff for Boys*, Dutton Children's Books)

2005

3/7/11: A Lincoln Heights Tale (commissioned by Cornerstone Theater, Los Angeles, California)
Aladdin, Jr., Dual Language Edition (commissioned for musical adaptation by Disney Theatrical Productions, Ltd.)
Fast and Loose (*Humana Festival, 2004: The Complete Plays*, Smith & Kraus, Inc.)
The Guitar Maker's Children (commissioned by Stages Theatre, Minneapolis, Minnesota)
* *Tomás and the Library Lady* (commissioned by Childsplay, Tempe, Arizona)
* *Two Donuts* (Dramatic Publishing; *Theatre for Children: Fifteen Classic Plays*, St. Martin's Press)

2004

Case-Tec and Kelso (10 by 10) (Dramatic Publishing)
Earth Songs (commissioned by Metro Theatre Company, St. Louis, Missouri)
Paz (series on The Learning Channel/Discovery Kids/Discovery Channel, 2002–2004)
Waking Up in Lost Hills (commissioned by Cornerstone Theater, Los Angeles, California)
Lessons of Language Learned (play reading at Pacific Conservatory of the Performing Arts, Santa Maria, California)

2003

The Red Forest (commissioned by Florida Stage, Manalapan, Florida)

2002

Always Running (commissioned by Cornerstone Theater, Los Angeles, California)

Cousin Bell Bottoms (commissioned by California Institute of the Arts, Community Arts Partnership program, Valencia, California)

Words from a Cigar Maker (Cock Tales) (presented at Edge Festival, Los Angeles, California)

2001

Harvest Moon (Dramatic Publishing)

* *The Highest Heaven* (Dramatic Publishing; *Dramatic Literature for Children: A Century in Review*, Anchorage Press Plays, Inc.)

* *The Magic Rainforest—An Amazon Journey* (commissioned by the Kennedy Center, Washington, D.C.)

Odysseus Cruz (commissioned by South Coast Repertory, Costa Mesa, California)

* *Salt & Pepper* (Dramatic Publishing)

Three Tuesdays (commissioned by Teatro Visión, San José, California)

2000

Manzi: The Adventures of Young César Chávez (commissioned by Teatro del Pueblo, St. Paul, Minnesota)

1999

* *Lily Plants a Garden* (commissioned by Mark Taper Forum, P.L.A.Y., Los Angeles, California)

Sirenas (commissioned by Crossroads Theatre, New Brunswick, New Jersey)

1998

Calabasas Street (Dramatic Publishing)

La Posada (Dramatic Publishing)

Spirit Dancing (Teatro Visión, San José, California)

1997

Mariachi Quixote (commissioned by L.A. Vision/L.A. Voices, A.S.K. Theater, and Cornerstone Theater, Los Angeles, California)
Mustang Angel (Rain City Projects, Seattle, Washington)

1994

Harvest Moon (Seattle Group Theatre, Seattle, Washington)

1991

Crossroads (film; Immigrant Rights Coalition, California)

1990

Common Ground (video; Orange County California Human Relations Commission)
* *Marisol's Christmas* (Teatro Cucucuévez, Santa Ana, California)

Collaborative Creation

Responses from Corey Madden, David Saar,
J. Richard Smith, and Graham Whitehead

In documenting the creation and development of new plays by González as he worked with professional playwrights, directors, and designers, the original plan was to have an actual round-table discussion with Corey Madden, David Saar, J. Richard Smith, and Graham Whitehead. Because of numerous scheduling and logistical difficulties it was impossible to have a group meeting; therefore, each person was asked to provide written answers to a number of questions. The responses of the four participants are combined here to suggest an actual group meeting; the individuality of each participant is clearly evident.

Corey Madden

Corey Madden was Center Theatre Group's (CTG) Producing Director of Performing for Los Angeles Youth (P.L.A.Y.) from 1999–2007 and CTG's Associate Artistic Director of the Mark Taper Forum from 1993–2005. Now an independent director and writer, she specializes in the creation of new works for diverse and younger audiences, interdisciplinary collaborations, and unique producing partnerships through her company, L'Atelier Arts. Madden was on the artistic staff of Actors Theatre of Louisville and has directed at the Kennedy Center; the Public Theatre, New York City; Ojai Playwrights Festival, Ojai, California; the Playwright's Center, Minneapolis; University of Washington, Seattle; and Summer Nights at the Ford, Washington, D.C. She has taught or guest-directed at the University of Texas at Austin; University of California, San Diego; University of Washington;

University of California, Los Angeles; California Institute of the Arts, Valencia; and North Carolina School of the Arts, Winston-Salem. Madden directed the world premiere of the opera *Keepers of the Night* in Los Angeles with the Los Angeles Children's Chorus. In residency at the University of California, San Diego, in 2007–2008, she adapted and directed *Surf Orpheus*. During the same season she co-created *The Imagi-NATION* at Childsplay, Tempe, Arizona. She conceived and directed *Animal Logic* for Center Theatre Group, Los Angeles, and the Getty Museum, Los Angeles. She is the author of the play *Worth*, which had its initial reading at Angels Gate Cultural Center, San Pedro.

David Saar is founder and Artistic Director of Childsplay, Tempe, Arizona. He has directed and taught for Childsplay since the company was formed in 1977. Among the many productions he has directed for Childsplay are *Still Life with Iris; A Year with Frog and Toad; Pero, or the Mystery of the Night; Afternoon of the Elves;* and *Cyrano.* Saar has also directed *The Origins of Happiness in Latin* for the Arizona Theatre Company; *Charlotte's Web* and *The Yellow Boat* for Seattle Children's Theatre; and *The BFG* for the Chicago Theatre for Young Audiences. David served on the roster of the Arizona Commission on the Arts Artist-in-Education program for nine

David Saar

years, was an adjunct faculty member for the Department of Theatre at Arizona State University, and worked for the Mesa Unified School District as a Drama Curriculum Specialist. He is a former board member of the U.S. Center of ASSITEJ (*Association International du Théâtre pour l'Enfance et la Jeunesse/* International Association of Theatre for Children and Young People). In 1989 he received the Governor's Arts Award for his contributions to the arts in Arizona; in 1991 he was the recipient of the national Winifred Ward Dare to Dream Fellowship; and in 1993 he received the Phoenix Futures Forum Dream Weavers Vision award. In 2002 he received the first Notable Achievement Award from the Herberger College of Fine Arts at Arizona State University. In March 2007 he was honored with the prestigious Thomas DeGaetani Award from the United States Institute for Theatre Technology (USITT). He currently serves as a site reporter for the National Endowment for the Arts.

J. Richard Smith

J. Richard Smith works as an actor, director, writer, illustrator, producer, and professional scenographic designer, having designed regionally for community, professional, children's, and academic productions throughout the Southwest and Pacific Northwest. For adult audiences he has either designed or directed *Les Liaisons Dangereuse*, *A Shayna Maidel*, *Man of La Mancha*, *Carousel*, *The Tempest*, *Much Ado About Nothing*, *All's Well That Ends Well*, *In a Room Somewhere*, *Blood Wedding*, *Guys and Dolls*, *Big River*, *Secret Garden*, *Beauty and the Beast*, *The Snow Queen*, *The Hobbit*, and *My Neighbor*. He was also responsible for more than thirty productions for Second Youth Family Theatre, a professional theatre company for young audiences that he co-founded in 1991 in Austin, Texas. He served as Producing Artistic Director for Second Youth from 1996 to 2005. Smith relocated to the Pacific Northwest in 2005, and subsequently directed *Two Rooms*, the inaugural production for the West of Brooklyn Theatre Company; designed the West Coast Premiere of *Black Water* for Off Center Opera Company; and *The Rocky Horror Show* for the Historic Everett Theatre. Smith holds a M.F.A. in Drama and Theatre for Youth and a professional certificate in Non-Profit and Philanthropic Studies from the University of Texas at Austin.

Graham Whitehead

Graham Whitehead was born in Egypt and raised in England, and lived in Canada for almost thirty years. He now resides in the United States. Since becoming a permanent resident of the U.S. he has taught at Arizona State University, served as Associate Artistic Director at Childsplay in Tempe, Arizona, and worked as a freelance actor and director. For adult theatre he has directed numerous plays and musicals, from *Driving Miss Daisy* to *A Chorus Line*. For young audiences at the Kennedy Center Whitehead directed *The Reluctant Dragon*, *East of the Sun, West of the Moon*, *The Emperor's New Clothes*, and, most recently, the new musical *Willy Wonka*, which also played at the White House during the Christmas holiday. As a playwright, he has written two plays, *Just So Stories* and *Peter and the Wolf*, that won awards as outstanding productions from the international puppetry organization, *Union Internationale de la Marionnette*. At Childsplay Whitehead has directed *Wolf Child*, *And Then They Came for Me*, *Wind in the Willows*, *Selkie*, *Boxcar Children*, *The Yellow Boat*, *Eric and Elliott*, and *Old Jake's Skirts*. He has appeared as Lincoln in *Lincoln's Log*, and as the Chair in Y York's *Portrait, Wind and Chair*. In addition he directed *Androcles and the Lion* for Free Space Theatre in Orel, Russia, and made a cameo appearance as the voice of God in *Castles in the Sky*, which he directed and co-created with Gayle LaJoie.

Coleman A. Jennings, onstage during development of *The Very Persistent Gappers of Fripp*, a collaboration between the Department of Theater and Dance at the University of Texas at Austin and the Center Theatre Group/Mark Taper Forum's Performing for Los Angeles Youth (P.L.A.Y.) program.

Jennings: *In studying the creation and development of new plays for children and family audiences, what is the optimum way to support playwrights in the writing of new works?*

Whitehead: Generalizations are dangerous; that is, I think that each playwright can be expected to work in an idiosyncratic fashion, and what one person would see as helpful is not necessarily going to be useful to another. Similarly, even the same playwright at different times or working on different scripts may want to relate to the director in an entirely different way. How I relate to a playwright depends entirely on what she or he feels is best for them at the particular time. In more general terms, the most obvious thing is to express faith and enthusiasm for the writing during the process and to try in production to give the playwright the play that he or she has in mind and not what's in mine.

Smith: Yes, first and foremost, we need to honor the playwright's vision. One must be especially cognizant of how a playwright reacts to suggestions. Some welcome constructive criticism, others immediately put up barriers that filter the feedback in ways that may alter the original intent. Suggestions that could be quite helpful may ultimately be ignored or misinterpreted.

Saar: Give the playwright space and time, and wait to be invited into the process, which is different for each playwright, and indeed, for each play. When invited, be honest, but tactful—questions, opinions should lead to a discussion, rather than shutting it off. Respond to the work on the page, not to what either side thinks should be on the page.

Madden: Take a leap of faith. That is to say, once you have identified a writer with whom you want to work, you should commit to their work, to the process that is best suited to their work and to a production. You should also pay them as well as you can, since they inevitably give considerably more of their time than you can ever hope to pay them for.

Jennings: *How have you worked with José in the development of new plays?*

Madden: We developed Lily Plants a Garden from commissioning through development and production. We also invited him to be a part of the Mark Taper Forum's Performing for Los Angeles Youth program, which allows artists to do early research and development on new projects in an atmosphere in which their colleagues can support and engage freely with them.

Smith: In 2003 I had the privilege of participating as a dramaturgical intern working on Lily Plants a Garden during the Bonderman Playwriting Workshop [Waldo M. and Grace C. Bonderman Playwriting for Youth National Symposium at Indiana Repertory Theatre]. I became a visual contributor to José's creative process by illustrating a number of his magical realism ideas through sketches, created during rehearsals and discussion sessions. José seemed to find inspiration in the sketches, written notes, and our "discussion walks" through the park near the theatre.

Saar: We have premiered five productions, beginning with *The Highest Heaven*. Our initial experience working on that project was so positive that we just kept it up. A grant from a local foundation enabled José to serve as playwright-in-residence for three years. During that time he developed and premiered several productions with our resident ensemble of artists and taught playwriting to the same group. In that context he served as teacher and dramaturg for others' writing, some of which we went on to produce. Several more projects were commissioned, including the dramatization of Pat Mora's book, *Tomás and the Library Lady*, which became our first national touring production.

Whitehead: I have been lucky enough to work with José on several projects, and there is a mutual respect and trust that helps in the process. The danger in this is that one might be too urgent in recommending ideas and changes; however, as José has grown in confidence and experience, the danger of letting others influence his work too much has faded. José is an incredibly creative and generous man; he listens and welcomes suggestions throughout his creative process.

Jennings: *How has your position as director or designer influenced José's writing and/ or rewriting?*

Whitehead: I really can't answer this. It is surely something that José might want to comment on, but I don't feel qualified to answer.

Madden: The community of artists who circulated through P.L.A.Y. from 1999 to 2006, when I was directing it, all influenced each other. I know that P.L.A.Y. was important in giving writers and other theatre artists the freedom and encouragement to experiment with form and process while striving to achieve new levels of artistry in programming for younger audiences.

Saar: As we have worked together over the past eight years, our relationship as writer and director has changed and evolved. A deepening trust and understanding by each of us as artists has blurred the traditional roles of writer and director. When we begin a new project, we now approach it as partners with the best possible production our shared aim. To get to that, we often work in each other's shoes, but we're comfortable with that based on our shared experiences over the years.

I think our work together has challenged his theatricality in a good way. He keeps asking for impossible stage moments—and then our designers deliver the goods! A cloud of Monarch butterflies ascending from an open suitcase? Piece of cake . . . !

Jennings: *What is unique about the way José works with others during play development?*

Saar: José is one of the most collaborative playwrights that I know. Some of that stems from the fact that he has worked with Childsplay artists for eight years, and we know and trust each other as creative artists. He has an artistic home here, and we count him as one of our own. He actively solicits feedback and encourages dialogue from anyone in the room—we are all equal at the discussion table. He certainly doesn't incorporate every idea, but he listens to them all. He listens, ponders, and then writes. And rewrites. And rewrites. And rewrites.

Whitehead: José likes to generate a universal enthusiasm for the project. He believes in the value and integrity of his work and invites others to join in that belief. He is very generous to his collaborators and invites comment and suggestions from everyone. He respects his audience and listens to comments from the invited audiences at play readings and workshop performances. He establishes a kind of creative loop. His enthusiasm and nonjudgmental approach stimulates other people's creativity, which in turn fosters his own. Working on a José Cruz González piece is always a joy for the whole company.

Madden: As we have all said, José is among the most generous and committed writers we know. He is a gentle leader in his process, welcoming others into the creative act along with him. He has the strength to trust others with his work. He begins with very evocative and personal imagery. In the case of *Lily Plants a Garden*, he talked about a girl whom he saw as trapped in a wasteland. He wanted to write a play about how she survived the trauma of losing her mother. It was very personal for José, who lost his father at a young age, and a very global play for him since we had just gone through 9/11 and had entered the second Iraq war.

Over the last five years José has become further engaged with collaborators, particularly designers and directors with strong dramaturgical skills. He is becoming increasingly more interested in creating work that is not simply about text, but also about imagery, poetry, and even a sense of the spiritual.

Jennings: *Any additional comments about your experiences of working with José?*

Whitehead: I don't know anyone who is kinder and more generous in his reactions to others than José. I have loved working with him—it's been a joy and a privilege; and the scripts that he has written are a wonderful contribution to contemporary theatre for young people.

Madden: José came to the Bonderman Playwriting Workshop having just completed a highly visual play with puppets and was excited to learn that Eric Johnson and I wanted to work with visuals as a way of charting his storytelling. We were lucky enough to have a classroom of schoolchildren who had drawn pictures about the story, as well as Richard Smith, a gifted designer, as an intern, who sketched moments from the piece. This gave us a storyboard which we used to better understand the plot; it guided us in the development of the play. José was wildly enthusiastic about this experience.

He works really hard, turning out a lot of ideas quickly, editing as he listens to actors, dramaturg, and director. José doesn't worry too much about whether the script-reading experience is perfect. He allows the play to be big and wild, and then later considers possible answers to the many challenges he has created. This is a major benefit of playwriting workshops. It is, however, essential that all participants understand from the outset of the workshop that the play is to be evaluated after the writer has had time to digest the experience, time to rewrite. Everyone needs to be patient, needs to trust the playwright and to withhold judgment until the play is produced. An essential follow-up premiere completes the play-development process as final touches are added. With José, the creative collaboration established during the playwriting workshop continues throughout the final phase of the premiere production.

Saar: Working with José has made me a better director, because I've had to dig deeper to create the possibilities that he so temptingly dangles in front of you. In addition, his dedication to bilingual theatre for young people has enabled us to better serve and represent a growing part of our audiences. And his mother's recipe for tamales is just the best!

Jennings: During an April 2005 "Horizonte" program of the Arizona Public Broadcasting System [see http://www.azpbs.org/horizonte/transcripts/2005/april/apr7_2005.html], José expressed his joy in new play development by collaboration, saying: "I love working with a lot of people. It's like familia to me. You bring in a director, designers, composers, actors, and you work together in the room trying to find a great way to tell this story. And so you've got a million ideas floating around, and as a writer, what a wonderful way to say, 'I'm going to take this idea and that idea,' and then weave them into, you hope, a wonderful story!"

The Playwriting of José Cruz González

Susan Vaneta Mason

Susan Mason has been professor of theatre arts and dance at California State University, Los Angeles, since 1989. She has also taught in Italy, New Zealand,

and the Netherlands, where she was a Fulbright lecturer in 1994. She studied dramaturgy at the Yale School of Drama from 1982 to 1983 and has worked with such playwrights as José Cruz González and Anna Deavere Smith. She has published articles on contemporary theatre in the United States and Europe as well as a piece on Ibsen. Her book, *The San Francisco Mime Troupe Reader*, published in 2004, is an anthology and company history. She is currently co-authoring a book of interviews with actresses from all over the world who have played Nora in *A Doll's House*.

Susan Mason

José Cruz González spent part of his childhood working in fields in the Salinas Valley in central California. Born in the Imperial Valley on the Mexico-California border near Arizona, his parents and grandparents were migrant workers who came from regions around both sides of the border. When he was very young, González and his brothers slept in the fields while their parents worked—his father and grandfather in lettuce, and his mother and grandmother in strawberries. In his first full-length play, *Harvest Moon* (1990), a family working in a field races to gather up their children while trying to outrun planes spraying pesticides—a recurring nightmare his family and millions of farm workers have had to endure.

When he was five his family moved north to Watsonville, where the climate and soil provided year-round work. There they lived in an old abandoned *bracero* barrack, the prototype of the humble *casitas* in many of his plays. González spent weekends, summers, and afternoons after school working in the fields that surrounded their house.

González returned to southern California in the mid 1970s to study at the University of California, San Diego. His major in Chicano Studies placed him among the first generation to graduate in what was, in the 1970s, a new academic discipline. His undergraduate minor in theatre led him to the Theatre Department at Arizona State University, where he earned an M.A. in 1982. It was there that he was introduced to theatre for youth, which has remained a central focus for his work.

He continued his professional theatre training at the University of California, Irvine, where he was awarded his M.F.A. in directing in 1985. From there he joined the artistic staff at the nearby South Coast Repertory (SCR), where he created the Hispanic Playwrights Project (HPP; 1986–1996), dedicated to nurturing Latino and Latina writers. Four years after launching HPP, he wrote his first play, *Marisol's Christmas*. Around this time he organized and attended a playwriting workshop at SCR facilitated by Cuban-American playwright María Irene Fornés, who has had a strong influence on his stream-of-consciousness approach to writing.

González's remarkably prolific playwriting career includes plays for adults as well as children. The nine plays in this volume offer a diverse range of his plays for youth that are as varied as his entire oeuvre, which includes twenty-two plays and three television, film, and video scripts to date. They cover fifteen years in his growth as a playwright, from *Marisol's Christmas* in 1990 to the three plays written in 2005. González's body of work is remarkable because he has created these stories and participated in the collaborations that developed many of them while teaching full-time at California State University, Los Angeles, where he has been a professor of theatre since 1989 and where he has created a playwriting program to develop young writers.

Seven of the plays presented here are original work and two, *Old Jake's Skirts* and *Tomás and the Library Lady*, have been adapted from books by others. All but two, *Marisol's Christmas* and *The Highest Heaven*, were commissioned by theatre companies that have become increasingly interested in González's rich storytelling and powerful visual imagination. Childsplay, an award-winning professional theatre company for young audiences in Tempe, Arizona, where González held a Theatre Communications Group Theatre Artist Residency in 2004–2005 and where he is a playwright in residence, has produced five of his plays, all of which are in this volume. Only one of the following plays, *Watermelon Kisses*, has yet to be produced.

Magical Realism and Mature Themes

Tomás Rivera, a part of whose biography González adapted from the book by Pat Mora in *Tomás and the Library Lady*, was a leader in Chicano literature in the burgeoning Chicano movement of the 1960s and 1970s. He wrote extensively about his childhood as a migrant worker and the intimate relationship most Chicanos have to nature:

> The Chicano, when he knelt upon the land and engendered love, gen-
> erated and gave it life. He thus felt a symbiotic existence with the
> land and if he did not understand the political, economic, and social
> situations that surrounded him and that tried to structure him, he did
> understand his own relationship with the realities of the land, the sun,
> the wind, and the water. (Rivera 365)

The rich and mysterious natural world, at the heart of most descriptions of magical realism, bridges what Seymour Menton, in his seminal book on the genre, describes as "the oxymoronic combination of realism and magic" (13), terms that are contradictory only from a rational European perspective.

Gabriel García Márquez, the Colombian Nobel Laureate whose novels are usually cited in descriptions of magical realism, was interviewed for an episode of *The South Bank Show* in 1989. When asked about magical realism, he explained that the amazing things in Latin America that he writes about happen all over the world, but Western people can't see them because of their cultural upbringing. He asserts that reductive Western values (*Cartesianismo*) have created a rigor of thought that doesn't allow the imagination to fly. Consequently, magical realism should be understood not as an exotic way of thinking about existence, but as a boundless vision undiminished by the rational borders of Western thought.

Note that in Rivera's description above, earth, sun, wind, and water constitute reality, rather than political, economic, and social "situations," a word implying their transitory nature. Similarly, Paul Hawken describes the ephemeral nature of what passes for history in the West in his book *Blessed Unrest*:

> Things come and go; conquests, ideas, and leaders arise and fall away.
> For indigenous people, in the time that defines one's life, the relation-
> ship one has to the earth is the constant and true gauge that deter-

mines the integrity of one's culture, the meaning of one's existence, and the peacefulness of one's heart. (22–23)

Hawken contends that indigenous people are also connected to the natural world by the exploitation each has endured: "Slaves, serfs, and the poor are the forests, soils, and oceans of society; each constitutes surplus value that has been exploited repeatedly by those in power" (22).

Thus magical realism may be described as a perspective of the oppressed whose lives are intricately bound to the natural world and may be understood in its terms. In Márquez's work, for example, blood flows through a town from an executed man to his mother, a woman hanging laundry is carried away by the wind in her sheets, an old man with enormous wings crash-lands in a poor village.

Chicanos are descendants of the indigenous people who inhabited North America's southwest for centuries before the European occupation compartmentalized the continent and drew a border across northern Mexico's Yaqui land. Poet Jimmy Santiago Baca summed up the paradox of Chicano identity in the title of his 1979 book of poetry, *Immigrants on Our Own Land*. Broken treaties and stolen land became causes in the Chicano Movement of the 1960s and 1970s. New Mexican poet Sabine Ulibarrí described the land as holy and sacred to Chicanos, not only because "your parents and their parents are buried there," but also because your "sweat, blood and tears have filtered into the land" (in Rosales, *Chicano!* 157).

González's experience as a farm worker in central California has grounded him in the earth as surely as it did John Steinbeck, who, like González, worked on farms among migrant workers. The fertile, loamy soil of the Salinas Valley infuses González's work with a rich fecundity, and nature has a powerful, magical presence in his plays. The conflicts arise when destructive human forces such as greed, violence, and ignorance attempt to plunder life in its remarkable abundance.

In the assault against nature and the bodies and souls of González's characters, the loss of childhood is collateral damage. But he has faith in the power of healing. Just as nature is resilient and renewing, the children in his plays overcome violence and personal loss by remembering the lessons of their elders. Their courageous journey toward adulthood, sometimes undertaken much too early, often begins by rediscovering their relationship to the land. "Your garden is a beginning," the father tells the despairing young heroine of *Lily Plants a Garden*, "and isn't that what hope is?"

Gardens are a central image in many of González's plays: flower gardens, vegetable gardens, cool, soothing grass. Lily's tiny garden, watered by her tears, fits into a wagon; El Negro's, in *The Highest Heaven*, is a sacred grove ("nature's church") where monarch butterflies breed and incubate. When gardens are in danger, so are their caretakers. In *The Magic Rainforest*, deforestation by human beings threatens all life in the Amazon. Even the plays without gardens have one in the wings. In *Salt & Pepper*, Salt's grandfather transports local produce in his truck and Pepper's unseen father is a migrant farm worker. In *Marisol's Christmas*, a small pine tree bounces off a truck and into the family's freeway off-ramp encampment.

Although gardens are sometimes the vocation of the young ("Are you an angel?" the Little Girl asks Lily. "No, I'm a gardener."), they are more often the legacy of the old. If there's an *abuela*, there's a garden. And seeds, like the children that populate González's plays, carry in them the promise of growth. Abuela in *Two Donuts* tells her grandson that when she fled Guatemala she brought only memories of her homeland and a pocketful of seeds. After her sudden death the neighborhood baker reminds Pepito that his grandmother's stories "are like seeds. They'll grow in your heart and bloom." Old Jake plants pumpkin seeds in his rocky garden and reaps "a bountiful harvest" the year he allows grace to unfold in his heart "as would a tender flower." In *Watermelon Kisses* a nine-year-old taunts his little brother about the danger of swallowing watermelon seeds: "They get planted in your stomach and then green vines start to rise up through your throat and ears and spill out everywhere."

González's characters communicate with nature. The boy's mother in *The Highest Heaven* tells her young son: "The earth has secrets. If you watch and listen closely, she'll share them with you." Hannah, the mother in *Salt & Pepper*, leaves home when she hears the wind call her name. Wakote, a tribal elder in *The Magic Rainforest*, tells his nephew that to become a shaman he will have to learn the language of animals and the secrets of plants. In *Marisol's Christmas*, the whole universe hears the girl sing. Nature smiles on Old Jake when he learns to open his heart.

The natural world makes González's plays timeless, even though some of them are set against specific eras. Salt's brother Andy leaves to fight in the Korean War. Pepito's grandmother in *Two Donuts* fled a military dictatorship in Guatemala, probably in the 1980s. Huracán in *The Highest Heaven* is separated from his parents during the forced repatriation of Mexican Americans in the 1930s. The real Tomás Rivera was nine in 1944, when Chicano schoolchildren were routinely punished for speaking Spanish. These "situations," to use Rivera's word—war, oppressive regimes, harassment of minorities, and intolerance—are the backdrop for most of González's plays.

Only one work in this volume is completely removed from external strife.

Watermelon Kisses, a chamber play about two little brothers with Aztec names sitting on the porch steps eating watermelon, takes place in the hot slowness of a summer day when everything is good. Dad is offstage mowing the overgrown lawn, and Mom kisses one of the boys before going to the store. Gentle moments like this drift through all González's plays, reminding us of abiding human kindness and oneness with nature.

No discussion of González's plays would be complete without mentioning the comedy that accompanies the serious journeys of his characters. His plays include a full range of comedy, from slapstick to gentle humor. Some draw on popular culture that young audiences can easily relate to: the Guatemalan worry dolls in *Two Donuts* are mafia hit men with Brooklyn accents; Potato, Squash, and Yam, three characters in *The Magic Rainforest*, are "the baddest veggies in the rainforest"; Gravity, a character in *Marisol's Christmas*, is a dude who raps.

González also creates comedy by ridiculing the powerful: Doña Elena in *The Highest Heaven* tries to maintain authority in a town where every shopkeeper and local official is one of her deceased husband's illegitimate offspring; Comandante Boots and Sergeant Botas in *Two Donuts* are a bumbling duo performing military maneuvers. Sometimes comedy results from Spanish-English confusion: Tomás thinks the Carnegie Library is a meat (*carne*) library; the singing of the "Star-Spangled Banner," which indicates a baseball game in *Marisol's Christmas*, begins with, "Oh, José, can you see." With several prepubescent characters in his plays, González finds humor in sexual confusion: Quetzal warns his younger brother that a kiss, even from his mother, can "activate" the watermelon seeds he's swallowed; El Negro shocks eleven-year-old Huracán by telling him, "Pretty soon you gonna be growin' hair in places you never thought you could!"

Just as transformation is a central action in most of González's plays, it is a fundamental aspect of the staging. Past and present must intertwine and merge because of the importance of memory in his plays. Furthermore, actual or metaphoric journeys and migrations suggest multiple settings. Consequently, the stage transforms into various periods and locations, usually simply by suggestion. Sound and light sometimes give a sense of place: a train whistle, a baseball game, a bus, a blue sky with white clouds, stars, the moon, fire. *Tomás and the Library Lady* uses projected scenery, such as the library and the houses of the migrant camp; even the character of Papá Grande is represented by a big white mustache projected on a screen.

González also employs movable structures that can transform into furniture or landscapes. *Salt & Pepper*, a play about illiteracy, uses an abstract setting of large letters of the alphabet strewn about the stage that actors play on and around. *Old Jake's Skirts* employs a large trunk filled with props, including a miniature version of Old Jake's cabin, his truck, and his dog, Shoestring. González likes large boxes that can be opened in various ways to reveal portions of settings or to hide surprises. His play *The Cloud Gatherer* (2007) uses a large rolling crate as a prop box, a landscape of Africa, and the small stage on which the puppet children play. The use of a stage within a stage increases the metaphorical possibilities in the plays since the theatre becomes all the world. In this regard theatre is an ideal medium for magical realism, because the dramatic dimensions of the world on stage are flexible and limitless. Time and space have no boundaries, and characters navigate through both as freely as migrating butterflies cross the U.S.-Mexican border.

Narration is another staging convention González uses often. Narration enhances the storytelling aspect of his plays while linking them to the Chicano oral tradition. Tomás Rivera described the importance of the oral tradition in the migrant camps of his childhood, where stories about Mexico, the revolution of 1910, supernatural characters, and spirits became part of "remembering, narrating, and retelling" (367). González remembers his grandfather telling stories while they worked in the fields. Grandparents in his plays are all storytellers. History, folklore, myth, and legend are carried in memory and transmitted from one generation to another through storytelling.

González's narrators are magicians: they can set the scene, influence the action, change the time or location, and transform into characters. Because other characters in González's plays rarely address spectators directly, narrators act as intermediaries, crisscrossing the boundary between the world of the audience and the world of the play.

González also writes his plays for adjustable cast sizes and dimensions. The fewer the actors, the more roles each plays. Consequently actors must transform from one character into another. In *Marisol's Christmas* three actors play all the roles, including a comet, a Christmas tree, a beach ball, and gravity. Actors play dolphins, birds, and vegetables in *The Magic Rainforest*, a play that intermingles puppetry with people. *Two Donuts* can be presented with as few as three actor-puppeteers or up to twelve actors. In *The Cloud Gatherer* five puppeteers and a narrator create shadow landscapes of Africa, elephant herds, and a journey into the sky.

In oral traditions music plays a significant role in committing stories to memory. Music is an important part of González's life (he plays guitar and writes music) and an important element in most of his plays. The plays in this volume use diverse styles of music: Negro spirituals in *The Highest Heaven*, Appalachian bluegrass in *Old Jake's Skirts*, a Spanish-language Christmas song in *Marisol's Christmas*. Sometimes González's young characters are budding musicians: Akí in *The Magic Rainforest* is learning to play the flute; Sanchi, the young girl in *Mariachi Quixote* (1999), is determined to become a mariachi musician; Chioniso, the African girl in *The Cloud Gatherer*, discovers she has been chosen to play the *mbira*, a sacred instrument of Zimbabwe used to communicate with the ancestors.

Music also contributes to the bridging devices in González's plays, providing transitions and supplying local color while communicating in a universal language that can transcend time and place, adding another element to the richly complex fabric of his stories.

González once told me about his visit to the Smithsonian Institution in Washington, D.C., where he discovered that Chicano history had been overlooked. "Where are we?" he asked, seeing the remarkable stories of his parents and grandparents and their vast community reduced to a low-rider car. If Chicano culture is, as Márquez suggests, invisible to Western eyes, then González has a vital role to play in the American theatre: to awaken the imagination of audiences through his stories so their profound lessons about tending the earth can be seen and heard.

Works Cited

Hawken, Paul. *Blessed Unrest: How the Largest Movement in the World Came into Being and Why No One Saw it Coming*. New York: Viking, 2007.

Menton, Seymor. *Magic Realism Rediscovered, 1918–1981*. Philadelphia: Art Alliance Press, 1982.

Rivera, Tomás. "Remembering, Discovery, and Volition in the Literary Imaginative Process." Translated by Gustavo Valadez. In *Tomás Rivera: The Complete Works*, edited by Julián Olivares, 365–370. Houston: Arte Público Press, 1992.

Rosales, F. Arturo. *Chicano! The History of the Mexican American Civil Rights Movement*. Houston: Arte Público Press, 1997.

The South Bank Show: Gabriel García Márquez. Directed by Holly Aylett. 85 minutes. London: Luna Films, 1989.

Considering the Design Process

J. Richard Smith

In the hope of stimulating the imagination of readers of this anthology, the editor invited scenic artist J. Richard Smith to study each of the plays, keep a record of his initial impressions, and create at least two sketches for each of the scripts. The first sketch was to be a visual, dramaturgical response to the script; the second, a hypothetical design that develops from the first image. In one instance—Lily Plants a Garden—his sketches are of scenes from a new script during rehearsals as it was first being developed. Smith documents his own creative process in comments and preliminary sketches following each script. Regarding his process, he writes:

> For me, some of the greatest joys of designing and directing theatre come during the journey to the final product. As I begin working on any design project I keep, as most artists do, a journal or log of ideas about the script and how the designs might be realized. For the artwork of this anthology the emphasis was to be on the settings rather than costumes or lighting, with notes about the process that governed the results.
>
> I spent the first several months prior to receiving word that this anthology had been approved for publication pondering how I would approach each of the plays as a designer rather than as an active participant in the development of a new play (as I had done for Lily Plants a Garden).
>
> My participation with the development of Lily was as a dramaturgical intern at the 2003 Indiana University-Purdue University Indianapolis/Indiana Repertory Theatre Waldo M. and Grace C. Bonderman National Youth Theatre Development Workshop and Symposium. After the framework for the development of Lily Plants a Garden was settled, and as I worked with dramaturg Corey Madden, director Eric Johnson, and the playwright, I formulated my own strategy for the best way to

contribute to the process of creating Lily. I rapidly sketched various scenes, especially those of climactic moments and of characters in crisis. My work was a form of visual dramaturgy in which an artist creates drawings to help the playwright in a complementary effort in the process of writing a new work.

My comments and sketches that follow each script here represent nine approaches to the first steps toward realization of setting designs for a production.

The Plays

The Magic Rainforest—
An Amazon Journey

José Cruz González

Originally commissioned by the John F. Kennedy
Center for the Performing Arts, Education Department

Oh, my dear, you want something impossible. You want to comprehend the Enchanted Beings through study, and that's not the way. Because you can capture them only through thought, through the force of concentration. A person has to risk his life to get to the Enchanted City, he has to undergo a transformation.

—Doña Marina, from "Dance of the Dolphin," Candace Slater

Our Lord in his goodness guide me that I may find this gold.

—Christopher Columbus, December 23, 1492

That night, I had a terrifying dream. An enormous jaguar strode into my hut and stared deeply into my eyes, as if trying to divine my thoughts. Powerful muscles tensed in its back as it arched its body to spring. So vivid was the apparition that I awoke with a scream. I sat upright in my hammock, trembling, my body soaked in a cold sweat. Carefully, I looked around the hut: I saw nothing—no footprints on the dirt floor, nothing disturbed or overturned, nothing to indicate the presence of an unwanted visitor. The only sound was the rustling of palm fronds as a gentle breeze blew through the village.

The next morning, just after sunrise, the young Indian who had served as our translator came to my hut. "Shall we go into the forest and look for more plants?" he asked.

"Before we do," I said, "find the old shaman and tell him that last night I saw the jaguar." I gave no details, and the Indian left. He returned a few minutes later. "Did you tell him?" I asked. "Yes." "What did he say?" I asked. "He broke into a big smile and said, 'That was me!'"

—"Tales of a Shaman's Apprentice," Mark J. Plotkin

Characters

AKÍ (ah-KEE): a young Amazonian Indian boy. He wants to be a warrior instead of a shaman.

UNCLE WAKOTE (wah-KOH-tey): a medicine man. AKÍ's uncle. A wise man. He also plays a VILLAGE WARRIOR, THE JAGUAR KING, TOUCAN, and POTATO PLANT.

PEREIRA (peh-REH-ra): a ruthless man who wears an eye patch. He is the FIRE DEMON.

MAURICIO (mao-REE-syo): Pereira's assistant. Superstitious and kind. A local.

ESTRELA (eh-STRAY-la): a star maiden. She also plays PIRA (PEE-ra), VILLAGE WARRIOR, GHOST #1, TURTLE, YAM PLANT, and FROG.

SQUASH PLANT: also plays PAXKE (PAHSH-kay), VILLAGE WARRIOR, GHOST #2, and an ENCANTADO, etc.

PINK DOLPHINS, MACAW, SLOTH, SNAKE, PIRANHA, BATS, and COBRA GRANDE (KO-bra GRAHN-djee) are manipulated by the actors.

Setting

The Amazon rainforest.

Words in Portuguese

caboclo (kah-BO-klo)
encantado (en-kahn-TA-doe)
encante (ehn-KAHN-tey)
pajé (pah-ZHEY)
piranha (pee-RAH-nya)
senhor (seh-NYOR)

The Portuguese "r" is softly rolled, similar to that in Spanish.

Scene 1

SCENE: *The Amazon rainforest.*

AT RISE: *The stage is scattered with etchings of indigenous human, plant, animal, and celestial imagery. The rustic etchings vary in size and detail. On stage lay a waterfall and a river that snakes through the forest. It is a magical transformational area.*

The echo of flutes is heard. It is as if the entire jungle has come alive with music. The river glows, transforming into a deep blue as several etchings of rainforest creatures glow to life. WAKOTE *appears in a pool of light.*

WAKOTE: Deep below the waters of the Amazon River lies a magical kingdom called the Encante. It is peopled by enchanted beings called Encantados. The Encantados swim freely with such joy in their hearts. If you listen you can hear their song.

(Several PINK DOLPHINS *emerge, swimming in the magical river. Their vocal sounds become musical.)*

WAKOTE: The Encantados have lived in the great river since the beginning of time. It is said that they can transform themselves into human beings. I know of one that did. He fell in love with an Indian maiden named Pira.

*(*PIRA*, a young Indian woman, appears.)*

WAKOTE: Each day Pira would collect water from the river and an Encantado would play his song for her. One night, while the tribe celebrated a prosperous hunt, a young man appeared out of nowhere.

(A young man, PAXKE*, stands beside* PIRA*.)*

WAKOTE: Pira recognized him. For it was the enchanted being now turned human. That night, under the moon's careful watch, they danced by firelight. They spoke in whispers and fell in love. And so it went that Pira and Paxke were soon married, and they returned to the river kingdom to live. But Pira became saddened.

PIRA: Husband?

PAXKE: Yes, wife?

PIRA: I miss my home.

PAXKE: Are you not happy living here?

PIRA: I am very happy but I miss my family. I wish to see them again.

WAKOTE: You see, *Pira* had been away for only three days, but in the human world it had been three years. *Pira* longed to see her village.

PAXKE: Very well, wife, you may go.

WAKOTE: *Paxke* gave to *Pira* an emerald necklace.

PAXKE: This will protect you from harm but you must never take it off.

PIRA: I understand, husband.

(*PAXKE exits.*)

WAKOTE: *Pira* was very happy to see her family. You see, she was with child. And one day, she gave birth to a pink baby boy.

(*A child's cry is heard. PIRA holds an imaginary infant in her arms.*)

PIRA: I will name you *Akí*, "great forest guardian."

WAKOTE: You will possess great magical powers.

PIRA: And even greater wisdom, my son.

WAKOTE: Soon after *Akí*'s birth, an evil creature descended into the rainforest. It was a beast far more cunning and dangerous than had ever been seen before. His arm was made of fire and he loved to watch things burn. He destroyed many villages. He is called the Fire Demon!

(*The FIRE DEMON appears. It is a villager wearing a large monstrous mask and carrying a giant thunder-lightning stick.*)

FIRE DEMON: *Wanetopa! Wanetopa!*

WAKOTE: We fought the Fire Demon, but his magic was too powerful. Our village went up in flames. *Pira* ran to the river and the Fire Demon pursued her. She put baby *Akí* in a small basket and placed her emerald necklace around him.

PIRA: This will protect you, my son!

WAKOTE: She sent the basket floating downriver but the Fire Demon set it on fire.

PIRA: No!

WAKOTE: *Pira* charged the Fire Demon and fought him but it was no use. She was engulfed in his fire and was never seen again.

(*PIRA exits.*)

WAKOTE: Tongues of fire rose up from baby *Akí*'s basket. Nothing could save him. But then the most magnificent thing happened. An *Encantado* leaped out of the water, putting out the fire and saving *Akí*.

(*The FIRE DEMON removes his mask. It is AKÍ. He is a teenage Indian boy. WAKOTE is his uncle. Their bodies are painted with geometric patterns and they are simply adorned with feather decorations.)*

AKÍ: Uncle *Wakote*, that's impossible! Dolphins can't do that!

WAKOTE: Well, this one did. You wouldn't be here if that *Encantado* hadn't saved you, Akí.

AKÍ: You're making all this up.

WAKOTE: No, it's true. It happened.

AKÍ: And I suppose this *Encantado* was my father?

WAKOTE: Yes, he was your father, *Paxke*.

AKÍ: Uncle *Wakote*, why must you keep telling me these silly stories? I'm not a kid anymore.

WAKOTE: They're not silly stories. They're lessons for you to learn. You are thirteen seasons old. And I have chosen you to be our tribe's next *pajé*.

AKÍ: I don't want to be a shaman. All they ever do is reenact dumb stories. Walk around the forest talking to plants.

WAKOTE: It is an honor for you to be a *pajé*. You must learn our history. Our myths. Learn the language of animals. And yes, study the secrets of plants too.

AKÍ: But I'd rather be a warrior instead! A warrior's life is filled with so much danger and fun!

(AKÍ lifts his bow, aiming at an imaginary foe.)

WAKOTE: What do you know of it?

AKÍ: I know plenty.

WAKOTE: Such as?

AKÍ: A great warrior is never afraid of anything.

WAKOTE: Is that so?

AKÍ: A great warrior places terror in the hearts of his enemy. He never misses what he shoots at and he can run, jump, and scream far better than anyone!

WAKOTE: I see.

(The JAGUAR KING is heard. AKÍ drops his bow and arrow and runs up to his uncle.)

AKÍ (frightened): What was that?

WAKOTE: Be quiet!

(A giant pair of luminous eyes appears in the jungle.)

WAKOTE (whispering): It's the Jaguar King.

AKÍ: What's he doing here?

WAKOTE: Be still. He's looking for his next meal.

AKÍ: Will he eat me?

WAKOTE: Shhh . . .

(The JAGUAR KING'S eyes fade away into the jungle.)

AKÍ: Is he gone?

WAKOTE: Yes.

AKÍ: Good. Lucky for him—if he had gotten any closer I would've shot him dead right between the eyes.

WAKOTE: I see you're still afraid of him.

AKÍ: No, I'm not!

WAKOTE: He roams your dreams at night.

AKÍ: Yes, I see his eyes glowing at me in the dark. I dream he chases after me and then eats me. There's nothing left but my teeth.

WAKOTE: Your teeth?

AKÍ: And my nose.

(Beat.)

WAKOTE: I must leave now.

AKÍ: Uncle, where are you going?

WAKOTE: Into the jungle, where I go to find a new place for our tribe to settle.

AKÍ: But why must you do that?

WAKOTE: Look there in the sky. What do you see?

AKÍ: Smoke as dark as a raven's feathers.

WAKOTE: It's the work of the Fire Demons.

AKÍ: Fire Demons? There's more than one?

WAKOTE: Many more. And soon they will be upon us.

AKÍ: May I go with you?

WAKOTE: Where I go a boy mustn't follow. The jungle is filled with much danger.

AKÍ: Danger is my middle name!

WAKOTE: You haven't got a middle name, and besides you are not ready.

AKÍ: Uncle, I can shoot far better than any warrior in the village.

WAKOTE: This journey requires something more than the straight shot of an arrow.

AKÍ: Uncle, I don't understand.

WAKOTE: *Akí,* I have tried teaching you to be a *pajé* but you have not taken it seriously. And now when I need you, you are not ready. Don't you see a *pajé* must summon greater courage than a dozen warriors going into battle? He must fight alone, and his foes are much more frightening. You're still afraid of your own shadow. I expected too much from you.

AKÍ: Uncle, I'm not of afraid of the Fire Demons.

WAKOTE: But you will be.

(WAKOTE *gives* AKÍ *an emerald necklace.*)

WAKOTE: This belonged to your mother. I have kept it safe for you. Here.

AKÍ: Uncle, please let me go with you!

WAKOTE: This flute was your father's. He played it magnificently. I wonder if you could play it just as well?

AKÍ: I'll listen to everything you say!

WAKOTE: You'll be safe as long as you stay near the village. Your grandfather and grandmother will watch over you. Goodbye, *Akí.*

AKÍ: Uncle!

(WAKOTE *exits.*)

AKÍ (*shouting*): Then I'll stand watch! My bow is mighty and all will fear my aim! Even the Fire Demons!

(A MACAW *puppet flies nearby, squawking.* AKÍ *pretends he is a warrior shooting the Fire Demons. He looks at the* MACAW.)

AKÍ: Are you a spy? Come to learn my secrets? Do you serve the Fire Demons? Take heed. I never miss!

(AKÍ *pretends to shoot the* MACAW. *The* MACAW *just watches. Bored,* AKÍ *begins to play his flute. He plays badly. The* MACAW *swoops down on* AKÍ's *head, pecking at him.*)

MACAW: Aw, aw, aw!

AKÍ: Hey!

MACAW: Awful!

AKÍ: What'd you say?

MACAW: Awful! Awful! Awful!

AKÍ: Hey, stop that! Stop that!

Scene 2

(*Drums are heard.* PEREIRA, *the* FIRE DEMON, *appears. He is a ruthless man who wears an eye patch. He carries a large torch in one hand and a machete in the other.*)

AKÍ: The Fire Demon!

(PEREIRA *sets the village on fire. The* VILLAGE WARRIORS *enter, battling him, but he defeats them.*)

AKÍ: No!

(AKÍ *charges the* FIRE DEMON *but the* FIRE DEMON *knocks* AKÍ *unconscious, sending him into the river.* AKÍ *descends to the river bottom. Music. The river glows a deep blue, and etchings of river life become luminous. Two* ENCANTADOS *appear. They are beautiful pink dolphins.*)

ENCANTADO #1: Chahhh . . .

ENCANTADO #2: Chahhh . . .

ENCANTADO #1: Chaah . . . Akí!

ENCANTADO #2: Chaah . . . Akí!

AKÍ: Wasowa . . .

ENCANTADO #1: Wake up!

ENCANTADO #2: Wake up!

AKÍ: Huh? Where am I?

ENCANTADO #1: In the river kingdom! Chaah . . .

ENCANTADO #2: Kingdom! Chaah . . .

AKÍ: Am I dead?

ENCANTADO #1: No, chaah . . .

ENCANTADO #2: No, chaah . . .

AKÍ: But how can this be? I'm underwater!

ENCANTADO #1: Come and play with us little brother, chaah . . .

ENCANTADO #2: Stay with us forever, chaah . . .

AKÍ: Yes, I want to play! Swim! Chaah!

ENCANTADO #1: Chaah!

ENCANTADO #2: Chaah!

(*The* ENCANTADOS *lead* AKÍ *through the river, where he sees an abundance of water spirits swimming by.*)

AKÍ: What is this place?

ENCANTADO #1: It is our home! Chaahh . . .

ENCANTADO #2: *Encante!* Chaahh . . .

AKÍ: Uncle spoke of it, but I never believed him. What's that there?

ENCANTADO #1: Don't go there, chaah . . .

ENCANTADO #2: Not there, chaah . . .

AKÍ: But why not?

ENCANTADO #1: *Cobra Grande* lives there, chaah . . .

ENCANTADO #2: Don't awaken him, chaah . . .

AKÍ: Who is *Cobra Grande?*

ENCANTADO #1: A giant serpent, chaah . . .

ENCANTADO #2: He'll devour you like he did your father . . .

ENCANTADO #1/ENCANTADO #2: Take you deep below, chaah . . .

(*Music is heard.* COBRA GRANDE *stirs.*)

AKÍ: Let's go! I want to go home!

ENCANTADO #1: You musn't go, chaah . . .

ENCANTADO #2: Only sorrow there, chaah . . .

AKÍ: Take me home now!

ENCANTADO #1/ENCANTADO #2: As you wish . . .

(*The* ENCANTADOS *lead* AKÍ *to shore, where his village appears.*)

AKÍ: This isn't my village. It can't be. There's nothing left but ashes. Grandmother? Grandfather?

(GHOSTS OF VILLAGERS *appear. They are tiny spots of light. They float about* AKÍ.)

GHOST #1 (*sadly*): Akí . . .

GHOST #2 (*sadly*): Akí . . .

AKÍ: Who are you?

GHOST #1/GHOST #2: Forest spirits.

AKÍ: But where are my grandmother and grandfather?

GHOST #1: We are they.

AKÍ: No, you can't be!

GHOST #2: You were taken from us.

GHOST #1: Taken far away.

AKÍ: Are you dead?

GHOST #1/GHOST #2: Yes.

AKÍ: I mustn't speak to you!

GHOST #1: The entire jungle rose up in flames against us.

GHOST #2: We couldn't escape.

GHOST #1: But you survived.

GHOST #1/GHOST #2: If only we had a hero to save us!

GHOST #1: Save us, Akí!

AKÍ: I don't know how! Where are my cousins? My aunts? The rest of the villagers?

GHOST #1: Scattered!

GHOST #2: Hiding in the jungle!

GHOST #1: Alone!

GHOST #2: Afraid!

GHOST #1/GHOST #2: Starving to death!

AKÍ: Go away! Leave me!

GHOST #1: Don't leave us, Akí.

GHOST #2: Take us with you!

AKÍ: Don't touch me!

GHOST #1: Akí . . .

GHOST #2: Akí . . .

AKÍ: I have to find my Uncle *Wakote*!

GHOST #1: Save us, Akí . . .

GHOST #2: Save us, Akí . . .

AKÍ: No, I can't!

Scene 3

(MAURICIO, PEREIRA'S *assistant, enters, fishing* AKÍ *out of the river.*)

MAURICIO: *Senhor Pereira*!

(PEREIRA *enters, dipping his handkerchief into the cool waters of the Amazon River and wiping his face.*)

PEREIRA: What do you want, *Mauricio*?

MAURICIO: I thought I was catching fish for dinner, but instead I caught a boy! Look!

PEREIRA: I don't have time, *Mauricio*. Don't you see I'm exhausted? Put him with the others.

MAURICIO: This is no ordinary catch, *Senhor Pereira*. He's a shaman's apprentice. Look at his adornments. His feathers.

PEREIRA: He looks like a savage to me.

MAURICIO: His symbols mean he's got powerful magic.

PEREIRA: There's no such thing.

MAURICIO: *Senhor*, I know about these voodoo guys. They can transform ordinary things into extraordinary things. I've seen it happen. Look for yourself.

(MAURICIO *holds up* AKÍ'S *flute.*)

PEREIRA: What is that?

MAURICIO: It's a magical flute, *senhor*.

PEREIRA: You've got to be joking.

MAURICIO: In the hands of a shaman it can become anything. Just watch and listen.

(The MACAW *flies in squawking.*)

PEREIRA: What an ugly looking bird.

MAURICIO: It's a macaw, *senhor*.

PEREIRA: Who cares!

MAURICIO: Okay, boy, see this leaf? Turn it into something valuable. Like diamonds! D-I-M— . . . Or silver! S-I-V— . . . How about gold! G-O-L— . . .

PEREIRA: Enough with the spelling contest!

MAURICIO: Go on! Play!

(MAURICIO *gives* AKÍ *the flute.* AKÍ *plays it badly. The* MACAW *swoops down, attacking* AKÍ.)

MACAW: Awful!

AKÍ: Aagghhh!

MACAW: Awful! Awful!

(The MACAW *flies off. The* LEAF *begins to move. It is a puppet insect*).

MAURICIO: Look! The boy did it! He turned the leaf into a gold bug!

PEREIRA: That's impossible! Let me see! Ouch! Does everything in this godforsaken country either bite or sting?

MAURICIO: It's magic!

PEREIRA: *Mauricio*, we live in a world of science and reason, of power and wealth, and you, my friend, know nothing. But what can I expect from a *caboclo?* Half-breed, you're lucky to be working for me. Enough with this mumbo jumbo!

MAURICIO: You're right, *senhor*. I am grateful to work for you.

PEREIRA: Jail him with the rest of the savages! And be done with it!

MAURICIO: But shouldn't we let him go? He's just a boy.

PEREIRA: We have an important job, *Mauricio*. Burn the forest down. Clear the land for cattle and farming. Those who get in the way we jail. Those who fight with us, well . . . it's called "progress." Everybody benefits.

MAURICIO: Except the Indians.

PEREIRA: Who cares about them? I've had to squeeze everything out of this land to make a living. I am a conqueror without a country to tame. Are there no more conquests to be made? Where are the great civilizations with pyramids and riches? What heroic stories will I tell my children and my good-for-nothing friends? Oh, this jungle exhausts me!

(AKÍ *tries to sneak away.* MAURICIO *grabs him.*)

MAURICIO: Where do you think you're going, boy?

(PEREIRA *takes notice of* AKÍ'S *necklace.*)

PEREIRA: What have we here?

MAURICIO: *Senhor?*

PEREIRA: What an interesting-looking necklace.

MAURICIO: Is it valuable?

PEREIRA: Hmmm . . .

MAURICIO: Well?

PEREIRA: You're in my light.

MAURICIO: Sorry.

PEREIRA: Perhaps this expedition hasn't been a complete failure.

MAURICIO: I knew it! We're gonna be rich!

PEREIRA: We?

MAURICIO: But I found the boy!

PEREIRA: You nitwit, you're working for me! Therefore, anything you find belongs to me!

MAURICIO: But—

PEREIRA: This is a very expensive-looking emerald.

MAURICIO: Is it worth a lot of money?

PEREIRA: Indeed it is. And I bet the boy knows where there's more. With a few of these emeralds I could live like a king. Live in a high-rise in the city. Eat caviar and sip champagne all day. All it'll take is two men and a few days work.

MAURICIO: What are you suggesting, *senhor*?

PEREIRA: You should join me.

MAURICIO: Join you?

PEREIRA: You could be very rich, you know?

MAURICIO: Me?

PEREIRA: I'll need a partner.

MAURICIO: Partner?

PEREIRA: Think of it as God's work.

MAURICIO: God's work?

PEREIRA: He made emeralds. He put them in the ground for man to dig up. What harm is there in that? What do you say?

MAURICIO. Very well, *senhor*. We'll do God's work.

Scene 4

(*At the* FIRE DEMON'S *camp.* TOUCAN, SLOTH, *and* TURTLE *are caged together. They are snoring.* AKÍ *enters. He is shackled in chains.*)

TOUCAN: Guys, guys, wake up! Who's the new guy?

SLOTH: Oh, don't start, Toucan. Can't a sloth ever get some—

(SLOTH *falls asleep, snoring.*)

TOUCAN: I don't know about you guys, but my idea of a good time isn't waiting for some human to eat me.

TURTLE: Is that what's going to happen?

TOUCAN: You ever heard of turtle soup?

TURTLE: Oooh!

(AKÍ *touches his injured leg.*)

AKÍ: Ouch! Will you be quiet? I'm trying to think!

TOUCAN: Who's he talking to, Turtle?

TURTLE: Not to me. 'Bye!

(TURTLE *sticks his head into his shell.* SLOTH *snores.*)

TOUCAN: Coward!

AKÍ: There's got to be a way out of here.

TOUCAN: Hey, New Guy? How is it you understand the language of animals?

AKÍ: I don't know, but I do.

TURTLE: Are you going to eat us?

AKÍ: No, I want to get out of here. This is an awful place. There isn't a living tree for miles.

TOUCAN: We haven't been outside in a long time. The man with the one eye captured and caged us.

TURTLE: But the other man feeds us and talks to us nicely.

AKÍ: I've got to free myself of these chains.

TOUCAN: If we helped you, would you take us with you?

AKÍ: Yes. We've got to distract the Fire Demon and take away his keys.

TURTLE: I could run and he'd have to chase after me. If I leave now I could get a head start.

TOUCAN: You're a turtle. How far can a turtle get?

TURTLE: Oooh . . .

AKÍ: I know! Toucan, you could fly around and distract him while I snatch his keys away.

TOUCAN: I don't think it's such a good idea.

AKÍ: It's our only chance.

TURTLE: Oh, please, Toucan, do it!

TOUCAN: Why don't you ask the Sloth to do something?

TURTLE: He'll be asleep before you —

(SLOTH snores.)

TOUCAN: Oh, all right, but if that loser of a human pulls my feathers I won't control myself. There's only so much a bird will take.

AKÍ: Great!

(MAURICIO enters.)

MAURICIO: Good morning, little fellows. I hope you slept well. I brought you some little cakes my wife made for you. I won't harm you, boy. I bet you're hungry, huh? Here. Eat.

(AKÍ takes a cake.)

MAURICIO: I'm sorry about your village. *Senhor Pereira* had me jail your villagers, but I let them go instead. I know what he does isn't so good. But what am I to do? I have a family to feed. I was once like you. I grew up in the rainforest. I wish you could understand me.

(*MAURICIO picks up* AKÍ'S *flute.*)

MAURICIO: Is this your flute? Maybe if I play it I can conjure something of value, and then *Senhor Pereira* will be pleased and he'll let you go.

(*MAURICIO plays the flute, but it turns into a small* SNAKE.)

SNAKE: Ssssshhhh!

MAURICIO: Aaaggghh, *Senhor Pereira! Senhor Pereira!*

(*MAURICIO drops the* SNAKE. AKÍ *grabs the keys.* TOUCAN *pecks* MAURICIO *in the head.* MAURICIO *exits while the* SNAKE *slithers away.*)

AKÍ: My flute turned into a snake!

TOUCAN: How'd he do that?

TURTLE: It must be magical.

TOUCAN: Did you get his keys?

AKÍ: Yes! Let's get out of here!

TURTLE: Hurry! They're coming!

AKÍ: It's too late!

(*MAURICIO and* PEREIRA *enter.* PEREIRA *carries his machete.*)

MAURICIO: *Senhor Pereira*, it was the biggest snake you ever saw!

PEREIRA: Was it a *cobra grande?*

MAURICIO: Yeah, a giant one! Almost twelve feet long!

PEREIRA: Well, where is it?

MAURICIO: It was here a minute ago. I barely escaped with my life.

PEREIRA: I hate *cobras grandes!*

TURTLE (*to* AKÍ): When do we run away?

TOUCAN: Now?

AKÍ: Not yet.

(*PEREIRA picks up the flute.*)

PEREIRA: What's this? It's the boy's flute.

MAURICIO: *Senhor Pereira*, it turned into a snake. Honest, it did! Maybe it wasn't a giant one, but—

PEREIRA: *Mauricio*, it never ceases to amaze me the power of your imagination.

MAURICIO: It even hissed at me!

PEREIRA: You've wasted enough of my time!

(*PEREIRA holds up AKÍ's emerald necklace.*)

PEREIRA: Tell me, boy, where did you find these emerald stones?

AKÍ: . . .

MAURICIO: *Senhor*, I don't think he can understand you.

PEREIRA: You're in my light.

MAURICIO: Sorry.

TOUCAN (*to AKÍ*): Now?

AKÍ: Not yet.

PEREIRA: Perhaps I should encourage our Indian friend to understand what I want more clearly. I saw this in an American movie once.

(*PEREIRA leans AKÍ over the river.*)

PEREIRA: I should warn you, boy, that falling into the river is not good. You see, it's filled with all sorts of dangerous creatures, very hungry creatures. I lost an eye to a *cobra grande*. He jumped right out of the river and took it from me.

(*A PIRANHA jumps out of the water, nipping at AKÍ. It falls back into the water.*)

PEREIRA: Steady now. Balance is good. Falling is bad. Now, boy, will you show me where I can find more of these precious stones?

AKÍ: . . .

MAURICIO: He doesn't understand you, *senhor*.

PEREIRA: Then it's time he did!

TOUCAN (*to AKÍ*): Now?

AKÍ: Not yet.

(*AKÍ is thrown into the river.*)

MAURICIO: Senhor Pereira, you threw him into the river!

PEREIRA: Did I?

MAURICIO: Please bring him up!

PEREIRA: Not just yet. Patience. All good things come to those who wait.

TURTLE: Toucan, he's not going to make it!

TOUCAN: Hang in there, boy!

SLOTH: Hold on!

MAURICIO: Please, *senhor?*

PEREIRA: Oh, all right!

(*MAURICIO pulls AKÍ out of the river. AKÍ spits a fish out of his mouth.*)

PEREIRA: Are you going to tell me now? Or do I need to persuade you again?

(*AKÍ points toward the jungle.*)

PEREIRA: That's more like it. You see, Mauricio, the boy and I see eye to eye now. Go ready my equipment. We're going on an expedition!

MAURICIO: Yes, *Senhor Pereira.*

(*They exit. AKÍ frees himself.*)

TURTLE: Are you all right?

AKÍ: I think so.

SLOTH: That was a very brave thing to do.

TOUCAN: Well, he had some help.

AKÍ: You're right, Toucan. I couldn't have done it without you.

(*AKÍ frees the animals. They don't move.*)

AKÍ: Now! Let's go before the Fire Demons return.

(*TOUCAN, TURTLE leave. SLOTH snores. AKÍ picks him up and exits.*)

AKÍ: Come on, sleepy head!

(*MAURICIO and PEREIRA enter. PEREIRA picks up AKÍ's chains.*)

PEREIRA: The boy's escaped!

MAURICIO: He stole my keys.

PEREIRA: He's smarter than I thought.

MAURICIO: But he can't be too far away. He went this way!

PEREIRA: Let's go!

(*They exit.*)

Scene 5

(*Dusk. In the heart of the jungle, AKÍ runs in, still carrying SLOTH. AKÍ is out of breath.*)

AKÍ: I think we lost them. I've got to rest. I'm so tired.

(*SLOTH awakens.*)

SLOTH: Is it dinnertime yet?

AKÍ: I wish it were. I'm starving.

SLOTH: Me too. And I could use a nap. Traveling exhausts me.

(*The* JAGUAR KING *is heard. His luminous eyes appear.* AKÍ *remains very still.*)

SLOTH: What is it?

AKÍ: Shhh . . .

(*The* JAGUAR KING'S *eyes fade away.*)

AKÍ: Good. He's gone.

SLOTH: Who was it?

AKÍ: The Jaguar King. He's hungry, too.

SLOTH: He hates your kind.

AKÍ: My kind?

SLOTH: Two-legged creatures.

AKÍ: Why?

SLOTH: Long ago, he shared the secret of fire with a boy just like you. He found him in the jungle alone and—

(SLOTH *suddenly falls asleep.*)

AKÍ: Sloth, wake up!

SLOTH: Are we there yet?

AKÍ: No! Tell me about the Jaguar King!

SLOTH: Well, he took the boy to his home. Taught him how to use a bow and arrow, and showed him the secret of—

(SLOTH *falls asleep again.*)

AKÍ: Sloth!

SLOTH: While the Jaguar King was away the boy killed the Jaguar's wife and stole his fire. The Jaguar King swore that all two-legged creatures would be his enemy. You better be—

(SLOTH *snores.*)

AKÍ: Great! Now I've got the Jaguar King after me too! I wish I could find my Uncle Wakote. But I don't even know where to begin.

YAM PLANT (*offstage*): Come on, boys!

AKÍ: What's that?

(AKÍ *exits. The Noisy Vegetables—* POTATO PLANT, SQUASH PLANT, *and* YAM PLANT*— enter. Actors play the Noisy Vegetables.*)

POTATO PLANT/SQUASH PLANT/YAM PLANT (*singing*):

Wate mari, mari
Ha ha,
Wate mari, mari
Ha ha.

Wate mari, mari
Ha ha,
Wate mari, mari
Ha ha.

AKÍ (*offstage*): Hello? Hello?

(POTATO PLANT, SQUASH PLANT, *and* YAM PLANT *freeze.* AKÍ *enters, carrying* SLOTH.)

AKÍ: Is anybody here?

(AKÍ *scratches his head and exits.* POTATO PLANT, SQUASH PLANT, *and* YAM PLANT *unfreeze.*)

POTATO PLANT/SQUASH PLANT/YAM PLANT (*singing*):

Wate mari, mari
Ha ha,
Wate mari, mari
Ha ha.

AKÍ (*entering*): Hello? Hello there?

(POTATO PLANT, SQUASH PLANT, *and* YAM PLANT *freeze once again.*)

AKÍ: Is anybody here? I know I heard singing.

(AKÍ *sits and rests. He plays his flute badly.* POTATO PLANT, SQUASH PLANT, *and* YAM PLANT *throw potatoes at him.*)

AKÍ: Hey, stop that!

POTATO PLANT: Man, you play awful!

AKÍ: You're talking plants!

SQUASH PLANT: Of course we are!

YAM PLANT: So what else is new?

AKÍ: You're the ones making all that racket.

POTATO PLANT: Racket?

SQUASH PLANT: Hey, man, we're the Noisy Vegetables!

YAM PLANT: We're the baddest veggies in the rainforest!

POTATO PLANT: We're loud and proud!

SQUASH PLANT: We were having a great time 'til you got here.

AKÍ: Look, I'm sorry.

YAM PLANT: You should be.

POTATO PLANT: No one invited you, man.

AKÍ: Look, I'm hungry. May I have something to eat?

POTATO PLANT: Don't give him a thing.

SQUASH PLANT: I don't trust him.

YAM PLANT: Why is your ankle bleeding?

AKÍ: I injured it escaping from the Fire Demons.

SQUASH PLANT/YAM PLANT/POTATO PLANT (*afraid*): The Fire Demons?

AKÍ: Yes, they're following me.

YAM PLANT: We've got to help him.

POTATO PLANT: He sorta looks familiar.

AKÍ: This was my grandmother's vegetable garden.

YAM PLANT: I knew it!

POTATO PLANT: We've been waiting for her.

SQUASH PLANT: We're ready to be picked and eaten!

POTATO PLANT: Yo, me first!

AKÍ: My grandmother is dead.

YAM PLANT: What?

AKÍ: It was the Fire Demons.

POTATO PLANT: That's sad, man.

SQUASH PLANT: We're sorry.

YAM PLANT: Here. This aloe plant will heal your wound.

AKÍ: I have to find my uncle, but I don't know how.

YAM PLANT: There's a magical canoe that could guide you to him.

AKÍ: Where is it?

YAM PLANT: Near the Meeting of the Waters. There is a great *kapok* tree at the river's edge. If you play your flute the *kapok* tree will reveal the magic canoe to you. All you have to do is climb aboard and paddle.

AKÍ: But I play awful.

POTATO PLANT: You should've practiced, man.

SQUASH PLANT: Yeah.

YAM PLANT: Just listen to what the mighty *kapok* plays and if you play it back, she will answer.

AKÍ: Why are you helping me?

YAM PLANT: We're afraid of the Fire Demons too.

AKÍ: Thank you.

(AKÍ *exits*)

POTATO PLANT/SQUASH PLANT/YAM PLANT (*singing*):

>*Wate mari, mari*
>*Ha ha,*
>*Wate mari, mari*
>*Ha ha.*

(AKÍ *crosses to the other side of the stage, where the* KAPOK TREE *stands.* PEREIRA *and* MAURICIO *enter. The scenes are taking place in different areas of the jungle, but are happening simultaneously onstage.*)

WAKOTE (*voice*): Akí, listen to the rainforest and learn. And one day it may teach you its power.

PEREIRA: He's around here somewhere.

MAURICIO: I thought I heard a party.

PEREIRA: In the middle of the jungle?

MAURICIO: There's the boy's footprints!

PEREIRA: We have him now!

MAURICIO: Look, there! Veggies!

(MAURICIO *reaches for a vegetable and he and* PEREIRA *are pummeled with vegetables. They exit.* AKÍ *stands before the* KAPOK TREE. *He plays badly.* MACAW *suddenly swoops down, striking* AKÍ.)

MACAW: Awful! Awful!

AKÍ: Hey, stop that! Stop that!

(MACAW *flies off.* AKÍ *tries again, but this time the* KAPOK TREE *plays a beautiful note, which* AKÍ *imitates. They begin to go back and forth until it becomes a musical moment. At last, the* KAPOK TREE *reveals a magic canoe to him.*)

AKÍ: The magic canoe! Thank you, Great Kapok.

(AKÍ *places* SLOTH *onto the* KAPOK TREE *and* SLOTH *snores peacefully.*)

AKÍ: Goodbye, old friend.

(*From the jungle canopy, the* JAGUAR KING'S *eyes appear. The* JAGUAR KING *chases after* AKÍ.)

AKÍ: Aagghhh!

(AKÍ *escapes in the canoe.*)

Scene 6

(*Night. The stars shine brightly. It is a peaceful night.* TWO BATS *fly by.* AKÍ *stops paddling.*)

WAKOTE (*voice*): *Akí, I have tried teaching you to be a pajé. And now when I need you, you are not ready. A pajé must fight alone, and his foes are much more frightening. You're still afraid of your own shadow.*

(*The* GHOSTS OF VILLAGERS *appear.*)

GHOST #1 (*voice*): Save us, Akí!

GHOST #2 (*voice*): Save us, Akí!

AKÍ: Grandmother? Grandfather?

GHOST #1: The entire jungle rose up in flames against us!

GHOST #2: We couldn't escape!

AKÍ: I mustn't speak to the dead!

GHOST #1: Don't leave us, Akí!

GHOST #2: Take us with you!

AKÍ: I can't! I don't know how!

PAXKE (*voice*): This emerald necklace will protect you from harm, but you must never take it off.

WAKOTE (*voice*): You are not ready—

ENCANTADO #1 (*voice*): Don't go there, chaah . . .

ENCANTADO #2 (*voice*): *Cobra Grande* lives there, chaah . . .

ENCANTADO #1 (*voice*): He'll devour you like he did your father . . .

GHOST #1: Join us, Akí!

GHOST #2: Join us!

AKÍ: Yes, I will!

(AKÍ *stands up in the canoe, ready to leap into the river.* ESTRELA, *the* STAR MAIDEN'S *face, appears in the moon.*)

ESTRELA (*singing*):

    Young Akí down below
    If you could wish
    What would you ask for?

AKÍ (*sadly*): I want everything as it was.

ESTRELA (*singing*):

    Young Akí down below

If you could wish
What would you ask for?

AKÍ (*sadly*): To be with my friends and family.

ESTRELA/AKÍ (*singing*):

The past remains behind us
The future lies ahead
There's nothing to hold onto
Let your dreams fly instead

ESTRELA: Akí, don't jump! Wait for me!

(*A star falls out of the sky. A* FROG PUPPET *appears, sitting on the edge of the canoe.*)

FROG PUPPET: Ribbit.

AKÍ: Who are you?

FROG PUPPET: I am Estrela, the Star Maiden.

AKÍ: Star Maiden?

FROG PUPPET: Yes, ribbit.

AKÍ: But you're a frog.

FROG PUPPET: Well, that's true, I am.

(*The* FROG PUPPET *zaps an imaginary insect with her tongue.*)

AKÍ: Are you an evil spirit or a good spirit?

FROG PUPPET: I'm a good spirit. I can change form. Shall I show you?

(*Music. The* FROG PUPPET *transforms into* ESTRELA, *the* STAR MAIDEN. *She is a beautiful young Indian girl.*)

AKÍ: You're a girl!

ESTRELA: Well, that's what Star Maidens are.

AKÍ: How'd you do that?

ESTRELA: I simply close my eyes, imagine what I want to become. And when I open my eyes that is what I am. Would you like me to change back?

AKÍ: No! I like you better this way. I mean, you look a lot nicer, you're not so slimy, and your eyes aren't on the side of your head.

ESTRELA: Thank you. Ribbit. Oh, excuse me. I've been watching you.

AKÍ: You've been watching me?

ESTRELA: Yes. From up there. There's a big hole where one can see below.

AKÍ: A hole in the sky? No.

ESTRELA: Yes. Long ago, an armadillo made it by burrowing so deeply into a cloud he fell through to your world. I've seen the awful things you've endured and I want to help you.

AKÍ: How can you? I'm doomed. The Fire Demons will make sure of that.

ESTRELA: Come with me to the sky world. There you can think clearly. Take my hand and leap up with me.

(ESTRELA and AKÍ leap into the sky world.)

ESTRELA: This is my home!

AKÍ: From up here everything is so clear, Estrela. The jungle looks so small and delicate, like a spider's web in the morning light.

ESTRELA: You can stay if you want.

AKÍ: Stay here?

ESTRELA: With me. No one ever goes hungry, lonely, or cold here.

AKÍ: And what of the Fire Demons?

ESTRELA: They'll never find us.

AKÍ (upset): But they'll find my Uncle Wakote, won't they? They'll burn more trees in the rainforest. And ruin more lives.

ESTRELA: What do you expect? That's what humans do.

AKÍ: But I'm human.

ESTRELA: Only half of you is.

AKÍ: What are you saying?

ESTRELA: Your father was an Encantado.

AKÍ: That's just a silly old story my Uncle Wakote made up.

ESTRELA: Are you sure? Hasn't the rainforest taught you anything?

AKÍ: I've learned lots of things. But how can I be an Enchanted Being? I don't even know how to become one.

ESTRELA: Simply close your eyes. Imagine what you want to become and that's what you will be.

AKÍ: That's it?

ESTRELA: Yup.

AKÍ: Estrela, I wish I could stay here. I couldn't live with myself if something were to happen to my Uncle Wakote. I have to go back.

ESTRELA: Then remember this. Your father's flute can summon the power of the river. Look there—

(WAKOTE enters.)

AKÍ: It's my Uncle Wakote!

(PEREIRA and MAURICIO stalk WAKOTE. The JAGUAR KING's eyes appear, scaring them.)

ESTRELA: The Jaguar King!

AKÍ: And the Fire Demons! I have to save my uncle!

ESTRELA: Okay, I'll come with you!

AKÍ: Estrela, it's too dangerous.

ESTRELA: It's my choice!

(ESTRELA kisses him on the lips.)

AKÍ: What's that for?

ESTRELA: For good luck. Let's go!

(AKÍ and ESTRELA leap back into the forest. Just then the JAGUAR KING enters, circling AKÍ. The JAGUAR KING leaps at AKÍ but is hurt.)

AKÍ: Aaagghhh!

ESTRELA: Akí!

AKÍ: It's the Jaguar King!

JAGUAR KING: Aagghh! Oooh . . .

(AKÍ pushes the JAGUAR KING off.)

AKÍ: He's burned.

ESTRELA: Akí, what are you doing?

JAGUAR KING: Get away from me!

AKÍ: I've got to help him.

(AKÍ begins to treat the JAGUAR KING's wound.)

AKÍ: If you don't let me heal you, you will die. I know how. Some very noisy vegetables taught me.

JAGUAR KING: Why are you doing this?

AKÍ: Because I know how it feels to be hunted.

JAGUAR KING: I remember you, boy.

AKÍ: You remember me?

JAGUAR KING: I saw your mother battle a Fire Demon once. You were placed on a river shore. I walked right up to you and looked into your eyes.

AKÍ: Why didn't you eat me?

JAGUAR KING: Because I understood your loss. I would not have harmed an orphan.

(Voices are heard off in the distance.)

ESTRELA: It's the Fire Demons!

AKÍ: We've got to go!

(AKÍ, ESTRELA, and the JAGUAR KING run off. PEREIRA and MAURICIO enter.)

MAURICIO: Senhor Pereira, it's the boy's footprints! They lead this way!

PEREIRA: Good. Ready my torch.

MAURICIO: But why, senhor?

PEREIRA: Because I'm going to burn this forest down. Nobody cheats me!

(They exit.)

Scene 7

(WAKOTE enters. He sniffs something in the air. MACAW flies while SLOTH holds on for dear life.)

MACAW: Awful! Awful!

SLOTH: Hurry, Macaw! Hurry!

MACAW: I'm going as fast as I can!

SLOTH: They'll soon be here!

WAKOTE: The Fire Demons have set the trees on fire!

(AKÍ and ESTRELA enter.)

AKÍ: Uncle Wakote!

WAKOTE: Akí, what are you doing here? Who is she?

AKÍ: This is Estrela.

WAKOTE: The Star Maiden.

AKÍ: Yes, she took me to the sky world. An armadillo made a—

WAKOTE: —Akí, there isn't time! We've got to warn the village!

AKÍ: Which village?

WAKOTE: The one near the river. The fire will reach them before they can escape! We've got to save them!

(PEREIRA enters, holding his torch and machete. He grabs ESTRELA, holding her as a hostage. MAURICIO follows.)

ESTRELA: Akí!

PEREIRA: Don't move!

MAURICIO: Senhor, you're scaring the girl!

PEREIRA: Take me to those emeralds, boy!

MAURICIO: Please let her go!

PEREIRA: Not until I get what's coming to me!

MAURICIO: You're hurting her!

(MAURICIO *charges* PEREIRA. PEREIRA *strikes* MAURICIO *down.*)

PEREIRA: You fool! Now you'll get nothing! You deserve to burn with all these savages!

(ESTRELA *transforms into a* FROG, *surprising* PEREIRA.)

ESTRELA: Ribbit!

PEREIRA: Aagghh!

(ESTRELA *transforms back.*)

ESTRELA: The fire's about to reach the village!

(WAKOTE *charges* PEREIRA *and they battle.*)

WAKOTE: Warn the villagers!

ESTRELA: Akí, play your flute!

AKÍ: Here goes nothing!

(AKÍ *begins to play his flute. He still plays badly. The echo of flutes begins and suddenly the river starts to glow. Several* ENCANTADOS *appear.*)

ESTRELA: Akí, you've summoned the Encantados!

AKÍ: Tell the villagers to grab hold! The Encantados will take them to safety!

(Meanwhile, PEREIRA *is just about to defeat* WAKOTE.)

PEREIRA: I want those emeralds!

WAKOTE: Akí!

(AKÍ *charges* PEREIRA.)

AKÍ: Aagghhh!

PEREIRA: Aagghhh!

(AKÍ *and* PEREIRA *fall into the river. The river transforms as* PEREIRA *and* AKÍ *battle deep below the waters. Just as* PEREIRA *is about to defeat* AKÍ, COBRA GRANDE *emerges, taking* PEREIRA *and* AKÍ *below into the abyss. As the lights fade an* ENCANTADO *is seen swimming away.*)

PEREIRA: *Cobra Grande, no!*

Scene 8

(WAKOTE *and* ESTRELA *enter. A* VILLAGE WARRIOR *looks on.*)

ESTRELA: Akí? Akí?

WAKOTE: We've searched everywhere.

ESTRELA: Akí?

WAKOTE: But he's nowhere to be found. *Cobra Grande* must have taken him.

ESTRELA: No!

WAKOTE: I'm sorry, *Estrela.*

(AKÍ *enters, coughing. He spits out a small fish.*)

ESTRELA: Akí!

WAKOTE: You're alive!

AKÍ: I had to fight the Fire Demon and then *Cobra Grande* too.

ESTRELA: How did you escape?

AKÍ: I turned into an *Encantado* and swam away as fast as I could!

WAKOTE: *Akí,* you saved the village! You saved us all!

ESTRELA: What a sight! *Encantados* everywhere!

WAKOTE: I was wrong about you. You have become a great *pajé.* Your mother and father would be proud.

(WAKOTE *gives to* AKÍ *his shaman's headdress.*)

AKÍ: You taught me, uncle, despite my foolishness.

WAKOTE: But where's your emerald necklace?

AKÍ: Right here. I got it back. *Estrela* saved my life.

ESTRELA: That's what Star Maidens do.

AKÍ: Thank you for helping me.

(AKÍ *places the emerald necklace on* ESTRELA.)

ESTRELA (*to* WAKOTE): What will you do now?

WAKOTE: We'll go back to our village.

AKÍ: The Fire Demons destroyed it. Grandmother and Grandfather didn't make it. Others are scattered throughout the rainforest.

WAKOTE: Then we must go find them. Start over again, but far away from the Fire Demons.

AKÍ: We will never escape them. They're part of the rainforest.

(MAURICIO *enters. He holds* AKÍ'S *flute.* VILLAGE WARRIOR *points his weapon at* MAURICIO.)

ESTRELA: A Fire Demon!

MAURICIO: Don't harm me. I'm sorry for causing you so much pain, boy. It isn't right what we did. Can you ever forgive me? This belongs to you.

(MAURICIO *hands the flute to* AKÍ.)

WAKOTE: I don't trust him.

(*He turns to leave, but* AKÍ *grabs* MAURICIO'S *shoulder.*)

MAURICIO: What is it?

(AKÍ *places his arm on* MAURICIO'S *shoulder.* MAURICIO *does the same thing.*)

MAURICIO: Thank you!

AKÍ: Fire Demons can change, Uncle.

WAKOTE: I do not understand their ways.

AKÍ: But I do. They need to listen to the music of the rainforest. Like I have.

WAKOTE: Will they learn?

ESTRELA: Look, there. Off in the distance. Smoke.

AKÍ: Another fire begins.

CURTAIN

Designer's Response

Immediately upon reading *The Magic Rainforest* I began to consider how best to support the central elements of the script: the forest, the river, and the flora and fauna of rainforests. The discovery of Margaret Mee's book, *In Search of Flowers of the Amazon Forests*—a collection of essays, delicate watercolors, and pencil sketches that record her expeditions to the Amazon rainforest—provided a range of images. In my mind these images quickly connected with the theme of the script: progress means one thing to those perpetrating it and something else entirely to those affected by it. Those who destroy the forest have a mistaken sense of entitlement that they feel gives them the right to interrupt the circle of life that maintains that environment.

Images

Rustic and luminous etchings
Pink dolphins as water spirits
Emerald necklace, a talisman of power
Fire demon mask
Luminous eyes
River and waterfall

Ghosts of villagers
Barren, dead trees
Fire
Kapok tree
Frogs, bats, insects
Cobra

To begin the design process with strong graphic textures and shapes I used origami paper to interpret the environment in a collage (plate A) before translating it into a preliminary design sketch (plates B and C).

Resources

Cardoza y Aragón, Luís. *Mexican Art Today.* Trans. Asa Zatz. Mexico: Fondo de Cultura Económica, 1996.

Mee, Margaret. *In Search of Flowers of the Amazon Forests.* Ed. Tony Morrison. London: Nonesuch Expeditions, 1988.

Plate A: Collage of an abstraction of forest.

Plate B: Forest setting (early).

Plate C: Forest setting (destruction).

Two Donuts

José Cruz González

Originally commissioned by Childsplay,
Tempe, Arizona

Where Do the Tears of Children Go?

Where do the tears of children go?
Are they wiped away by a mother's loving hand?
Do they become absorbed in a father's shirt sleeve?
Or do they evaporate in the warm sunlight of day?

Maybe the tears of children fall on earth
Turning into little water streams capturing light
Or maybe they become great rivers flowing towards the open sea

Into an ocean of tears, maybe?

—José Cruz González

Characters

PEPITO: a small boy. He has dark curly hair and loves eating donuts.

ABUELA: PEPITO's grandmother. She loves to sing and tell stories.

PANADERO: our storyteller and local barrio baker. He wears a mustache, a baker's hat, and an apron.

MADRE: PEPITO's mom. She looks a lot like ABUELA, only younger.

MODESTO and RIDÍCULO: two Guatemalan worry dolls dressed in Armani suits and ties.

LITTLE GIRL FOOTSTEPS: a girl with the gift of being able to transform into a coconut and rock, or just about anything, by holding her breath. She is a Super Agent Spy and Protector of the Last Flower in *Cuate-Malo*.

COMANDANTE BOOTS: the evil dictator of *Cuate-Malo*. He wears sunglasses, a military uniform, boots, and lots of medals.

SERGEANT BOTAS: an army sergeant. He is COMANDANTE BOOTS' sidekick.

TIRADO: a single tire. That is all that is left of him. He is a very nervous type.

THE GREAT SEA TORTUGA: a wise, giant sea turtle. She leads the resistance against COMANDANTE BOOTS.

and . . .

ARM, EYE, NOSE, BI-PLANE PAIR OF SHOES, BABY MANATEE, LUNA, BUMBLE ZAPPER, and other characters seen throughout the play.

Production Note

The play may be presented several ways: with three actor-puppeteers (two male and one female), or with a larger cast of up to twelve actors with some double casting (seven males and five females).

SCENE: *A bakery in the heart of the barrio.*

AT RISE: *Mambo music plays as* PANADERO, *the local barrio baker, appears.*
He wears a big mustache, a baker's hat, and an apron.
He balances a stack of pink donut boxes.

PANADERO: ¡Quihubo! I'm *Panadero*, the local baker. Each morning before the sun rises, I'm busy baking *pan dulce*. That's sweet bread. My customers have got to have their *pan dulce* with their *leche* or *cafecito* at breakfast. When I bake I listen to the radio in *español*. I love to sing loudly, and sometimes even the neighborhood dogs join in. Every now and then I even dance the *mambo*! I can't help it. It starts at my feet and everything else follows. ¡*Mambo*!

(PANADERO *presents an old wooden house with porch and steps. The house sits in the old part of town. A tire hangs from a tree and an old bucket rests in the garden, while a used pair of shoes, newly shined, rest nearby.*)

PANADERO: I have a story to tell you. It's about a little boy named *Pepito*. *Pepito* loved eating donuts. My delicious donuts, baked fresh—the scent would reach him next door where he lived and he would instantly arrive at my bakery.

(PEPITO *appears.*)

PEPITO: ¡Hola, Señor *Panadero*!

PANADERO: ¡Buenos días, *Pepito*! He was a small boy with black curly hair and eyes as dark as a moon's eclipse. He would always order—

PEPITO: ¡Dos *donas, por favor*!

PANADERO: Two donuts.

PEPITO: ¡Gracias!

PANADERO: ¡De nada! One for him and the other for his *abuela*.

(ABUELA, *Pepito's grandmother, appears.*)

ABUELA: *Pepito*, ¿qué me trajiste hoy? [What did you bring me today?]

PEPITO: What else, *Abuela*?

ABUELA: Oh, yummy, ¡una *dona*!

PANADERO: *Pepito* and *Abuela* would sit on their porch steps and delight in my sweet creations. (*Admiring the garden.*) Oh, what a lovely garden *Abuela* has.

PEPITO: Mmm, good!

ABUELA: Mmm, ¡muy buena!

PANADERO: His *abuela* would tell him stories of the old country, where jaguars roamed, eagles soared, and rivers flowed endless like a poet's imagination. They shared a language all their own.

ABUELA: *Pepito*, there's a tale about how *la luna* came to be. Have you heard it?

PEPITO: No, *Abuela*.

ABUELA: Then I'll tell it to you. Long ago there was a God of Lightning who became very hungry.

(The GOD OF LIGHTNING *appears. He may be played by* PANADERO.)

ABUELA: His stomach rumbled like the earth when it shakes. He searched the heavens for something to eat, but found only—

GOD OF LIGHTNING: ¡Masa!

PEPITO: That's dough!

ABUELA: ¡Muy bien! The God of Lightning wasn't sure what do with the *masa*. So he rolled it into a ball, but it accidentally fell.

GOD OF LIGHTNING: Oh-oh.

ABUELA: So he spread it flat like a pancake, using a giant redwood tree—

PEPITO: —Abuela, a redwood tree so big?

ABUELA: And threw it onto *el sol* to cook! Soon the *masa* began to bake.

GOD OF LIGHTNING: ¡Masa, masa, masa!

ABUELA: The smell was so delicious. The hungry god couldn't wait so he reached for it, but he burned his hand instead, yelling a great *grito*.

GOD OF LIGHTNING: Aaaghhh!

ABUELA: He threw the *tortilla* high into the sky, where it stuck.

PEPITO: No way!

ABUELA: And that's how *la luna* came to be. But every now and then, that God of Lightning still gets hungry and takes a giant bite out of that big *tortilla* moon. That's why you sometimes see it half-eaten!

PEPITO: Abuela, is your story true?

ABUELA: ¿Tú qué crees? [What do you think?]

PEPITO: I think eating *donas* is always fun with you!

PEPITO and ABUELA: Breakfast of *campeones*! [Champions!]

(PEPITO *burps*.)

ABUELA: *¡Ese es mi nietecito!* [That's my little grandson!]

PANADERO: *Pepito* loved his *abuela* very much.

(ABUELA *crosses into an empty lot. She picks up garbage and an old boot, throwing it into the trash can.*)

ABUELA: Oh, look at this neighborhood. *Necesita mucho amor.* [It needs a lot of love.]

PEPITO: *Abuela*, don't start. We've got enough work to do already.

ABUELA: Once we've fixed up our *casita*, I bet we could make the whole neighborhood *bonito* with a little paint and *flores*.

PEPITO: *Abuela*, our street has got too many potholes. Most of the houses are boarded up, and the people living here are all strangers. What's the use of fixing things up if they're only going to get wrecked anyway?

ABUELA: This is our new home. *Debemos estar muy orgullosos.* [We should take pride in it.]

PEPITO: Don't say the "T" word, *Abuela*.

ABUELA: *Bueno*, moving into an old *casa* does take a lot of *trabajo*.

PEPITO: You said the "T" word! *Trabajo*, work, yuck!

ABUELA: A little *trabajo* doesn't hurt anyone.

PEPITO: But a lot of *trabajo* does. It's not good for little kids to work so much.

ABUELA: *Es verano y no hay escuela.* [It's summer and there's no school.]

PEPITO: But by the time I start third grade, I'll be all used up! No good for *nada*! An empty shell.

ABUELA: *Trabajo* makes you an *hombre*!

PEPITO: *Trabajo* makes you an old *hombre*!

ABUELA: *Quizás tienes razón.* [Maybe you're right.] Maybe I have been working you a little—

PEPITO: —too much? *Abuela*, I think it's time we went to the beach.

ABUELA: *¿La playa?*

PEPITO: Please just say "yes"! *¡Por favor!*

ABUELA: *Bueno pues*, okay! [Well]

PEPITO: You really mean it?

ABUELA: *¡Es una promesa!* [It's a promise!]

PEPITO: Hurray, *Abuela*! Maybe I'll even get to see my little *tortuga* turtle swimming in the sea!

ABUELA: I'm glad you and your *papá* let her go free.

PEPITO: I bet she's all grown up. Well, I'm ready!

ABUELA: *Pepito, tenemos un poco de trabajo que hacer. Las flores necesitan agua.* [Pepito, we've got a little work to do. The flowers need watering.]

PEPITO: Okay. *Flores.* Water.

(PEPITO *waters the garden with an old bucket, while* ABUELA *gathers flowers.*)

ABUELA: I brought two things with me when I left my beloved homeland.

PEPITO: Memories of your country . . .

ABUELA/PEPITO: . . . and a pocketful of seeds.

PEPITO: *Abuela,* did you feel sad leaving *Guatemala?*

ABUELA: Oh, *sí.* When I was a little girl I could run barefoot everywhere and pick flowers whenever I wanted, but then *soldados con armas y botas* came and took everything away.

PEPITO: Soldiers with guns and boots?

ABUELA: I never looked at their faces, just their shiny new *botas.* I was always hiding from them. They stole my country and they broke my heart.

PEPITO: I would have fought them.

ABUELA: Many of our people tried, but the soldiers made them disappear.

PEPITO: Did they use magic?

ABUELA: No. They used the cover of *la noche* to come into people's homes and take them away.

PEPITO: I would've run out of there as fast as I could.

ABUELA: *Eso es lo que yo hice.* [That's what I did.] I listened to my heart and I came here so our *familia* would have a better future. That's why it's important you water these sweet *flores.* They remind me of the good things we brought with us. Always remember, *Pepito,* to trust what's inside your heart.

PEPITO: I'm all done watering!

ABUELA: *Ándale.* [Go on.] Go get your shorties and towel and I'll pack us a *lonche.*

PEPITO: I'm going to build the biggest sand castle ever!

(PEPITO *rushes into the house.* ABUELA *sweeps the porch steps and sings a lively song in Spanish.* ABUELA *stops sweeping.*)

ABUELA: Oh, my . . .

(*She sits on the porch to catch her breath.*)

PANADERO: Pepito and Abuela never did get to the beach that day. You see, Abuela became very ill. (PANADERO *covers* ABUELA *with a piece of fabric.*) And soon she didn't even get out of bed. Days passed and nights came, and Abuela died. She left behind a very sad, *triste*, Pepito.

(ABUELA *and* PANADERO *exit.* PEPITO *enters in a white shirt and clip-on tie. He holds one of* ABUELA's *flowers. He sits on the porch steps and covers his face. A silhouette of Pepito's* MADRE *appears in the doorway.*)

MADRE: ¿Pepito?

PEPITO: . . .

MADRE: Pepito, where are you?

PEPITO: I'm out here, 'Amá.

MADRE: Come inside the house.

PANADERO: Pepito's mother and father were away at work most of the time. Abuela had always looked after him, since he was a baby. Now he would have to take care of himself.

MADRE: Pepito, it isn't safe out there.

PANADERO: Abuela would always give him a dollar on Friday mornings and send him to my bakery to buy two donuts, but now that would change too. (*To* PEPITO.) Buenos días, Pepito.

PEPITO: Hi, Panadero.

PANADERO: I'm sorry about Abuela.

PEPITO: . . .

PANADERO: Her garden still looks beautiful.

PEPITO: . . .

PANADERO: I brought you two donuts. I thought you might want to share one with your *mamá*. I bet she'd love to hear one of your *abuela's* stories.

PEPITO (*to himself*): My 'amá and papá are too busy for stories.

(PANADERO *places the donut bag near* PEPITO.)

PANADERO: Well, I—

PEPITO: Panadero, when you die, where do you go?

PANADERO: That's difficult to answer. Some people believe you go to heaven.

PEPITO: Is that where my *abuela* went?

PANADERO: Isn't that where you want her to be?

PEPITO: No. No, I want her here with me.

PANADERO: Well, maybe she is.

PEPITO (*sarcastically*): I don't see her anywhere.

PANADERO: That's because she's inside you in your *corazón*. You've got so many good memories of her. And you have her *cuentos* too.

PEPITO: Her stories?

PANADERO: Her stories are like seeds. They'll grow in your heart and bloom. And when you share them with others it will be like *Abuela* is sitting on the porch steps right beside you listening.

PEPITO: She shouldn't have left me.

PANADERO: She didn't have a choice.

PEPITO: She was going to take me to the beach.

PANADERO: I bet she would have if she could.

PEPITO: But she never did. She lied. She broke her promise!

PANADERO: Well, I better go. I've got tomorrow's bread to bake. Goodbye, *Pepito*. Over the next few days, *Pepito* kept to himself. You could see a dark cloud forming over his head. Thunder and lightning too.

MADRE: *Pepito*, if you're staying outside then water *Abuela's* garden.

PEPITO: . . .

MADRE: Answer me, young man!

PEPITO: Okay! (PEPITO *kicks a bucket. He then picks it up and begins to water the garden. A bumblebee buzzes by, circling and annoying* PEPITO.) Get out of here, you dumb bumblebee! Get! (PEPITO *gets stung.*) Ouch! You stung me, you dumb bug! What's the use of watering this stupid old garden! She's not even here to see it! Everything in this garden is *estúpido*! This neighborhood is *estúpido*! These flowers are *estúpidas*! ¡Estúpidas!

(PEPITO *stomps on the garden flowers, crushing them. He runs into the house.*)

PANADERO: That night, *Pepito* sat on the couch all by himself reading a book and watching TV before bedtime.

(*The glow of a television appears, illuminating* PEPITO's *face. He looks at a book with a picture of a manatee on the cover. The sound of sirens and gunfire is heard.*)

MADRE (*offstage*): *Pepito*, turn off the TV!

PEPITO: Okay, 'Amá!

(PEPITO *turns the television off, but the sound of gunfire and sirens continues.*)

MADRE: Didn't I tell you to turn that thing off?

PEPITO: But I did!

MADRE: ¡Ay, Dios mío! Pepito, get down! Get down now!

(PEPITO *sits on the floor.*)

PANADERO: Pepito sat in the darkness as the sound of gunfire and sirens grew louder. Most nights in the neighborhood are peaceful and calm, but on occasion violence can strike, deadly like a rattlesnake's bite. Pepito and his family turn out the lights and TV and sit in the darkness, waiting until it is safe. That night Pepito went to sleep with a troubled heart.

PEPITO: Estúpido neighborhood!

(PEPITO *falls asleep on the couch. The television fades up as* ABUELA *appears on its screen.*)

ABUELA: Pepito . . .

(PEPITO *turns over in his sleep.*)

PEPITO: Masa . . .

ABUELA: Pepito . . . (PEPITO *turns over again and snores.*) Pepito . . . (PEPITO *releases a little gas.*) ¡Ese es mi nietecito! [That's my little grandson!]

PEPITO: ¡Abuela! What are you doing in the TV?

ABUELA: I've come to give you something.

(*A small Guatemalan pouch magically appears in* PEPITO's *hand.*)

PEPITO: Wow! What is it?

ABUELA: Un regalo. A gift. Now, come give me a kiss.

PEPITO: I don't want to. (PEPITO *opens the pouch, removing two small figurines.*) What are they?

ABUELA: They're Guatemalan worry dolls. They're supposed to help you when you're worried about something.

PEPITO: I'm not worried about anything.

ABUELA: You place them under your pillow before you go to sleep and in the morning all your worries will be gone.

PEPITO: Can they bring you back to life?

ABUELA: No.

PEPITO: Then what good are they?

ABUELA: Make a wish and you'll see.

(*The television fades out.* PEPITO *throws the* WORRY DOLLS *to the floor; a moment later he places them under his pillow. He goes back to sleep, talking to himself and snoring. Music. The moon appears over the house. From under* PEPITO's *pillow appears a* WORRY DOLL *named* RIDÍCULO. *He wears a Guatemalan Armani suit and tie, a New Yorker–type.*)

RIDÍCULO: Free at last! Yo, Modesto, hurry up!

(PEPITO turns over in his sleep, smashing MODESTO as he enters.)

MODESTO: I'm right behind—agghhh! Ridículo, get this kid off of me!

RIDÍCULO: I got your back!

(RIDÍCULO pulls PEPITO's hair.)

PEPITO: Ouch! ¿Abuela?

(MODESTO, Ridículo's brother, appears. He also wears a Guatemalan Armani suit and tie.)

MODESTO: Do we look like your abuela?

RIDÍCULO: Yeah, do we?

PEPITO: Who are you?

RIDÍCULO: I'm Ridículo.

MODESTO: I'm Modesto.

MODESTO/RIDÍCULO: And we're the Worry Doll Brothers!

(They high-five each other.)

RIDÍCULO: Oh, yeah!

MODESTO: Lookin' good!

PEPITO: So?

RIDÍCULO: So?!

MODESTO: So?!

RIDÍCULO: Are youse for real, kid?

MODESTO: Youse ain't playing with a full deck, are youse?

PEPITO: What are you talking about?

RIDÍCULO: Spell it out for him, Modesto.

MODESTO: Okay, kid, this is how it works. You make a wish and we make the worry go away. No questions asked.

RIDÍCULO: Nobody gets hurt.

MODESTO: Nobody sees nothing. Capiche?

PEPITO: Capiche?

RIDÍCULO: So what's your first wish gonna be?

PEPITO: You mean I have more than one?

RIDÍCULO: You got three.

MODESTO: So youse want somebody rubbed out?

PEPITO: Rubbed out?

RIDÍCULO: Youse want somebody to sleep with the fishes?

PEPITO: Sleep with the—

MODESTO: Kid, we ain't got all day!

RIDÍCULO: Time is money!

PEPITO: I . . . I . . . I wish to go to *Guatemala!*

RIDÍCULO/MODESTO: Guatemala?

PEPITO: That's right: *Guatemala.*

RIDÍCULO: You ever heard of it, *Modesto?*

MODESTO: Not on your life, *Ridículo.*

PEPITO: I'd rather go there than stay in this crummy old neighborhood.

MODESTO: Let me explain this to you, kid.

RIDÍCULO: It's real simple—

MODESTO/RIDÍCULO: We don't go to Guatemala!

PEPITO: But aren't you Guatemalan worry dolls?

RIDÍCULO: Whoa, hold on there, paisano!

MODESTO: Who says we're from Guatemala?

PEPITO: Well, aren't you?

RIDÍCULO: We may look like we're from Guatemala . . .

MODESTO/RIDÍCULO: But we're from New York.

(MODESTO's *cell phone rings.*)

MODESTO: Hold it there, cowboy. Hello?

RIDÍCULO: Who is it?

MODESTO: The boss.

(MODESTO *and* RIDÍCULO *listen to the phone together.*)

RIDÍCULO: He's right here.

MODESTO: You want him to—

RIDÍCULO: Right now?

MODESTO: But he's got three—

RIDÍCULO: Consider it done.

MODESTO/RIDÍCULO: No problemo.

(MODESTO *puts his cell phone away.*)

MODESTO: So we're on a mission, kid.

PEPITO: A mission?

RIDÍCULO: We gotta take you to *Cuate-Malo*.

PEPITO: *Cuate-Malo?* I don't want to go to there.

MODESTO: It's just like Guatemala. Right, *Ridículo?*

RIDÍCULO: Oh, yeah, youse could say that. They're like identical twin countries.

MODESTO: Yeah, tropical and stuff.

RIDÍCULO: Coconuts and grass skirts.

PEPITO: But doesn't *Cuate-Malo* mean "the bad twin"?

MODESTO: Look, kid, you gotta save a country.

PEPITO: Me?

RIDÍCULO: Except, you're gonna have to be real careful.

PEPITO: Careful?

RIDÍCULO: 'Cause it's risky.

PEPITO: Risky?

MODESTO: And dangerous.

PEPITO: Dangerous?

MODESTO: Get ready, kid.

PEPITO: But I don't want to go to *Cuate-Malo!*

RIDÍCULO: Don't forget your donuts!

(Thunder and lightning. PEPITO, MODESTO, and RIDÍCULO are sucked into the television set. It sprouts wings and flies away.)

PANADERO: Pepito was swept up into the sky on a chariot with wings heading toward a mysterious land called *Cuate-Malo*, The Bad Twin! He didn't know what he'd find. He didn't know what they wanted from him. He didn't even know how dangerous it would be.

(The television set crash-lands. PEPITO stands in a tropical jungle. Behind him is a volcanic mountain, which occasionally releases rings of smoke and a little gas.)

PEPITO: Modesto? Ridículo? Where am I?

(LITTLE GIRL FOOTSTEPS' face appears in a coconut hanging from a palm tree.)

LITTLE GIRL FOOTSTEPS: Be quiet, you!

PEPITO: Who said that?

LITTLE GIRL FOOTSTEPS (her face appears on a rock): Shhh!

PEPITO: How do you do that? (Her face disappears. PEPITO lifts up a rock. A flower springs up instantly.) Wow!

(LITTLE GIRL FOOTSTEPS' *face reappears in the coconut. She holds out an old bucket and starts to water the flower.*)

LITTLE GIRL FOOTSTEPS: I'll tell you my secret but you can't tell anyone. I hold my breath and disappear!

PEPITO: Yeah, right!

LITTLE GIRL FOOTSTEPS: That way they won't find me.

PEPITO: Who?

LITTLE GIRL FOOTSTEPS: Put that rock back this instant!

PEPITO: Not until you tell me what I'm doing here!

(*The sound of boots marching is heard off in the distance.*)

COMANDANTE BOOTS/SERGEANT BOTAS: Your left. Your left. That's why your mother packed up and left. Your left. Your left.

LITTLE GIRL FOOTSTEPS: Oh, no, they know you're here!

PEPITO: Who cares!

LITTLE GIRL FOOTSTEPS: You better hide!

PEPITO: I'm not moving 'til you start talking!

LITTLE GIRL FOOTSTEPS: Oh, you're a stubborn *muchacho*! The Great Sea *Tortuga* made a big mistake choosing you! How are you going to save *Cuate-Malo*?

PEPITO: I'm not saving *Cuate-Malo*!

LITTLE GIRL FOOTSTEPS: Hide! They're here!

(LITTLE GIRL FOOTSTEPS *places the rock back, covering the flower. She disappears.*)

PEPITO: Wait! Come back, you! Oh-oh!

(PEPITO *hides. Fanfare.* COMANDANTE BOOTS—*wearing sunglasses, military uniform, large boots, and lots of medals—and* SERGEANT BOTAS—*wearing a large pair of army boots—march in together.*)

COMANDANTE BOOTS: Halt!

SERGEANT BOTAS: Attention!

COMANDANTE BOOTS: Sound-off!

SERGEANT BOTAS: One! *Comandante* Boots, I'm ready and accounted for, sir!

COMANDANTE BOOTS: Good! Where is the boy, Sergeant *Botas*?

SERGEANT BOTAS: Boy, *Comandante*?

COMANDANTE BOOTS: Our mortal enemy, *idiota*! Go find him now, you!

SERGEANT BOTAS: Yes, sir! Hut! Hut! Hut!

(SERGEANT BOTAS *marches out.* PEPITO *pops up his head.* COMANDANTE BOOTS *sniffs the air.*)

COMANDANTE BOOTS: I smell boy. Boy?

PEPITO: . . .

(PEPITO *quickly hides somewhere else as* COMANDANTE BOOTS *searches for him.*)

COMANDANTE BOOTS: Boy?

PEPITO: . . .

COMANDANTE BOOTS: Come out, come out, wherever you are! (COMANDANTE BOOTS *finds nothing.*) I know you're hiding somewhere! Why must you play this silly game? It's only a matter of time, you know? I'll find you, and when I do, you'll wish you had never wished to come to *Cuate-Malo!* Boy? (COMANDANTE BOOTS *kicks the rock. The beautiful flower springs up.* COMANDANTE BOOTS *has a panic attack.*) Oh, no! A flower! Sergeant Botas! Sergeant Botas! (COMANDANTE BOOTS *walks around in a daze, almost kicking the old water bucket.*) I almost kicked the bucket!

(SERGEANT BOTAS *runs in.*)

SERGEANT BOTAS: What is it, *Comandante* Boots?

COMANDANTE BOOTS: It's a— It's a—

SERGEANT BOTAS: Oh, a flower! It's so beautiful!

COMANDANTE BOOTS: ¡*Exactamente!* Step on it, *idiota!*

SERGEANT BOTAS: ¡*A sus órdenes, Comandante!* ¡*Estúpida!* [At your orders, Commander! Stupid flower!]

(SERGEANT BOTAS *quickly stomps on the flower, crushing it.*)

COMANDANTE BOOTS (*to himself*): This boy is cleverer than I thought. He must have planted that flower to trick me, leaving that bucket for me to kick! (*To* SERGEANT BOTAS.) I want this whole field swept for buckets and seeds!

SERGEANT BOTAS: Seeds, *mi Comandante?*

COMANDANTE BOOTS: *Sí,* seeds!

SERGEANT BOTAS: ¡*Sí, mi Comandante!* [Yes, Commander!]

COMANDANTE BOOTS: Double the patrols, triple the defense budget, ask for more foreign aid! I want this boy captured immediately!

SERGEANT BOTAS: More patrols are on their way, sir!

COMANDANTE BOOTS/SERGEANT BOTAS: Your left. Your left. That's why your mother packed up and left. Your left. Your left—

(*They march off together.* LITTLE GIRL FOOTSTEPS *appears as a rock.*)

PEPITO: That guy's messed up. Who is he?

LITTLE GIRL FOOTSTEPS (*appears as a coconut*): A very bad pair of boots. He hates everything that's beautiful. Like white clouds against a blue sky, magnificent spider webs, and flowers. Especially flowers. (LITTLE GIRL FOOTSTEPS *appears as a rock.*) Oh, this one's stomped to bits, which means there's only one left in the whole country. Thanks to you! The Great Sea *Tortuga* shouldn't have picked you!

(LITTLE GIRL FOOTSTEPS *appears as a coconut.*)

PEPITO: Hey you, stop that! You're making me dizzy! Who are you, anyway?

LITTLE GIRL FOOTSTEPS: I'm Little Girl Footsteps, Protector of the Last Flower in *Cuate-Malo* and Super Agent Spy!

PEPITO: You're on my complaint list, Footsteps Girl!

LITTLE GIRL FOOTSTEPS: Oh, I'm scared!

(LITTLE GIRL FOOTSTEPS *appears as a rock for a moment and then disappears.*)

PEPITO: Hey! Where'd you go? (*Shouting.*) I want to see this Great Sea *Tortuga* now! I got some things to say, like, why am I here?

LITTLE GIRL FOOTSTEPS (*appears as a coconut*): You don't have to shout. The Great Sea *Tortuga* is hiding where *Comandante* Boots' navy can't find her. You've got a long and dangerous journey ahead of you. I hope you can swim real good.

(LITTLE GIRL FOOTSTEPS *appears as a rock.*)

PEPITO: Swim? Like in the sea?

LITTLE GIRL FOOTSTEPS: Yup.

PEPITO: I changed my mind. I'm not going. I want to go back home now.

LITTLE GIRL FOOTSTEPS: There's no time. (*She whistles.*) Tirado, our local taxi, will take you to the Sea of Tears.

(*A single black tire rolls in, screeching to a stop. The tire is* TIRADO, *the local taxi. He's got lots of tire patches all over his body. Whenever* TIRADO *speaks he stutters.*)

TIRADO: Wh-wh-what an honor!

PEPITO: What did he say?

LITTLE GIRL FOOTSTEPS: "What an honor."

TIRADO: T-t-to seat you!

LITTLE GIRL FOOTSTEPS: This is *Tirado.*

PEPITO: Is that all of him?

TIRADO: Th-th-that's it! Swizzle-stick!

LITTLE GIRL FOOTSTEPS: When *Comandante* Boots took power he imprisoned all those resisting him and sent them to Smoking Mountain Compound. *Tirado* was one of them. He came back that way.

TIRADO: Ha-ha-hop on, son!

PEPITO: I don't think this is a good idea.

LITTLE GIRL FOOTSTEPS: For heaven's sake, get in!

TIRADO: Si-si-sit! Lickety-split!

(*Marching is heard.*)

LITTLE GIRL FOOTSTEPS: Oh, no, the *Monstruo Botas*!

PEPITO (*climbs into* TIRADO): Aren't you coming?

LITTLE GIRL FOOTSTEPS: I can't! I've got to guard the last remaining flower in *Cuate-Malo.* It's hidden nearby. Get in! Don't fail us, *Pepito*!

TIRADO: To-to-to the sea! Pep-eee!

(TIRADO *screeches off as* PEPITO *spins.*)

PEPITO: Aaagghhh!!!

(PEPITO *and* TIRADO *journey across the countryside.*)

PANADERO: *Pepito* and *Tirado* traveled across *Cuate-Malo*. It was a tiny country with big mountains, deep valleys, and bumpy roads.

PEPITO: Ouch!

PANADERO: *Pepito* saw what *Comandante* Boots had done to the country. He had transformed it into a land of fear and sorrow, where even laughter was outlawed.

(*At a military checkpoint. A long* ARM *appears with a sign that reads,* "ALTO." TIRADO *screeches to a stop.* PEPITO *falls out.*)

ARM: ¡Alto!

PEPITO: Aaagghhh!

TIRADO: Shhh!

PEPITO: What is it now?

TIRADO: Ch-ch-checkpoint! D-d-danger! Stranger!

(*A large* NOSE *appears, sniffing everything in sight. It behaves like a bulldog, barking occasionally. The* ARM *holds the* NOSE *by a leash.* PEPITO *and* TIRADO *hide behind a fern.*)

PEPITO: We've got to get past them, don't we?

TIRADO: ¡Ay! ¡Ay! Eye!

(*A large single* EYE *appears, searching. It's like a searchlight.*)

PEPITO: We're sitting ducks! We've got to find a way!

(*In silhouette* ANIMAL REFUGEES *are seen leaving. A* BABY MANATEE *is left behind. The* NOSE *barks loudly at the* BABY MANATEE.)

BABY MANATEE (*terrified*): ¿Mamá? ¿Mamá?

PEPITO: Look, it's a baby manatee!

BABY MANATEE: ¿Dónde está mi mamá? [Where's my mommy?]

ARM: ¡Dámelo! [Give it to me!]

(*The* ARM, NOSE, *and* EYE *surround the* BABY MANATEE, *confiscating her little book.*)

PEPITO: They're taking her picture book away!

(*The* NOSE *barks loudly at the* BABY MANATEE, *scaring her away.*)

BABY MANATEE (*crying*): ¡Mamá!

PEPITO: They can't do that!

(*The* NOSE *goes sniffing toward* PEPITO *and* TIRADO.)

TIRADO: Hi-hi-hide! (*It begins to rain.* TIRADO *opens a small umbrella.*) Wh-wh-what sadness.

PEPITO: It's raining.

TIRADO: Ch-ch-children's tears.

PEPITO (*whispering*): Why is *Comandante* Boots doing these horrible things?

TIRADO: Wh-wh-when *Comandante* was a small pair of baby boots he played rough and s-s-sometimes cheated —

PEPITO: That's awful.

TIRADO: —we never th-th-thought that he'd leap from a size four to a size twelve and become—

PEPITO: So evil?

TIRADO: Ye-ye-yes.

PEPITO: Somebody's got to stop him.

TIRADO: You, you, you.

PEPITO: No, no, no. I'm just a little kid. I wouldn't know what to do.

TIRADO: R-r-rain gone!

(*The sun appears and a beautiful rainbow follows.*)

PEPITO: ¡Mira, un arco iris! [Look, a rainbow!]

(*The* EYE *screams and* NOSE *barks.*)

EYE: ¡Ay, ay, ay!

PEPITO: I know their weakness!

TIRADO: Wha-what? Chowchow?

PEPITO: They can't look at beautiful things! This is our chance! ¡Vámonos!

(TIRADO picks up speed as the rainbow shines. Sirens and gunfire erupt. The large ARM tries to catch them but can't. The NOSE chases after them but gives up. And the EYE just watches. The sounds of the seashore are heard.)

TIRADO: We-we-we made it! Se-Se-Sea of Tears, Pepito!

PEPITO: But where's the Great Sea Tortuga?

TIRADO: Ou-ou-out there.

PEPITO: But I can't swim too good!

TIRADO: F-f-find way! Me-me-me help Little Girl Fo-Fo- Footsteps.

PEPITO: Tirado, don't go! I don't want to be alone! (TIRADO exits, screeching.) What can I do? How can I save a country when I can't even take care of myself? I bet Abuela would know what to do. (PEPITO sits, opens his donut bag, and removes his two donuts. He bites into one.) Ouch!

(He strikes both donuts and they chime. PANADERO appears. He may also play EL SOL.)

PANADERO: Poor Pepito sat there alone on the beach while El Sol baked him all day like masa.

PEPITO: El Sol, it's so hot today. I'm so thirsty. The sea looks like a big cool glass of water.

EL SOL: I wouldn't drink from there if I were you.

PEPITO: Why not?

EL SOL: Because it'll make you sad and then sadder.

PEPITO: I don't care. Go away!

EL SOL: Very well.

(PEPITO drinks from the Sea of Tears. EL SOL is replaced by LA LUNA. LA LUNA is the moon. PEPITO cries softly.)

LUNA: Pepito.

PEPITO: Hello, Luna.

LUNA: You must be hungry?

PEPITO: Yes, I am. My tummy won't stop growling.

LUNA: How would you like to eat a tortilla moon?

PEPITO: Won't the God of Lightning be angry?

LUNA: Oh, no, he can always make another for himself.

PEPITO: I'll just take a bite.

(LUNA *descends toward* PEPITO. *He reaches up and tears a small piece.* LUNA *returns to the sky.*)

LUNA: Well?

PEPITO: It tastes good, but I'd rather have a donut instead.

LUNA: Rest your little eyes. Tomorrow is a new day.

(*A musical underscore.* LUNA *sings in Spanish.*)

PEPITO: *Abuela*, I miss your words in Spanish. I miss your soft hands when we'd cross a street. I miss your songs when I couldn't sleep. I miss your smile when you'd look at me. I miss everything about you and how life used to be. *¿Abuela?*

(PEPITO *lies down to sleep. A moment later he is softly snoring. The next day.* PEPITO *is sound asleep.* RIDÍCULO *and* MODESTO *pop out from behind him.*)

RIDÍCULO/MODESTO: Hey, kid, wake up!

PEPITO: *Ridículo, Modesto,* what are you doing here?

MODESTO: We go where youse go.

RIDÍCULO: We watch your back. Capiche?

MODESTO: What's on your mind, kid?

PEPITO: I've got to find the Great Sea Tortuga. Since I don't swim so good I need something to float in like a boat or an ocean liner or even a battleship!

MODESTO/RIDÍCULO: A battleship?

PEPITO: Yeah.

RIDÍCULO: Time-out. Conference. (MODESTO *and* RIDÍCULO *whisper to each other.* PEPITO *strikes the donuts repeatedly and they chime.*) Cut that out, kid—

MODESTO: —we're trying to think here.

(PEPITO *continues to strike the donuts.* RIDÍCULO *and* MODESTO *suddenly look at each other.*)

RIDÍCULO: Wo!

MODESTO: Wo!

RIDÍCULO: *Modesto,* are you thinkin' what I'm thinkin'?

MODESTO: I'm thinkin' that!

RIDÍCULO: Okay, kid, make your second wish.

PEPITO: What happened to my first?

MODESTO: We brought youse here.

PEPITO: But I wanted to go to *Guatemala!*

RIDÍCULO: *Guatemala. Cuate-Malo.* Same difference.

MODESTO: Make your wish, kid!

PEPITO: I wish for a—

(*Thunder and lightning.* MODESTO *and* RIDÍCULO *disappear.* PEPITO *sits on a large donut floating in the middle of the sea.*)

PEPITO: Hey, what's this? A donut! *¿Modesto? ¿Ridículo?* This isn't fair!

(*A* BI-PLANE PAIR OF SHOES *enters flying.*)

PEPITO: It's a plane! I'm going to be rescued! Hello! (*The* BI-PLANE PAIR OF SHOES *drops a* SHARK TORPEDO *into the sea.*) Oh, no, it's one of *Comandante Boots'* planes! And a torpedo's coming right at me! Paddle! (*The* SHARK TORPEDO *circles* PEPITO *while he desperately tries to paddle away. The* SHARK TORPEDO *takes a bite out of* PEPITO'*s donut, deflating it.*) Help! I'm sinking! *¡Ayúdame!*

(PEPITO *struggles to stay afloat, but he descends below the water. Suddenly out of nowhere* THE GREAT SEA TORTUGA *appears. She is a giant sea turtle. She brings* PEPITO *back to the surface on her shell.* THE GREAT SEA TORTUGA *has a magnificent voice.* PEPITO *awakens.*)

THE GREAT SEA TORTUGA: Hello, old friend.

PEPITO (*coughing*): You saved my life.

THE GREAT SEA TORTUGA: I was afraid I had lost you.

PEPITO: You're the Great Sea *Tortuga!*

THE GREAT SEA TORTUGA: *Pepito,* you are so brave to come here. You don't recognize me, do you?

PEPITO: No.

THE GREAT SEA TORTUGA: Well, I was a lot smaller then.

PEPITO: Did your shell have a sandy beach, a palm tree, and a coconut painted on it?

THE GREAT SEA TORTUGA: Yes.

PEPITO: We used to play for hours together.

THE GREAT SEA TORTUGA: You do remember me!

PEPITO: Oh, I missed you, my little *tortuga!*

(*He tries to hug her shell.*)

THE GREAT SEA TORTUGA: And I you, *Pepito.*

PEPITO: Why am I here, *Tortuga?*

THE GREAT SEA TORTUGA: Because I need your help. We've tried to stop *Comandante Boots* but he has become too powerful and dangerous.

PEPITO: But I don't know what to do. I don't have an army of Monstruo Botas. I'm not even in the third grade yet.

THE GREAT SEA TORTUGA: You're our last hope. You must find a way to stop him. Trust your heart.

PEPITO: My heart?

THE GREAT SEA TORTUGA: Look to the beauty inside. We're here. *Adiós, amigo.*

PEPITO: Goodbye! (PEPITO *steps onto the beach.* THE GREAT SEA TORTUGA *disappears into the sea.*) What did she mean by the "beauty" inside? ¡Ridículo! ¡Modesto! Anybody?

(RIDÍCULO *and* MODESTO *suddenly appear.*)

RIDÍCULO/MODESTO: What is it, kid?

PEPITO: I need your help.

MODESTO: Youse want us to take care of that no good *Comandante* Boots?

RIDÍCULO: Yeah, youse want us to fit him with a nice pair of concrete shoes?

MODESTO: Know what we mean?

PEPITO: That's not right. There's got to be a better way to beat him. I just don't know what it is yet.

(MODESTO's *cell phone rings.*)

MODESTO: Hold it there, cowboy. Hello?

(MODESTO *and* RIDÍCULO *listen to the phone together.*)

RIDÍCULO: Kid, the news on the home front ain't good.

MODESTO: *Comandante* Boots' secret police found the last remaining flower in *Cuate-Malo.*

PEPITO: They did?

MODESTO: They arrested Little Girl Footsteps and *Tirado* too.

RIDÍCULO: They've been taken to *Comandante* Boots' Smoking Mountain Compound.

PEPITO: We've got to save them!

RIDÍCULO: What are you, crazy?

MODESTO: The only way to get past *Comandante* Boots' army is to fly over them. Last time I checked I didn't have no aeroplane in my pocket. Do you, *Ridículo?*

RIDÍCULO: No, I don't.

MODESTO: It's hopeless, kid. We'll take you back home. Make your third wish.

PEPITO: I wish for a balloon made out of your suits!

(Thunder and lightning. RIDÍCULO and MODESTO's suits fly off. They wear only their ties and underwear. A colorful balloon instantly appears.)

RIDÍCULO: Hey, look what you did to our fine suits!

MODESTO: Nobody said nothin' about slicin' or dicin' —

PEPITO: Boys, we're on a mission. Capiche?

(PEPITO climbs aboard. The balloon flies off.)

MODESTO: Hey, kid, where you going?

RIDÍCULO: Bring back our suits!

MODESTO: They cost us a bundle!

PEPITO: I can see everything from up here! There's the Sea of Tears! (A gust of wind carries him higher.) Wo! Guys, I don't feel so good. Guys?

RIDÍCULO: That's pretty low!

MODESTO: Ungrateful, I say!

RIDÍCULO: What's a worry doll without his suit!

MODESTO: Exactly! Come on!

(They exit. PANADERO appears.)

PANADERO: A half-shaped moon appeared that night, casting giant shadows across the Land of Sorrow and the Sea of Tears. Pepito flew over Tierra City; the once-vibrant capitol of Cuate-Malo was now reduced to rubble and ash. And finally, there before him was Smoking Mountain. He was almost there.

(The balloon flies on toward Smoking Mountain Compound. A now visible LITTLE GIRL FOOTSTEPS is held in a glass jar, while TIRADO hangs in the air. SERGEANT BOTAS stands near a bucket full of seeds. COMANDANTE BOOTS looks on.)

SERGEANT BOTAS: Comandante Boots, these are the last seeds we swept up. And the only flower left in Cuate-Malo is underneath that rock there.

COMANDANTE BOOTS: Excelente, Sergeant Botas! Now, Tirado, where is the boy?

LITTLE GIRL FOOTSTEPS: He won't say a thing!

COMANDANTE BOOTS: All I have to do is click my heels and orders are carried out. Things get done. Who here values their life?

SERGEANT BOTAS: I do!

COMANDANTE BOOTS: Not you, *idiota!*

LITTLE GIRL FOOTSTEPS: We're not afraid of you!

COMANDANTE BOOTS: But you should be. What do you say, *Tirado?*

TIRADO: D-d-don't hurt me!

COMANDANTE BOOTS: Ah, someone who understands their situation.

TIRADO: Wh-wh-what do to me?

COMANDANTE BOOTS: Well, now, that depends on what you've got to tell.

TIRADO: N-n-nothing.

COMANDANTE BOOTS: Sergeant *Botas,* what shall we do with *Tirado?*

SERGEANT BOTAS: String him up, sir!

COMANDANTE BOOTS: We've already done that, you *idiota!* No, we need something a little more persuasive. Sergeant *Botas,* prepare the secret weapon!

SERGEANT BOTAS: Not the Bumble Zapper, sir!

COMANDANTE BOOTS: Yes, it's time we show him the power of my military.

SERGEANT BOTAS: But it's never been field-tested.

COMANDANTE BOOTS: Go on!

(SERGEANT BOTAS *removes a box, which now and then rattles terribly.*)

SERGEANT BOTAS: Oh-oh . . .

COMANDANTE BOOTS: Tirado, tell me where that confounded boy is to be found!

TIRADO: N-n-no, Colombo!

COMANDANTE BOOTS: Release the Bumble Zapper!

(SERGEANT BOTAS *releases the* BUMBLE ZAPPER. *It is a mechanical bumblebee with spiked hair, tattoos, and a bad attitude. He buzzes around madly.*)

BUMBLE ZAPPER: Buzz off!

(*The* BUMBLE ZAPPER *fires a stinger missile, striking* COMANDANTE BOOTS *on his behind.*)

COMANDANTE BOOTS: Ou-ou-ouchy!

SERGEANT BOTAS: Come here, you!

(SERGEANT BOTAS *grabs him, putting him back in his box.*)

COMANDANTE BOOTS: Medic! (SERGEANT BOTAS *quickly reveals a medic insignia.*) I need a band-aid!

SERGEANT BOTAS: But I don't have one, sir!

COMANDANTE BOOTS: In that case, I deserve a medal! A big one!

(COMANDANTE BOOTS *reveals a big shiny medal.*)

SERGEANT BOTAS: Oh, it's such a beautifully ugly medal, *Comandante* Boots!

COMANDANTE BOOTS: It's *Generalísimo* Boots! I just promoted myself. (*To* SERGEANT BOTAS.) Oh, get out of the way! Now, *Tirado*, shall I place the Bumble Zapper in Little Girl Footsteps' jar?

TIRADO: I— I— I—

COMANDANTE BOOTS: Are you ready to tell me what I want to know?

LITTLE GIRL FOOTSTEPS: *Tirado*, don't say a thing!

TIRADO: ¡Sí-sí-sí!

COMANDANTE BOOTS: Did you say "sea"?

TIRADO: No-no-no!

COMANDANTE BOOTS: Of course! The boy is with the Great Sea *Tortuga*! I'll send my warships there to destroy them! No one can stop me now! (*Fanfare.* COMANDANTE BOOTS *steps onto a soapbox.*) At ease. Victory is ours! Ugly statues will be erected! Long and boring speeches will be written! Major motion pictures will be made! I decree that all things beautiful be deemed WRONG against the state. And if BEAUTY appears anywhere it will be STOMPED OUT by my legion of *Monstruo Botas*! Sergeant *Botas*?

SERGEANT BOTAS: ¿Sí, mi general?

COMANDANTE BOOTS: I will dispose of the last flower now.

SERGEANT BOTAS: But won't that harm you, *mi general*?

COMANDANTE BOOTS: I won't look! I'll let my boots do the talking! Remove the rock! (SERGEANT BOTAS *lifts a rock and a flower instantly springs up.* COMANDANTE BOOTS *steps on the flower, crushing it.*) Oh, that feels so good!

(*The balloon descends into the compound.*)

SERGEANT BOTAS: Look!

COMANDANTE BOOTS: Don't interrupt me.

SERGEANT BOTAS: But . . . but . . .

LITTLE GIRL FOOTSTEPS: It's *Pepito*!

COMANDANTE BOOTS: There you are, boy! Finally, we meet!

PEPITO: Let my *amigos* go free, Boots!

COMANDANTE BOOTS: Or you'll do what?

PEPITO: I got backup, see?

SERGEANT BOTAS: Yeah, you and whose army, pal?

PEPITO: Me and—¿Ridículo? ¿Modesto? Guys? Oh, oh!

COMANDANTE BOOTS: En garde!

LITTLE GIRL FOOTSTEPS: Watch out, Pepito! (COMANDANTE BOOTS *tries to stomp on* PEPITO. PEPITO *tries to avoid him, but he is finally pinned to the ground.*) Oh, no!

SERGEANT BOTAS: Hurray, *Generalísimo!*

COMANDANTE BOOTS: The Great Sea *Tortuga* shouldn't have sent a boy to do a man's job!

PEPITO: I can't move!

COMANDANTE BOOTS: You got anything to say before I finish you off, boy?

LITTLE GIRL FOOTSTEPS: Trust what's inside your heart, Pepito!

PEPITO: What did you say?

COMANDANTE BOOTS: Nothing can stop me now!

LITTLE GIRL FOOTSTEPS: Beauty isn't dead yet!

COMANDANTE BOOTS: I crushed the last flower and all that remains is that bucket of seeds!

PEPITO: Seeds?

COMANDANTE BOOTS: Sí, seeds. And I'll stomp them out just like I will you, boy!

LITTLE GIRL FOOTSTEPS: You can't destroy what's inside us!

PEPITO: Stories are like seeds!

LITTLE GIRL FOOTSTEPS: That's right, Pepito!

COMANDANTE BOOTS: Victory will be mine!

PEPITO: They can flower in the heart!

LITTLE GIRL FOOTSTEPS: Go on!

PEPITO: And they'll grow beautiful like my *abuela's* stories!

(*The pounding of a drum is heard.* COMANDANTE BOOTS *becomes disoriented.* PEPITO *is freed.*)

COMANDANTE BOOTS: Stories? What stories?

PEPITO: The ones I got in my *corazón!*

(*Another drumbeat is heard.*)

COMANDANTE BOOTS: I hate beautiful stories!

SERGEANT BOTAS: Oh-oh!

PEPITO: A God of Lightning once threw *masa* onto the sun to cook!

(*Another drumbeat.*)

COMANDANTE BOOTS: Get away from me!

LITTLE GIRL FOOTSTEPS (*escapes from the jar*): It's working, *Pepito!*

PEPITO: It smelled so delicious he couldn't wait!

(*Another drumbeat.*)

COMANDANTE BOOTS: What's happening to me?

PEPITO: He burned himself and yelled a great *grito*—

COMANDANTE BOOTS: Aagghhh!

PEPITO: And that's how *la luna* came to be!

(*The final drumbeat is heard.* COMANDANTE BOOTS *literally kicks the bucket and drops to the ground.*)

SERGEANT BOTAS: *Dios mío,* he really did kick the bucket! Retreat!

LITTLE GIRL FOOTSTEPS: Freeze, soldier! (SERGEANT BOTAS *freezes.*) *Pepito,* you defeated *Comandante* Boots and his army! You saved us! You saved our country!

(*A tiny pair of baby boots crawl out of* COMANDANTE BOOTS' *boots. They run around, crying hysterically.*)

LITTLE GIRL FOOTSTEPS: Look, *Comandante* Boots isn't a general anymore! He's a pair of baby *botas!*

PEPITO: You've been very naughty!

(COMANDANTE BABY *cries again.*)

LITTLE GIRL FOOTSTEPS: What are we going to do with him?

PEPITO (*to* COMANDANTE BABY): As punishment, you and Sergeant Botas are going to plant every seed in this bucket all across *Cuate-Malo.* Not only that, you're going to water and weed, and like it too!

(COMANDANTE BABY *cries louder.*)

SERGEANT BOTAS: Oh, I like planting *flores.* Come on, Baby Botas!

(SERGEANT BOTAS *and* COMANDANTE BABY *exit with a bucket of seeds. Music. The crushed flower rises and blooms.*)

PEPITO: Look there! It's growing back!

LITTLE GIRL FOOTSTEPS: The last remaining flower in *Cuate-Malo* will now become our first. The whole country will transform into beauty once more. *Pepito,* I never have to be afraid or disappear again. I can run barefoot on the beach and play all I want.

PEPITO: This place is just like how *Abuela* described her homeland. She was right, you can make things better wherever you live.

LITTLE GIRL FOOTSTEPS: Thank you.

PEPITO (*embarrassed*): Well, I better go.

TIRADO: P-P-Pepito!

PEPITO: What is it, *Tirado?*

TIRADO: T-t-take these seeds to-to-to remember us!

PEPITO: *Gracias, amigos.* [Thank you, friends.]

LITTLE GIRL FOOTSTEPS/TIRADO: Goodbye!

(LITTLE GIRL FOOTSTEPS *and* TIRADO *exit.*)

PEPITO: *Adiós!* It's time for me to go home. My home. *Ridículo? Modesto?*

(MODESTO *and* RIDÍCULO *appear in their underwear.*)

MODESTO/RIDÍCULO: We're ready to rumble, kid.

PEPITO: It's all over.

RIDÍCULO: It looks like you didn't need our help after all.

PEPITO: But I still do. How will I find my way back?

MODESTO: The way we see it—

RIDÍCULO: —We owe youse one good wish.

(*The balloon flies in.*)

PEPITO: My donut balloon! Then I'm ready! Thanks, guys! *¡Vámonos!*

MODESTO: I tell you what my wish is, *Ridículo.* I want my suit back. The dry cleaning is gonna cost me a bundle. Am I right?

RIDÍCULO: You sure are, *Modesto.* Hey, is that kid leaving without us again?

MODESTO: After all we've done for him.

RIDÍCULO: I tell youse what, I'm going back to New York.

MODESTO: In your underwear? You're going to have to move to the Village!

(*They exit. A moment later,* PEPITO *lies sleeping on his couch.* MADRE *appears. She looks a lot like* ABUELA, *except younger.*)

MADRE: *Pepito.*

PEPITO: . . .

MADRE: *Pepito,* wake up!

PEPITO: ¿'*Amá?* (*Recognizing her.*) *¡'Amá!*

(PEPITO *hugs her.*)

MADRE: Oh, my, what's that for?

PEPITO: 'Amá, you're not going to believe what happened to me!

MADRE: What?

PEPITO: I went to *Cuate-Malo* and there was this very bad pair of boots—

MADRE: Boots? *Pepito*, you're just like *Abuela*. Such an imagination.

PEPITO: He captured my *amigos* and I had to free them!

MADRE: I've got so much to do today.

PEPITO: Well, I've got such a story to tell you!

(*Beat.*)

MADRE: Why don't you go to *Panadero's* bakery and buy us two *donas*!

PEPITO: Really?

MADRE: Yes, really. The laundry and shopping can wait. I want to hear all about your adventure. What do you say?

PEPITO: Okay, 'Amá! (*PEPITO crosses to the garden. He looks in his pocket and finds three seeds.*) It wasn't a dream! (*PEPITO looks up into the sky.*) Abuela, these seeds are for your garden. Thank you for your beautiful stories.

(*PEPITO kisses the seeds and plants them. PANADERO enters.*)

PEPITO: ¡Hola, Señor Panadero! ¡Dos donas, por favor!

PANADERO: Two donuts coming right up!

(*PANADERO hands PEPITO a small donut bag. PEPITO crosses to his MADRE, who waits for him on the porch steps.*)

PEPITO: 'Amá, I saved Cuate-Malo!

MADRE: Did you?

PEPITO: Ah-huh, and I met all sorts of strange creatures like a taxi tire, a coconut-girl rock, a talking *tortuga*—

MADRE: A turtle?

(*PANADERO now holds a paintbrush and a bucket of paint.*)

PANADERO: ¡Buenos días, señora!

MADRE: ¡Buenos días, Panadero! What a lovely morning it is.

PEPITO: Are you going to paint something?

PANADERO: I'm going to brighten up our little *barrio* with a mural on my bakery wall.

PEPITO: May I help, Panadero?

PANADERO: Bueno, pues, I can always use help!

PEPITO: Okay!

PANADERO: Well, *Pepito* came and helped me paint my mural. But first he had to tell his *'amá* all about his adventure.

PEPITO: There was *Ridículo* and *Modesto*, a television set with wings—

MADRE: Wings?

PEPITO: Yeah, and—

PANADERO: They sat on their porch steps eating their two *donas*. And what a beautiful morning it was. The sun was shining, and the garden flowers were blooming, and the spiders were spinning their magnificent webs, while children laughed and played throughout the neighborhood. And for a brief moment it was paradise. Just like the distant country *Abuela* loved to remember.

CURTAIN

Glossary of Spanish Words
and Phrases

abuela: grandmother
adios: goodbye
¡alto!: stop
amigo: friend
arco iris: rainbow
ayúdame: help me
barrio: neighborhood
bonito: pretty
bueno, pues: well
buenos días: good morning
cafecito: a little cup of coffee
comandante: commander
campeones: champions
corazón: heart
cuentos: stories
Dios mío: my God
dos donas: two donuts
el sol: the sun
escuela: school
español: Spanish
estúpido/a: stupid
exactamente: exactly
excelente: excellent
familia: family
flores: flowers
generalísimo: general
gracias: thank you
grito: a shout, scream
Guatemala: country in Central
    America

hola: hello
hombre: man
idiota: idiot
la luna: the moon
la noche: the night
la playa: the beach
leche: milk
lonche: lunch
mambo: a dance from Latin America
masa: dough
monstruo botas: monster boots
muchacho: boy
muy bien: well done; very good
panadería: bakery
pan dulce: sweet bread
por favor: please
quihubo: an informal greeting,
    something like "hello!"
regalo: gift
tirado: dirt cheap; or something
    thrown away
tortilla: a thin, flat, round Mexican
    bread made from corn meal or
    wheat flour
tortuga: turtle
trabajo: work
triste: sad
vámonos: let's go

Designer's Response

Two Donuts offers some of the most difficult design challenges of all the scripts within this anthology. Well aware of this, I pondered the problems of creating the visual magical realism of the play with its varying scale in size of characters, props, and locations, as well as the seemingly random characters and animals who appear after Pepito, the protagonist, arrives in *Cuate-Malo.*

After struggling with this for some time, I decided that my hypothetical production would have essential financial and production resources and sufficient rehearsal time to allow the play to be performed with both actors and *Bunraku*-style puppets, operated by fully visible manipulators who stand close to them.

When he enters the imaginary country of *Cuate-Malo,* Pepito becomes one of these puppets. The other characters of *Cuate-Malo* are also *Bunraku* puppets of various sizes. The setting is first Pepito's house (plate A), and then, with minimal changes and projected images, the jungle in *Cuate-Malo* (plate B). The two drawings for this script illustrate how a single setting accommodates both locations. The setting is transformed by scenic elements and characters who are *Bunraku* puppets.

Resources

Clip art images of donuts
Guatemalan cultural resource materials
Internet images of Guatemalan "worry dolls"
Jungle images from *National Geographic* magazine

Plate A: Pepito's house.

Plate B: Cuate-Malo.

Marisol's Christmas

José Cruz González

Marisol's Christmas premiered at Teatro Cucucuévez,
Santa Ana, California.

Characters

MARISOL: an eight-year-old Latina girl. She also plays SEÑORITA SATURNO, and SEÑORITA TIERRA.

PAPI: MARISOL's father. He also plays OLD VIEJO SOL, C. T., GLOBO, SOSA, and GRAVITY.

MAMI: *Marisol*'s mother. She also plays COMETA.

Setting

Near a freeway. Cars can be heard zooming by.

Time

Christmas Eve.

AT RISE: MARISOL, PAPI, and MAMI *appear in a pool of light.*
They have been walking all night. They carry their belongings.

PAPI: Come on, you two. We mustn't lag behind.

MARISOL: *Papi, are we there yet?*

PAPI: No, Marisol, we have a long way still to go.

MAMI: *Amor,* she's tired. We've been traveling all night. We need to rest.

PAPI: All right. We'll stop here before we cross the highway.

MAMI: It looks so dangerous. *Peligroso.*

PAPI: We have no choice, *corazón.* We'll wait for the right moment to cross. Don't you worry. Just think—by tomorrow we'll be in a new place. Our home. Heaven.

(*They put down their belongings.* MARISOL *sits by her mother.* PAPI *looks off toward the freeway.*)

MAMI: It's Christmas Eve, Marisol. And you know good things happen on Christmas Eve. Let's huddle together to keep warm.

MARISOL: Okay, Mami.

(*Music.* MAMI *sings "Paz en la tierra" ["Joy to the World"]. Then afterward—*)

PAPI: It's time! We've got to cross now!

(MAMI, PAPI, *and* MARISOL *gather their belongings as they try to cross the freeway. They hold hands. The crossing becomes a horrific moment of cars, trucks, and lights zooming past them.* MAMI *becomes separated from them. She disappears into the darkness.*)

MARISOL: ¡Mami! ¡Mami!

(*Blackout. In silhouette the downtown L.A. skyline can be seen and above the stars shine brightly. The glow of a fire—* PAPI *and* MARISOL *sit near it.*)

MARISOL: Where are the angels, Papi?

PAPI: What angels?

MARISOL: The angels of Los Angeles.

PAPI: Angels live in heaven, Marisol.

MARISOL: This isn't heaven?

PAPI: No.

MARISOL: *Papi,* where's Mami?

PAPI: She's on her way. I told her this is where we'd meet if we were separated.

MARISOL: I don't like *Los Angeles*. I want to go back home!

PAPI: *Los Angeles* is our new home.

MARISOL: I don't like it here. It's dark and dirty.

PAPI: Not all of *Los Angeles* is like this, *Marisol*. It's beautiful too. You just have to look for it.

MARISOL: I don't want to.

PAPI: It's Christmas Eve, *Marisol*. Good things happen on Christmas Eve, remember?

MARISOL: Like what?

PAPI: Well, if you look up into the night sky, pick a star and make a wish—

MARISOL: It'll come true?

PAPI: You see, you just have to have a little faith and work hard to make it happen.

(MARISOL *looks up into the sky. She closes her eyes and makes a wish.*)

MARISOL: Okay, Papi.

PAPI: Good. I'll tell you a secret—*un secreto*? I didn't like *Los Angeles* when I first came. *No me gustó*. I missed you and *Mami* a lot.

MARISOL: You did?

PAPI: Ah huh, I used to make up stories to pass the time. *Cuentos*. Like the ones your grandma, *Nana Mayo*, used to tell.

MARISOL: What kind of stories?

PAPI: All kinds. Funny ones, sad ones, even magical ones.

MARISOL: Magical?

PAPI: Ah huh.

MARISOL: *Papi*, would you tell me a story?

PAPI: Yes, if you promise to go to sleep after I tell you. It's late, you know?

MARISOL: Okay, I promise.

PAPI: Where do we start?

MARISOL: We?

PAPI: *Pos sí*. You've got to help me tell it.

MARISOL: Okay!

PAPI: *Marisol*, think of any five things! *¡Piensa en cinco cosas!*

MARISOL (*searching*): Okay, a fire!

PAPI: *¡Un fuego!*

MARISOL: A comet!

PAPI: ¡Un cometa!

MARISOL: A Christmas tree!

PAPI: ¡Un árbol de Navidad!

MARISOL: And the Dodgers of Los Angeles!

MARISOL/PAPI: Go Dodgers!

(They do a wave.)

PAPI: Uno, dos, tres, cuatro—but that's only four things, mija.

MARISOL: Oh, yeah . . . and Mami.

PAPI: Tu mami no debe tardar, mija. She won't be long.

MARISOL: We gotta have a little faith.

PAPI: That's right! Okay, a fire, a comet, a Christmas tree, the Dodgers of Los Angeles, and Mami.

(Music begins underscoring PAPI's tale.)

PAPI: Once upon a time there was a little girl named Marisol!

MARISOL: ¡Esa soy yo!

PAPI: And Marisol lived in the City of Angels. She had a very special gift. Un regalo de Dios.

MARISOL: What was it?

PAPI: Marisol could sing the most beautiful songs in Spanish!

(MARISOL sings "Cascabel" ["Jingle Bells"].)

PAPI: When Marisol sang the whole universe would listen. The stars and planets became awakened by her sweet voice. One such star was Señorita Saturno.

(PAPI places a blanket on MARISOL that has stars and planets and MARISOL puts on bracelets. She has now transformed into SEÑORITA SATURNO.)

PAPI: Señorita Saturno believed she was the most beautiful star in the whole universe.

MARISOL (as SEÑORITA SATURNO): Well, I am the most beautiful star, don't you think?

PAPI: Oh, yes, very beautiful.

MARISOL (as SEÑORITA SATURNO): Thank you!

PAPI: Among the stars was a tiny comet that heard Marisol sing.

(Music. MARISOL drops the blanket and sings once again as COMETA enters, racing around the stage on roller-skates. COMETA is played by MAMI.)

COMETA: Zooom! Zooom! Zoom!

PAPI: Her name was *Cometa!*

(*COMETA suddenly stops to listen to the music.*)

COMETA: What's that beautiful noise?

PAPI: *Cometa* was a comet who could circle the universe in seconds.

COMETA: Zooom! (*Suddenly stopping. To audience.*) ¿De dónde viene ese ruido hermoso? Where is that beautiful noise coming from?

PAPI: *Cometa* began searching the universe . . .

COMETA: Zooom!

(*COMETA races about, circling around the stage as MARISOL transforms back into SEÑORITA SATURNO. She now stands, sleeping and snoring loudly.*)

PAPI: . . . asking the stars and planets if they were creating the beautiful "ruido."

COMETA: Excuse me, Señorita Saturno, are you making the beautiful noise? ¿Es usted quien hace ese ruido hermoso?

MARISOL (*as SEÑORITA SATURNO, awakening*): ¡Yo no hago ruido! I just wear rings and things!

(*SEÑORITA SATURNO stretches her arm out, showing COMETA her many bracelets.*)

COMETA: Rings and things!

MARISOL (*as SEÑORITA SATURNO*): Don't touch!

COMETA: Don't touch?

MARISOL (*as SEÑORITA SATURNO*): Aren't I pretty? ¡Superestrella!

COMETA: Super star! Oh, *Señorita Saturno,* you are very pretty!

MARISOL (*as SEÑORITA SATURNO*): Good answer! I think it's Old *Viejo Sol* who lives down the street from me that's making all that noise. He's always mumbling about something or other.

COMETA: ¡Gracias, Señorita Saturno! Zooo . . .

MARISOL (*as SEÑORITA SATURNO*): Stop!

COMETA: Stop?

MARISOL (*as SEÑORITA SATURNO*): My rings and things, you'll mess them up with your zooming. Slow down!

COMETA: Oh . . . (*Quietly.*) Zooom . . .

(*COMETA circles the stage, searching for OLD VIEJO SOL.*)

PAPI: "Zooom," went *Cometa* . . .

COMETA: Zoom, zoom, zoom, zoom, zooom!

PAPI: . . . searching for Old Viejo Sol!

MARISOL: He went thataway!

(PAPI transforms himself into OLD VIEJO SOL by using found objects. He sort of resembles Don Quixote with a helmet, breastplate, and staff.)

COMETA (to OLD VIEJO SOL): Excuse me, are you Old Viejo Sol?

PAPI (as OLD VIEJO SOL): ¿Sancho?

COMETA: Yo soy Cometa.

PAPI (as OLD VIEJO SOL): Oh, you're one of those bilingual comets, huh?

COMETA: Sí, are you making the beautiful ruido?

PAPI (as OLD VIEJO SOL): No, but I like smiling a lot, see?

(PAPI sets off a flash of intense light when he smiles.)

COMETA: ¡Ay, mis ojos! Your teeth are very bright!

PAPI (as OLD VIEJO SOL): They're brand new! A knight's gotta have teeth! ¿¡Ves!?

(PAPI sets off another flash.)

COMETA: ¡Ay, mis ojos! If you're not making the beautiful noise, then who is?

PAPI (as OLD VIEJO SOL): The beautiful ruido se llama "singing" and it comes from my neighbor, Señorita Tierra.

COMETA: Earth?

PAPI (as OLD VIEJO SOL): Yes, Miss Earth.

COMETA: ¿Dónde está?

PAPI (as OLD VIEJO SOL): Señorita Tierra's down the block, towards the Milky Way, past la Luna. You can't miss her.

COMETA: Thank you, Old Viejo Sol!

PAPI (as OLD VIEJO SOL): ¡De nada! A knight's duty is never done. Where was I? Oh, yes, ¿Dulcinea? ¿Dulcinea?

COMETA: Zooom!

PAPI: So Cometa raced toward earth, going faster and faster so that everything became a blur.

COMETA: Zoom! Zoom! Zoom!

PAPI: She arrived there so quickly, before you could say "¡Adiós!"

MARISOL: ¡Adiós!

(Music. Now MARISOL has transformed into SEÑORITA TIERRA. She dances and stomps like a flamenco dancer. MARISOL claps rhythmically.)

MARISOL (as SEÑORITA TIERRA): ¡Olé!

PAPI: ¡Olé!

(COMETA *crosses to* SEÑORITA TIERRA.)

COMETA (*suddenly stopping*): Con permiso, Señorita Tierra, are you singing the beautiful *ruido*? *¿Es usted quien canta?*

MARISOL (*as* SEÑORITA TIERRA, *opera-like*): Sí, do you like it?

COMETA: *¡Me gusta mucho!*

MARISOL (*as* SEÑORITA TIERRA): It's called music! *¡Música!*

COMETA (*imitating* SEÑORITA TIERRA): *¿Música?*

MARISOL (*as* SEÑORITA TIERRA): My neighbors here on Earth love to sing and so do I!

COMETA (*imitating* SEÑORITA TIERRA): May I hear more *música*, please?

MARISOL (*as* SEÑORITA TIERRA): *Ten mucho cuidado* . . . be careful . . . not to come too close . . . otherwise you'll fall to Earth . . . and never leave!

COMETA: Why?

SEÑORITA TIERRA: *¡Wátchele!*

(SEÑORITA TIERRA *sings to the music of* "Carmen.")

SEÑORITA TIERRA (*singing*):

I am Tierra
I am the Earth
Gravity is my friend
From birth

Don't come too close
Stay far away
You'll fall to Earth
And there you'll stay

I love to sing
I love to dance
Soy peligrosa
Don't come too close!

SEÑORITA TIERRA: *¡Lo que se cae . . . se cae!* Anything near me is pulled toward me. It's called Gravity!

COMETA (*imitating* SEÑORITA TIERRA): *Gracias* for the warning!

(COMETA *accidentally bumps into* SEÑORITA TIERRA. COMETA *falls to Earth*).

COMETA: Oh, no, I'm falling!

MARISOL: It's Gravity!

COMETA: *¡Me estoy cayendo! ¡Ayúdame!*

PAPI: "¡Ayúdame!" screamed *Cometa* as she fell toward Earth—

COMETA: Help!

PAPI: —spinning and tumbling out of control, falling so fast that she began to glow bright red, lighting up the entire heavens until . . .

(COMETA *crashes to the ground, landing on* MARISOL.)

PAPI: She landed!

COMETA: Ouch! (*Looking around.*) *¿Dónde estoy?*

MARISOL: In *Los Angeles.*

COMETA: Are you an angel?

MARISOL: No, are you?

COMETA: No. Oh, I don't belong here.

MARISOL: Neither do I.

COMETA: *¡No debería estar aquí!*

MARISOL: I shouldn't be here either.

COMETA: I'm from up there. The universe. *¿Usted es de allá, del otro lado?*

MARISOL: Ah huh. I'm *Marisol.*

COMETA: *Me llamo Cometa.*

(*They shake hands. A musical touch.*)

MARISOL: You speak Spanish?

COMETA: Yes, of course, *claro que sí.*

MARISOL: Is your *otro lado* up there among the stars?

COMETA: Ah huh . . .

MARISOL: I thought only angels lived in heaven?

COMETA: And I thought they lived here.

MARISOL: What do you mean?

COMETA: Anyone who can sing so beautifully must be an angel.

MARISOL: How did you know it was me singing?

COMETA: I heard you. From up there. Earth is a pretty place, but standing here it's dark, cold, and lonely. I don't like it. *Me siento solita.*

MARISOL: Don't be afraid, *Cometa.* I'm here.

COMETA: I need to get back into the sky so I can zooom away *al cielo.*

MARISOL: Why?

COMETA: So I can help people on Earth find their way home. It's Christmas Eve. Something special is going to happen tonight. But I can't go anywhere because Gravity won't let me.

MARISOL: I've got an idea!

COMETA: What is it?

MARISOL: I'll lift you up!

COMETA: Why?

MARISOL: To get you back into the sky!

COMETA: Will it work?

MARISOL: We won't know until we try.

COMETA: Okay!

(*MARISOL tries lifting* COMETA *up, but nothing works. They fall to the ground.*)

COMETA: It didn't work! I'm still here. I'll never ever help people find their way home for Christmas now. (*Closing her eyes.*) I wish . . . quisiera . . . I wish . . . *quisiera volver a mi casa* . . . Am I still here?

MARISOL: Ah huh . . .

COMETA: Wishes aren't real, are they? They're just make-believe. They never come true and I'll never get home.

(*COMETA crosses to the campfire and sits alone.*)

PAPI: "They never come true and I'll never get home." *Cometa* sat by the fire alone, wondering what to do. Wondering if she'd ever see her family. Wondering if she'd ever zoom into the sky again.

(*MARISOL crosses to* PAPI.)

MARISOL: ¿Papi?

PAPI: What, *Marisol*?

MARISOL: Do you think Mami's afraid wherever she is? ¿*Tendrá miedo*?

PAPI: I think she's being brave like you and *Cometa*.

MARISOL: I don't think we're doing too good.

PAPI: I think you are.

MARISOL: ¿*De veras*?

PAPI: Sí, *de veras*. Well, suddenly *Marisol* and *Cometa* heard cars screeching and horns honking. Out in the middle of a big freeway a little pine tree had fallen out of a pickup truck. "Help!" yelled C. T.

(*PAPI transforms into* C. T. *by picking up a small leafless tree branch. He tumbles onto the stage, trying to avoid the imaginary cars.*)

MARISOL: We gotta save him, *Cometa*!

COMETA: But how?

PAPI (*as* C. T.): I'm gonna get smooshed!

MARISOL: We have to get him off the freeway before he gets run over by a car, or truck, or a Winnebago!

PAPI (*as* C. T.): Help!

COMETA: Okay, let's go!

MARISOL (*stopping* COMETA): No, it's too dangerous to cross the freeway! *¡Es muy peligroso!*

COMETA: But you just said we have to save him!

MARISOL: I know!

COMETA: If only I could zoom!

MARISOL: That's it! (*Interrupting* PAPI.) *¡Papi!*

PAPI: *¿Qué?* What?

MARISOL: *Necesitamos un globo.* We need a balloon for our story. *Un fuego,* a Christmas tree, the Dodgers, Mami, and now a *globo.*

(PAPI *searches on the ground and finds a deflated beach ball.*)

PAPI: Will an old ball do?

MARISOL: Yes!

PAPI: Suddenly from nowhere a balloon named *Globo* appeared!

(PAPI *inflates the ball, creating* GLOBO.)

COMETA: *¡Mira, un globo!*

GLOBO: Whoa, who turned on the lights?

MARISOL: *¿Globo?*

GLOBO: Is this heaven?

MARISOL: No, it's *Los Angeles.*

GLOBO: The last thing I remember I was in a car headed for the beach. Someone rolled down a window and I was sucked right out. I danced with a dozen cars before everything went black. Are you sure this isn't heaven?

(*Cars are heard screeching and honking.*)

PAPI: "Help!" screamed C. T.!

MARISOL: Come on, *Globo!*

(MARISOL *and* COMETA *grab hold of* GLOBO.)

GLOBO: Where are we going?

MARISOL: To the freeway!

GLOBO: Oh, no, I'm scared of heights! *¡No quiero hacer esto!*

COMETA: *Ándale, Globo, zooom!*

(MARISOL *and* COMETA *take* GLOBO *and float over to* C. T.)

PAPI (*as* C. T.): Help!

(MARISOL *and* COMETA *save* C. T. *and return to the campfire.*)

PAPI (As C. T.): Oh my, I've never, ever been sooo scared! I can't look—am I in one piece? ¿Estoy entero?

(*They pat him down quickly and loudly.*)

MARISOL: Yes, what about me?

(*They pat her down loudly and quickly.*)

COMETA: And me?

(*They pat her down quickly and loudly too.*)

PAPI (*as* C. T.): Thank you for saving my *vida!*

MARISOL/COMETA: De nada.

PAPI (*as* C. T.): ¿Hablan español?

MARISOL/COMETA: Sí, claro.

PAPI (*as* C. T.): My name's C. T. What's yours?

MARISOL: Marisol.

COMETA: Cometa.

MARISOL: What do the letters C. T. mean?

PAPI (*as* C. T.): C. T. is my nickname. My real name is Christmas Tree.

MARISOL: ¡Un árbol de Navidad! You're welcome to stay with us, C. T., but we gotta help Cometa back into the sky.

PAPI (*as* C. T.): Why?

MARISOL: So we can get her back to her *casa!* Cometa, all you have to do is hold on to Globo and he'll take you up into the sky!

(PAPI *picks up a piece of a hose, which creates a wind sound.*)

PAPI: Suddenly, from nowhere, came a strong wind blowing.

MARISOL/COMETA: What wind?

PAPI: It began as a whisper, then turned into a twister.

(*The wind sound begins to intensify.*)

COMETA: What's that noise?

PAPI: Around and around it formed a mighty storm.

GLOBO: What's happening?

PAPI: A monstrous wind had come! It began lifting everything off the ground, including Globo!

MARISOL: Hold on, Globo!

(MARISOL and COMETA are spun around in circles as the wind blows through.)

PAPI: The wind lifted Globo high into the night sky. "Help!" screamed Globo.

(PAPI tosses GLOBO away.)

PAPI: And Globo was no more.

MARISOL (to PAPI): But that's not fair, Papi!

PAPI: La vida is never fair, mija.

COMETA: What are we going to do?

MARISOL: I don't know.

COMETA: Now I'll never get home.

MARISOL (to C. T.): Cometa belongs up there where the stars twinkle.

COMETA: ¡Estoy estuck!

PAPI (as C. T.): Gravity keeping you down, huh?

COMETA: ¿Cómo sabes que es la gravedad?

PAPI (as C. T.): Everybody knows about gravity. What goes up must come down. I learned about it in school.

MARISOL: I got an idea!

COMETA/PAPI (as C. T.): What is it?

MARISOL: The Dodgers are from Los Angeles, right?

PAPI (as C. T.): Yeah?

MARISOL: Okay, pues they're playing baseball tonight!

PAPI: But, Marisol, the Dodgers don't play on Christmas Eve!

MARISOL: I know that, Papi, but it's my cuento, remember?

PAPI: Okay, but Fernando is pitching!

MARISOL: ¿Fernando Valenzuela?

PAPI: Why not?

MARISOL: Papi, Fernando Valenzuela ya no juega para los Dodgers.

PAPI: I know he doesn't play baseball anymore but he's my hero.

MARISOL: Okay, Papi, we'll put him in MY story.

PAPI: Goody! I miss Fernandomania!

MARISOL: Cometa, can you hold onto the seams of a baseball?

COMETA: Ah huh! What's a baseball?

PAPI (as C. T.): It's a round thing you throw that flies in the air.

COMETA: *¡Como un cometa!*

MARISOL: Exactly. All you gotta do is hold on and when somebody hits the baseball that should launch you into space, *¿ves?*

PAPI (*as C. T.*): It could work. Who's batting tonight?

MARISOL: *Sammy Sosa!*

PAPI (*as C. T., to* COMETA): Sammy Sosa will get you back into the sky, easy!

COMETA: Okay, let's go!

MARISOL: But how do we get to Dodger Stadium?

PAPI (*as C. T.*): I didn't think of that. I'm *estumped!*

MARISOL: *¡Yo sé!*

PAPI: *¿Qué?*

MARISOL: Follow my lead!

(*Suddenly the National Anthem is heard.* MARISOL *begins singing it.*)

MARISOL: Oh, José, can you see—

(*Crowd sounds are heard.*)

COMETA: We're at Dodger Stadium! How'd you do that?

MARISOL/PAPI: *¡Magia!*

(PAPI *transforms into* SAMMY SOSA *by placing a letter "C" on his cap. He picks up an old pipe as a baseball bat.*)

MARISOL: There's Sammy Sosa!

PAPI (*as* SOSA): *¡Quihubo! ¡Yo soy* Sammy Sosa! Baseball has been bery bery good to me!

MARISOL: And he's going to bat!

(MARISOL *picks up an old newspaper and crumples it into a baseball.*)

MARISOL: Hold on tight, *Cometa!*

COMETA: Okay!

MARISOL (*winding up to pitch*): Fernando looks in for the sign. He winds up and—

(MARISOL *pitches as* COMETA *streaks across the stage toward* SOSA. *He swings and misses.*)

MARISOL: Strike one!

PAPI (*as* SOSA): How'd she do that?

MARISOL: A spitball! This next pitch is it, *Cometa!* Fernando looks in for the sign. He winds up and—

(SOSA *swings and misses.*)

MARISOL: Strike two!

PAPI (*as* SOSA): Strike two?

COMETA: He missed again?

PAPI (*as* SOSA): That's it! To the moon, *Fernando! ¡Hasta la luna!*

MARISOL: *Ahora sí, Cometa,* Sammy is digging in! *Fernando* looks in for the sign. He winds up and—

(*Crowd sounds are heard.* SOSA *swings and misses.*)

MARISOL: Strike three! You're out!

COMETA: What happened?

MARISOL: El Sammy struck out!

PAPI (*as* SOSA): I was robbed!

COMETA (*disappointed*): Now I'll never get home.

MARISOL: There's gotta be a way, *Cometa.* Papi, you gotta help me find a way.

(PAPI *creates a hip-hop beat.*)

COMETA: What's that noise?

PAPI:

> He was from the street.
> Got himself a beat.
> Thought himself sweet.
> A neat super-freak!

(PAPI *transforms into* GRAVITY. GRAVITY *is hip. He wears a pair of sunglasses. He carries the planet Earth, which is the size of a basketball.* GRAVITY *speaks like a mix between a California surfer and a Spanish 101 student.*)

PAPI (*as* GRAVITY): *Oye,* dudes!

MARISOL/COMETA: Dudes?

MARISOL: *¿Quién eres tú?*

PAPI (*as* GRAVITY): *Gravedad,* Gravity, at your service, *amigos!*

COMETA: You're Gravity?

PAPI (*as* GRAVITY): Yeah, Gravity, man! What goes up must come down, *¿sabes?* What can I do for you?

MARISOL: You gotta let go of your gravity so *Cometa* can get back into the sky.

PAPI (*as* GRAVITY): Whoa! I can't do that! *Imagínate,* if I let gravity go everything would float away! There'd be dolphins flying and babies crying!

COMETA: I knew it wouldn't work!

MARISOL: There must be a way.

PAPI (*as* GRAVITY): There's only one way. *¡Hay una sola manera!*

MARISOL. What is it?

PAPI (*as* GRAVITY, *he holds basketball above the fire*): Someone has to hold Earth away from the Sun.

MARISOL: I'll do it!

PAPI (*as* GRAVITY): It could be *peligroso.* Someone has to hold Earth just right. If that could be done then I could bat *Cometa* into the sky!

COMETA: What do you mean, dangerous?

PAPI (*as* GRAVITY): The Sun *es un gran fuego!* (*Holding the ball over the fire.*) A great big ball of fire, and if you don't hold Earth just right, you could become a chicharrón!

COMETA: A *chicharrón?*

PAPI (*as* GRAVITY): A *chicharrón!* In other words, burnt toast!

MARISOL: I don't care! I want to help *Cometa!*

COMETA: He's talking burnt toast *chicharrones* here and I don't want to leave you *solita.*

MARISOL: I won't be alone.

COMETA: Will you come with me?

MARISOL: *Cometa,* my *mami* is going to be here real soon.

COMETA: But I'm scared.

MARISOL: I am too.

COMETA: You are?

MARISOL: Ah huh. Make a wish.

COMETA: What for?

MARISOL: Close your eyes and just do it.

COMETA: But they don't come true.

MARISOL: Sure they do. You just have to have a little faith and work hard to make it happen.

COMETA: Will you wish with me?

MARISOL: Okay. I'm a good wisher.

(*They close their eyes and wish.*)

MARISOL/COMETA: I wish . . . *quisiera* . . .

COMETA: Did it work?

PAPI (*as* GRAVITY): Órale, ya estuvo, time's up! *Vámonos* with the goodbyes!

(GRAVITY *gives Earth to* MARISOL *to hold over the fire. She struggles to hold on. It is very heavy.*)

PAPI (*as* GRAVITY): Hold on tight!

MARISOL: Get ready, *Cometa*!

(GRAVITY *picks up the bat.* COMETA *streaks across to the other side of the stage.*)

COMETA: I'm ready!

PAPI: Fernando looks in for the sign—

MARISOL: Hurry, it's getting hot!

PAPI: —he winds up and—

(COMETA *streaks towards* GRAVITY. *He swings, launching* COMETA *into the sky. A small, lighted piñata is seen flying into the sky. The sound of a stadium crowd roaring.*)

PAPI (*as* GRAVITY): Es . . . es . . . es un home run!

COMETA (*exiting*): My wish came true! Thank you!

MARISOL: ¡Adiós, *Cometa*!

PAPI (*as* GRAVITY): ¡Órale, dude, tú tienes mucho corazón!

(*A hip-hop beat is heard again as* GRAVITY *transforms into* PAPI. *The busy freeway is heard once again.*)

PAPI: So *Cometa* flew back into heaven on the seams of a baseball. C. T. found a Christmas *fiesta* and a child who would love him just the way he was.

MARISOL: And *Globo*?

(*Hawaiian music is heard.*)

PAPI: *Globo* landed on a beach.

MARISOL: ¿Una playa?

PAPI: The monster wind carried him all the way to Hawaii! Aloha!

MARISOL: Aloha!

PAPI: The end. ¡El fin!

(MARISOL *yawns.*)

PAPI: Time for sleep. It's been a long night. Acuéstate, Marisol.

(MARISOL *looks out across the city.*)

PAPI: ¿Qué haces, Marisol?

MARISOL: Waiting for Mami to come home.

PAPI: Home?

MARISOL: Ah huh.

(PAPI *wraps* MARISOL *in her old blanket.*)

PAPI: You just wait and see. There's a future for us here in Los Angeles. *El futuro es nuestro.* We crossed mountains and deserts to get here. Anybody who can do that deserves to live here, *¿que no?*

MARISOL: *¡Que sí!* I feel better, Papi. Will you sing me to sleep?

PAPI: *Seguro que sí.*

(MARISOL *lies down near the fire as* PAPI *sings "Noche de paz" [Silent Night].* MARISOL *falls asleep. A moment later* MAMI *enters. She joins him singing.*)

PAPI: *¡Corazón!* I was afraid I'd never—

MAMI: I'm here, *amor.*

PAPI: *Gracias a Dios.*

(*They embrace.* MARISOL *awakens.*)

MARISOL: *¡Mami!*

MAMI: *¡Marisol!* Oh, I missed you, *mijita.*

MARISOL: Mami, what took you so long?

MAMI: I got lost.

MARISOL: How did you find us?

MAMI: You wouldn't believe me if I told you.

PAPI: Tell us.

MAMI: I followed a comet, like the Three Wise Men who followed the Star of Bethlehem. A little comet showed me the way home to you.

MARISOL (*looking skyward*): Cometa . . .

MAMI: *Viejo,* have you been telling your stories again? *¿Tus cuentos?*

PAPI: *Pos* . . .

MARISOL: *¡Esta es nuestra primera Navidad en Los Angeles!* This is our first Christmas in Los Angeles together!

MAMI: Happy Christmas!

PAPI: Mari Christmas!

MARISOL: Merry Christmas!

(*They all look at one another, not sure whether they pronounced it correctly. Then . . .*)

ALL: *¡Feliz Navidad!*

(*Lights fade.*)

CURTAIN

Designer's Response

As I began to think about the environment and situation of the characters in the script, I recalled images from memories of my own few trips to Los Angeles, with its remarkable landmarks and crowded roads.

Los Angeles is a strange amalgam of Mediterranean climate with old versus new, clean versus dirty, bourgeois versus lower class. And into this is thrust a family struggling to survive and make a better life for themselves in living quarters under a highway. They are isolated and overwhelmed by the unfamiliar surroundings.

I wanted images that would capture the modern city of Los Angeles. In my library search I was coming up with little. I began to look online and found a wealth of images of the city in the work of John Humble, an L.A. photographer. His images spoke volumes about the bold contrasts and vistas of the city: the Los Angeles River, the skyline, and the L.A. County freeway system. Images of highway overpasses, buildings, and billboards were amazing and provided the sense of scale and isolation that I knew I would want to use in my design.

I began to play with shape and scale and settled on the one preliminary image seen here in the simple sketch (plate A). This one led me to the final drawing, in which the perspective is somewhat altered (plate B). It also brings together billboard, highway, skyline, palm trees, and chain-link fence, which immediately reveal where these characters are located. The short introductory scene could be staged with a realistic soundscape along with some dramatic lighting effects that identify the swiftly moving traffic on the highway above the scene.

Resources

A Place in the Sun: Photographs of Los Angeles by John Humble. Exhibit, the J. Paul Getty
    Museum, the Getty Center, March 27–July 8, 2007.
Numerous Internet image searches

Plate A: Simple sketch combining elements.

Plate B: Preliminary design further realized.

Tomás and the Library Lady

Adapted for the stage by
José Cruz González

Based on the book Tomás and the Library Lady by Pat Mora,
illustrated by Raul Colón

Tomás and the Library Lady was originally commissioned by
Childsplay, Tempe, Arizona.

Love is necessary in the classroom. A teacher should realize that if he has love for children he will be creating lasting happy individuals. A degree of love brings security to a child and makes him feel worthwhile. A child realizes he is loved and in turn will respond as a unique individual to that love.

—Tomás Rivera, 1961

It is impossible to imagine Chicano literature without the migrant worker.

—Tomás Rivera, "The Great Plains as Refuge in Chicano Literature"

The Great Plains have a special attraction to me as a person and as a fiction writer. I spent half of my first twenty years in one or another mid-western or Great Plains state. As a child and as a young man, I lived in Iowa, the Dakotas, Minnesota, Michigan, Wisconsin, and Ohio.

—Tomás Rivera, "The Great Plains as Refuge in Chicano Literature"

Characters

MALE ACTOR: our storyteller. He will transform into YOUNG TOMÁS
(age nine), ADULT TOMÁS, 'APÁ (FLORENCIO), and the voice of PAPÁ
GRANDE.

FEMALE ACTOR: our storyteller. She will play NIGHTMARE TEACHER, 'AMÁ
(JOSEFA), LIBRARY LADY, and ENRIQUE.

Setting

The play takes place in various locations in Hampton, Iowa,
and in Tomás' imagination.

Note on Casting

Roles may be divided to increase cast size
by assigning each actor a specific character.

AT RISE: *Upstage is a framed structure that serves as a projection area. At center is a small movable structure that may serve as a bench, bookshelf, or table. MALE ACTOR and FEMALE ACTOR enter, carrying suitcases.*

MALE ACTOR: Tomás—

FEMALE ACTOR: —and the Library Lady!

MALE ACTOR: Many years later he would fondly speak of the little library lady who introduced him to the wonderful world of books.

(FEMALE ACTOR *opens an umbrella.*)

FEMALE ACTOR: And every now and then, on a quiet summer afternoon, she often wondered what ever happened to the little boy who loved to read.

(MALE ACTOR *opens a book.*)

MALE ACTOR/FEMALE ACTOR: This is their story.

(*Music. They transform into* FLORENCIO *and* JOSEFA.)

MALE ACTOR/FEMALE ACTOR (*singing*):

Vámonos p'al Norte
Caminando con mucha fe
A buscar un jale
Qué Dios nos cuide

Pisca, pisca, pisca
Pisca, pisca, pisca
Betabel,
Espinaca

MALE ACTOR (*whistling*): ¡Vámonos p'al norte!

FEMALE ACTOR: ¡Tomás! ¡Enrique!

MALE ACTOR: ¡Métanse al carro!

FEMALE ACTOR: ¡Ándale, muchachos!

(*They load their suitcases into an imaginary car.*)

MALE ACTOR/FEMALE ACTOR (*singing*):

We're going to the northland
We're working with our hands
We're traveling a road paved with strife
In search of a better life

We pick, pick, pick
Pick, pick, pick
Pick, pick, pick
Pick, pick, pick
Beets,
And spinach too

(On the screen a shadow image of a small car traveling on the road at night appears.)

MALE ACTOR: Era medianoche.

FEMALE ACTOR: It was midnight.

MALE ACTOR: En una carretera larga y llena de baches.

FEMALE ACTOR: On a long and bumpy road.

MALE ACTOR: La luz de la luna llena seguía un viejo carro cansado.

FEMALE ACTOR: The light of the full moon followed a tired old car.

MALE ACTOR: Y una familia de campesinos dormía en la parte de atrás.

FEMALE ACTOR: And a farm worker family slept in the back.

MALE ACTOR: Dreaming of bright tomorrows.

FEMALE ACTOR: While a young mother—

MALE ACTOR: —and father—

FEMALE ACTOR: —worried over their son.

MALE ACTOR: En su mundo sólo hablaban español.

FEMALE ACTOR: In their world they only spoke Spanish.

MALE ACTOR/FEMALE ACTOR: This is what they said.

(They sit as if driving in a car. They place a blanket over a suitcase, making it appear as if someone is sleeping underneath.)

'AMÁ: Florencio, we shouldn't have taken Tomás out of school.

'APÁ: We had no choice.

'AMÁ: I want his life to be far better than ours.

'APÁ: Don't you think I want that for both our sons?

'AMÁ: If only we had stayed in Tejas—

'APÁ: —we would have starved. My compadre says there's plenty of work in Iowa. I promise you when we've earned enough money we'll go back home and Tomás can start school in the fall again.

'AMÁ: He's going to be so far behind when he returns.

'APÁ: Maybe we can help prepare him somehow.

'AMÁ: ¿*Cómo?*

'APÁ: I don't know how, but we'll ask *Papá Grande* when he wakes up. He'll think of something.

'AMÁ: I just wish—

'APÁ: *Josefa*, what's troubling you?

'AMÁ: *Tomás* has been tossing and turning in his sleep again.

'APÁ: You needn't worry. He'll be fine.

'AMÁ: Something's haunting him in his dreams—I know it.

(*An old school bell is rung, echoing into an ominous sound.* MALE ACTOR *transforms into* YOUNG TOMÁS *while* FEMALE ACTOR *opens a suitcase, disappearing behind it.* YOUNG TOMÁS *has a nightmare. Inside the suitcase a frightening image of the* NIGHTMARE TEACHER *appears.*)

NIGHTMARE TEACHER: I pledge allegiance to the flag—

YOUNG TOMÁS: ¿*Maestra?*

NIGHTMARE TEACHER: How many times have I told you to speak English, young man?

YOUNG TOMÁS: ¿*Qué dices?*

NIGHTMARE TEACHER: I'm putting a stop to this behavior once and for all!

YOUNG TOMÁS: ¡*No entiendo!*

NIGHTMARE TEACHER: I won't stand for this in my classroom! Do you understand me?

YOUNG TOMÁS: ¿*Maestra?*

NIGHTMARE TEACHER: Say it, Tommy: "I will not daydream, be lazy, or speak Spanish!" Say it, say it, or I'll get you!

YOUNG TOMÁS: ¡'*Amá!*

(*The suitcase is slammed shut by* JOSEFA. *She is now driving the old car.* YOUNG TOMÁS *awakens. A horn is heard from a passing car.*)

'AMÁ: *Tomás, tuviste un mal sueño.*

YOUNG TOMÁS: It felt real, 'Amá.

'AMÁ: What was your nightmare about?

YOUNG TOMÁS: I don't want to talk about it.

(YOUNG TOMÁS *drinks from a canteen.*)

'AMÁ: *Tomás*, slow down before you make yourself sick!

YOUNG TOMÁS: I'm so thirsty!

'AMÁ: *Despacio.*

YOUNG TOMÁS: If I had *un vaso de agua fría* I would drink it *todo!*

'AMÁ: Slow down.

YOUNG TOMÁS: I would suck the ice and pour the last *gotitas* of water on my face.

'AMÁ: Better?

YOUNG TOMÁS: No.

('AMÁ *hugs* YOUNG TOMÁS.)

'AMÁ: Hugs are the best thing, you know? They make you feel better and they cost nothing.

YOUNG TOMÁS: I feel better.

'AMÁ: Good. Your *'apá* and I feel awful for taking you out of school—

YOUNG TOMÁS: *'Amá,* I don't want to talk about it anymore.

'AMÁ: But in the fall you'll return to the same teacher and—

YOUNG TOMÁS: Please *'Amá!*

'AMÁ: Fine, I won't bring it up anymore unless you want.

(PAPÁ GRANDE *is heard snoring loudly.*)

YOUNG TOMÁS: *Papá Grande* is snoring again.

'AMÁ: I don't think anyone is going to get much sleep tonight.

YOUNG TOMÁS: He sounds like a big old giant.

YOUNG TOMÁS / 'AMÁ: *Papá Grande,* you're snoring again!

'AMÁ: Turn over!

(PAPÁ GRANDE *snorts and then sleeps quietly.*)

'AMÁ: You know, your *Papá Grande* is always reminding your father and I how smart and talented you are.

YOUNG TOMÁS: He does?

'AMÁ: Your *Papá Grande* thinks that someday you're going to be a great writer or a famous painter.

YOUNG TOMÁS: *¿De veras?*

'AMÁ: He's always saying—

(PAPÁ GRANDE's *big white mustache appears on the screen.*)

PAPÁ GRANDE: *Un escritor* writes great thoughts and *un pintor* paints great paintings. Some say that *artistas* are *locos* but I say they are touched by God's own brilliant madness.

'AMÁ: My *papá* is wise but I sure wish he'd trim that big, bushy mustache of his. I can't bear to watch him eat—

(PAPÁ GRANDE *sneezes loudly.*)

PAPÁ GRANDE: Achooo!

'AMÁ: —or sneeze!

YOUNG TOMÁS: *¡Salud, Papá Grande!*

PAPÁ GRANDE: *¡Gracias, Tomasito!*

(PAPÁ GRANDE's *image fades away. A car tire is heard exploding.*)

'AMÁ: *¡Ay, la llanta!*

YOUNG TOMÁS: Is it a flat tire?

'AMÁ: Ah huh. *¡Florencio!*

(YOUNG TOMÁS *and* 'AMÁ *step out of the car. On the screen is an image of a full moon and an old car on a hill with a man working to repair a flat tire. We hear crickets and the car being repaired.*)

YOUNG TOMÁS: Where are we now, *¿'Amá?*

'AMÁ: Somewhere in Iowa. Far away from *Tejas.*

YOUNG TOMÁS (*under his breath*): And school.

'AMÁ: What?

YOUNG TOMÁS: Nothing. We've been driving forever.

'AMÁ: It won't be much longer before we're at the camp.

YOUNG TOMÁS: How can 'Apá even tell where we're going when it's night?

'AMÁ: Your *'apá* can see *muy bien* because of the light of a full moon, and the headlights of the *carro* shine on the passing road signs.

(YOUNG TOMÁS *yawns.*)

YOUNG TOMÁS: 'Amá, what do you think about when you don't sleep?

'AMÁ: Mostly it's about you and your brother Enrique. And you?

YOUNG TOMÁS: I think about lots of things. Sleeping isn't one of them.

'AMÁ: I think about what you'll grow up to be. Will you live near your *'apá* and me when we're old? Will you laugh and be silly like your *Papá Grande?* Will you be happy?

YOUNG TOMÁS: 'Amá, you don't have nothing to worry about 'cause I'm never going to grow up, or move away. I'll live with you, 'Apá, and *Papá Grande* forever.

'AMÁ: When I was your age I said the same thing to my *mamá* and *papá.* Then I sprouted into a young lady. I met your *'apá* and fell in love.

YOUNG TOMÁS: Yuck!

'AMÁ: We got married.

YOUNG TOMÁS: Yuck! I'm never, ever going to marry a girl!

'AMÁ: Never say never, and forever is a long time.

'APÁ (offstage): ¡Vámonos!

('APÁ waves to them. YOUNG TOMÁS waves back. YOUNG TOMÁS and 'AMÁ sit in the front seat of the car. She continues driving. YOUNG TOMÁS plays with his toy car. On the screen we see a little old car on the road as the moon trails behind. YOUNG TOMÁS looks back.)

YOUNG TOMÁS: I think the moon is following us, 'Amá.

(She stops the car. The moon stops moving. They look back.)

'AMÁ: ¿La luna?

(She starts driving again. The moon follows.)

YOUNG TOMÁS: Yeah, when we left Tejas, the moon was in the sky right behind us.

'AMÁ: That was days ago.

(She stops the car again. The moon stops. They look back once again. Nothing. She drives on as the moon follows.)

YOUNG TOMÁS: And each night la luna is still in the same place. I think the moon is a lost puppy.

(YOUNG TOMÁS barks at the moon.)

'AMÁ: Silly boy.

(The moon howls back.)

YOUNG TOMÁS: I like the quiet of night, and how the tires make the road hum, and that our familia stays together. I bet that you and me are the only people in the whole world awake tonight.

'AMÁ: It feels that way, doesn't it?

('AMÁ yawns.)

YOUNG TOMÁS: 'Amá, don't you ever get sleepy?

'AMÁ: Yes, I do, but it's my turn to drive. I wouldn't want to fall asleep while driving, ¿qué no?

YOUNG TOMÁS: Yeah, 'cause we might end up falling off a giant cliff, or into a fiery lava pit, or maybe even get swallowed up by the earth and never be found!

'AMÁ: ¡Ay, no!

YOUNG TOMÁS: 'Amá, what's Iowa like?

'AMÁ: It's a big country with lots of work. Your *'apá* and I and *Papá Grande* are going to pick crops there.

YOUNG TOMÁS: Like what?

'AMÁ: *Elotes,* corn.

YOUNG TOMÁS: Yuck!

'AMÁ: *Betabeles,* beets.

YOUNG TOMÁS: Double yuck!

'AMÁ: *Espinaca,* spinach.

YOUNG TOMÁS: I'm never eating that!

'AMÁ: There'll be plenty of it and you'll eat it all, *¡señor!*

(YOUNG TOMÁS *yawns and lays his head down. On the screen we see the little old car passing through a migrant camp. Music.* YOUNG TOMÁS *falls asleep.*)

'AMÁ (*singing*):

    Duerme, duerme, duerme, niño,
    Sueña, sueña, sueña, mi lindo,
    Duerme, duerme, duerme, hijo,
    Sueña, sueña, sueña, mi ángel,
    En paz, en paz, en paz—

'AMÁ: We're here.

(FLORENCIO *and* JOSEFA *stand looking at an old, rundown wooden shack. The moon glows brightly above. A single chicken is heard.*)

'APÁ: *Bueno, Josefa, este es nuestro hogar.*

'AMÁ: Florencio, it's a chicken coop.

'APÁ: I know it isn't much.

'AMÁ: We're not chickens. Shoo!

'APÁ: It could be worse.

'AMÁ: How?

'APÁ: We could be living in a car, or a tent, or out in the open air. This is the only housing there is in Hampton for migrant workers like us. It's all the *patrón* can provide.

(*A single chicken is heard.*)

'AMÁ: I would like to see his house. I bet it isn't a chicken coop. Shoo!

'APÁ: We're one of the lucky families.

'AMÁ: If this is luck then I don't want it.

'APÁ: It's the best I can do, *amor. Lo siento.* There's nowhere else.

'AMÁ: I bet it isn't even clean.

'APÁ: I asked some of the *muchachos* in the camp to sweep it before we arrived.

(*They enter the rundown shack.*)

'AMÁ: I bet there're salamanders and spiders.

'APÁ: If there are I'll take care of them. *Te lo prometo.*

'AMÁ: I bet it isn't even big enough for two families.

'APÁ: I think it could be.

'AMÁ: Well, it's going to take a lot of work.

'APÁ: *Papá Grande* and I can put up a divider to make two rooms, one room where we, our aunts, and our uncles can sleep, and the other room for a kitchen.

'AMÁ: We could use some scraps of wood and cardboard to fill up the cracks to keep the cold and salamanders and spiders out.

'APÁ: That's a good idea. I'll do that. You'll see, *Josefa*, once we're through fixing up this *casita*, it'll be just like our—

'AMÁ: Don't even say it! My house in *Tejas* is not a chicken coop!

'APÁ: I'll fix it the way you want.

(*He embraces her.*)

'AMÁ: *Gracias a Dios* we made it safely to Iowa.

'APÁ: It pays to have *el padre* bless the *carro*. We only broke down once and we had enough gas rations to get us here.

(*A window appears and moonbeams pour into the wooden shack.*)

MALE ACTOR: *Tomás* curled up on the floor in the small house that his family shared with the other workers. He opened his eyes momentarily to see the moon shining brightly through the wooden slats of the shack as if waiting for him to come out and play.

FEMALE ACTOR: He thought he heard the moon howl but his eyelids slowly closed and he floated off to sleep.

MALE ACTOR: The chill of the air kept everyone huddled together and they slept peacefully for the first time in days.

FEMALE ACTOR: And *Tomás* dreamed of *pan dulce*, sweet bread his 'Amá would make and that he loved to eat.

(*Music.* JOSEFA *carries a suitcase, giving it to* YOUNG TOMÁS. *He opens it, holding up a sweet bread pig. Pieces of* pan dulce *with little wings fly across the upstage screen.*)

'AMÁ: I've got ¡cochinitos!

YOUNG TOMÁS: *¡Cochinitos!*

'AMÁ: *¡Elotitos!*

YOUNG TOMÁS: *¡Elotitos!*

'AMÁ: *¡Cuernitos!*

YOUNG TOMÁS: *¡Cuernitos! ¡Un cochinito!*

(*More and more little sweet bread pigs appear until they transform into the shadow of the* NIGHTMARE TEACHER.)

NIGHTMARE TEACHER: Say it, Tommy: "I will not daydream, be lazy, or speak Spanish!" Say it!

YOUNG TOMÁS: *¡Maestra!*

NIGHTMARE TEACHER: Say it!

YOUNG TOMÁS: *¡No entiendo!*

NIGHTMARE TEACHER: Say it or I'm going to get you!

YOUNG TOMÁS: *¡No! ¡'Amá!*

(YOUNG TOMÁS *awakens as* JOSEFA *enters, shutting the suitcase closed.*)

'AMÁ: *Tomás, tuviste un mal sueño.* Do you want to tell me about it?

(YOUNG TOMÁS *steps away.*)

FEMALE ACTOR: This nightmare intruder troubled *Tomás* greatly.

MALE ACTOR: You see, he worried about going back to his school and to his Nightmare Teacher.

FEMALE ACTOR: He didn't want to be yelled at—

MALE ACTOR: —or laughed at—

FEMALE ACTOR: —because he didn't understand English so well.

MALE ACTOR: But he didn't know what to do.

FEMALE ACTOR: So he kept it to himself.

MALE ACTOR/FEMALE ACTOR: Hoping it would just go away.

(*A rooster is heard. Dawn. On the screen the migrant camp begins to emerge in the vast Iowa landscape. Trucks are heard starting up, voices of men and women, trucks rumbling off into the distance. A cornfield appears on the screen.*)

FEMALE ACTOR: Early the next morning, *Tomás' familia* went out to pick corn, *elotes,* in the green fields.

MALE ACTOR: *¡Ándale, vámos a piscar elotes!*

FEMALE ACTOR: All day they worked in the hot sun.

(*The sun arcs across the sky as farm workers toil in the fields.* MALE ACTOR *and* FEMALE ACTOR *work on stage.*)

MALE ACTOR/FEMALE ACTOR (singing):

> Elotes are what we pick all day
> Elotes help us earn our pay
> Green fields of *elotes*
> Many, many fields of *elotes*
> Elotes are what we pick all day
> Will life get better someday?

MALE ACTOR: *Tomás* and Enrique carried water to the workers.

FEMALE ACTOR: And when they tired they slept under the shade of swaying cornstalks.

MALE ACTOR: At lunch the boys played with a ball their 'Amá had sewn from an old teddy bear.

MALE ACTOR/FEMALE ACTOR (singing):

> Elotes are what we pick all day
> Elotes help us earn our pay
> Green fields of *elotes*
> Many, many fields of *elotes*
> Elotes are what we pick all day
> Will life get better someday?

(PAPÁ GRANDE's *big white mustache appears on the screen. The glow of a fire.*)

PAPÁ GRANDE: ¡Ay, tengo mucha sed!

YOUNG TOMÁS: Have some cool water, *Papá Grande!*

(*He drinks from a canteen. Water drips off his mustache.*)

PAPÁ GRANDE: ¡Ay, qué buena el agua fría! Thank you, mijito.

(*He sneezes loudly.*)

YOUNG TOMÁS: Hey!

PAPÁ GRANDE: ¡Ay! Lo siento, Tomasito.

ENRIQUE: Papá Grande, tell us the *cuento* about the man in the forest!

PAPÁ GRANDE: En un tiempo pasado, once long ago on a windy night—

(ENRIQUE *creates the wind.*)

PAPÁ GRANDE: —a man, un hombre, was riding a horse through a forest.

(YOUNG TOMÁS *creates the hooves of the horse galloping.*)

PAPÁ GRANDE: The wind was howling, whooooooooo, and the leaves were blowing, whish, whish . . .

YOUNG TOMÁS: All of a sudden something grabbed the *hombre*.

PAPÁ GRANDE: He couldn't move.

ENRIQUE: He was so scared to look around.

PAPÁ GRANDE: All night, *toda la noche*, he wanted to ride away.

YOUNG TOMÁS: But he couldn't!

PAPÁ GRANDE: How the wind howled, whoooooooo. How the leaves blew.

ENRIQUE: How his teeth chattered!

PAPÁ GRANDE: *Finalmente*, the sun came up. Slowly the *hombre* turned around. And who do you think was holding him?

YOUNG TOMÁS: A thorny tree!

ENRIQUE/PAPÁ GRANDE: *¡Tomás!*

(ENRIQUE *exits.*)

PAPÁ GRANDE: You know all my *cuentos*! *Tomasito*, you're going to have to learn some new ones!

YOUNG TOMÁS: New ones?

PAPÁ GRANDE: *Ándale.*

MALE ACTOR: The next day Young *Tomás* had a job to do. He was going into town all by himself—

(*'AMÁ enters and hands* YOUNG TOMÁS *a letter.*)

'AMÁ: Tomás, you come home right after you've delivered this letter to the post office.

YOUNG TOMÁS: Yes, 'Amá.

'AMÁ: Don't wander staring at the big buildings like you do.

YOUNG TOMÁS: No, 'Amá.

'AMÁ: People in town are going to think the sun has baked your *cabeza* and call you *loco*. *¿Me entiendes?*

YOUNG TOMÁS: Yes, 'Amá.

'AMÁ: I don't want anyone thinking that you haven't been raised proper.

YOUNG TOMÁS: No, 'Amá.

'AMÁ: Keep your hair combed, clothes clean, shoes dry, and behave yourself just like if you were at school with your teacher.

(*Beat*)

'AMÁ: What is it, *mijo?*

YOUNG TOMÁS: *Nada.*

'AMÁ: You've turned pale as if you saw a ghost. Are you all right?

YOUNG TOMÁS: I'm fine.

'AMÁ: Ándale pues. Hurry now.

(YOUNG TOMÁS starts running. He runs through town. We see the rundown migrant camp, then pristine houses and stores on the screen behind him.)

YOUNG TOMÁS: Oh, it's so hot! ¡Qué calor!

(A tall brick building appears. YOUNG TOMÁS looks up to see in giant letters "Carnegie Library." The letters "Carne" become more pronounced.)

YOUNG TOMÁS: Huh. ¿Carne? Meat library?

(He scratches his head.)

YOUNG TOMÁS: No.

FEMALE ACTOR: Tomás just stood there speechless.

(The building zooms up close until he is standing right in front of its very doors. He peeks through the glass.)

FEMALE ACTOR: He didn't even notice when the lady holding an umbrella appeared right behind him.

(A tall, silhouetted figure appears on the screen. FEMALE ACTOR opens an umbrella and becomes the LIBRARY LADY. She taps YOUNG TOMÁS on the shoulder.)

LIBRARY LADY (Slight German accent): Hey!

YOUNG TOMÁS: Aagghhh!

LIBRARY LADY: I see you!

YOUNG TOMÁS: I have to go!

LIBRARY LADY: You come here every day!

YOUNG TOMÁS: Back to el campo!

LIBRARY LADY: Wait!

YOUNG TOMÁS: ¡Perdóneme!

LIBRARY LADY: What are you saying?

YOUNG TOMÁS: I'm sorry! So sorry!

LIBRARY LADY: It's all right, boy.

YOUNG TOMÁS: Am I in trouble?

LIBRARY LADY: No, of course not. I scared you, didn't I? I'm so sorry. You look like you could use a cool drink of water. Why don't you come inside the library?

YOUNG TOMÁS: Library?

LIBRARY LADY: That's right.

YOUNG TOMÁS: The sign on it says *Carne-gi-eh.*

LIBRARY LADY: It's pronounced "Carnegie," not "carnay-gee-eh" —

YOUNG TOMÁS: *Carne.*

LIBRARY LADY: What?

YOUNG TOMÁS: *Carne* means meat in Spanish.

LIBRARY LADY: Carnay is "meat."

YOUNG TOMÁS: Yes.

LIBRARY LADY: Carnay —

YOUNG TOMÁS: *Carne.*

LIBRARY LADY: *Caar-nay!*

YOUNG TOMÁS: *Carne.*

LIBRARY LADY: *Car-naay!*

YOUNG TOMÁS: *Carne.*

LIBRARY LADY: *Carne!*

YOUNG TOMÁS: Yes!

(*She imagines a side of beef. We see it on the screen.*)

LIBRARY LADY: Oh, my!

YOUNG TOMÁS: What is it?

LIBRARY LADY: I understand now! A meat library!

(*A cow is heard mooing!*)

YOUNG TOMÁS: It isn't really a meat library, is it?

LIBRARY LADY: Come and see for yourself.

YOUNG TOMÁS: Am I allowed?

LIBRARY LADY: Of course. This is a public library and everyone is welcome. I should know, I work here. I'm sure you must be parched!

YOUNG TOMÁS: Parched?

LIBRARY LADY: That means "thirsty."

YOUNG TOMÁS: Parched. I like the sound of that word. Yes, I'm "parched."

LIBRARY LADY: What's your name?

YOUNG TOMÁS: *Tomás Rivera.*

LIBRARY LADY: It's a pleasure to meet you, *Tomás Riviera.*

YOUNG TOMÁS: *Rivera.*

LIBRARY LADY: *Rrreviera!*

YOUNG TOMÁS: *Rivera. Rrr-rrr—rrr.*

LIBRARY LADY: *Rrr-rrr—rrr.* I'll have to practice that new word!

MALE ACTOR: *Tomás* broke into a smile.

FEMALE ACTOR: And so did the library lady.

MALE ACTOR: He understood what she was talking about.

FEMALE ACTOR: She understood what he was talking about.

LIBRARY LADY: Come, *Tomás!*

(*The interior of the library appears on the screen. She reveals a shelf filled with books.*)

YOUNG TOMÁS: They're *libros!* Lots and lots of *libros!*

LIBRARY LADY: What are "leebros"?

YOUNG TOMÁS: *Libros* are books.

LIBRARY LADY: *Libros.*

YOUNG TOMÁS: Where did they all come from?

LIBRARY LADY: Everywhere you can imagine. This section here is for grown-ups, and this place, my favorite place, is for children. Why don't we pick something for you to read?

YOUNG TOMÁS: For me?

LIBRARY LADY: Yes, and later you can borrow some to take with you.

YOUNG TOMÁS: "Borrow?"

LIBRARY LADY: It means you can take them with you and when you're through you just bring them back. I'll check them out for you in my name.

YOUNG TOMÁS: *¡Oh! ¡Pedir prestado!*

LIBRARY LADY: We'll start with this book.

(*YOUNG TOMÁS opens the book.*)

YOUNG TOMÁS: "The jello cat eh-sleeps."

LIBRARY LADY: That's a very good start. The sound of "Y" in yellow is "yuh." Try sounding it out again.

YOUNG TOMÁS: Yuh, yuh, yellow. "The yellow cat eh-sleeps."

LIBRARY LADY: Good! Now, this word is "sleeps" and it begins with the letter "s."

YOUNG TOMÁS: "Eh-sleeps."

LIBRARY LADY: I mean that the sound of "s" is "s-s-s." Now you try.

YOUNG TOMÁS: S-s-s . . . s-s-sleeps . . . sleeps! "The yellow cat sleeps. The yellow cat sleeps. The yellow cat sleeps."

LIBRARY LADY: Well done!

YOUNG TOMÁS: My tongue is tired!

LIBRARY LADY: Good reading takes a lot of practice.

MALE ACTOR: Young *Tomás* decided he'd practice and practice.

FEMALE ACTOR: He was thirsty to learn new things.

(*The* LIBRARY LADY *hands* YOUNG TOMÁS *two books.*)

LIBRARY LADY: Goodbye!

YOUNG TOMÁS: 'Bye!

(YOUNG TOMÁS *freezes in place as the town buildings and pristine houses zoom by. He arrives at the migrant camp. 'AMÁ is drying her hands with a towel as he enters.*)

YOUNG TOMÁS: ¡'Amá! ¡'Amá!

'AMÁ: Shhh, you'll wake your brother Enrique. He's taking a nap. Do you want to draw some pictures together before I start dinner?

(*She pulls out his drawings on scraps of paper.*)

YOUNG TOMÁS: 'Amá, look what I got!

'AMÁ: ¿Dónde encontraste estos libros?

YOUNG TOMÁS: At the *Carne* Library, 'Amá!

'AMÁ: *Carne* Library?

YOUNG TOMÁS: At the *Carne-gi-eh* Library, 'Amá!

'AMÁ: *Carne-gi-eh* Library? ¿Qué es eso?

YOUNG TOMÁS: ¡Una señora me prestó los libros! ¡Mira!

'AMÁ: She gave you these books?

YOUNG TOMÁS: No. She let me "borrow" them.

'AMÁ: ¿Qué es "borrow?"

YOUNG TOMÁS: *Prestar.*

'AMÁ: Ah!

YOUNG TOMÁS: The library lady said that when I finished reading these I could go back for more!

'AMÁ: No me digas.

YOUNG TOMÁS: And the library is filled con muchos libros. All kinds, all sizes, all colors with big letters and little letters, some with pictures and some without pictures and they all smell so good. And it's real clean and quiet there so you can read as long as you want.

'AMÁ: Which book are you going to read first?

YOUNG TOMÁS: This one! No! This one! ¡No sé! ¡Ay, estoy tan confundido!

'AMÁ: And the letter? Did you deliver it?

YOUNG TOMÁS: Oh, no!

'AMÁ: ¡Ay, Tomás! One day your head is going to float off into the clouds and you won't even know it! Bueno pues, mañana you deliver the correo.

YOUNG TOMÁS: Okay, 'Amá.

('AMÁ exits.)

MALE ACTOR: Young Tomás liked visiting the library. There were so many interesting things to read. The library lady was always there to help him.

(Music. The LIBRARY LADY enters. As the song progresses dinosaurs, horses, and baseball images appear on the screen in the bookshelves.)

YOUNG TOMÁS: The big, tall, deeno-sour—

LIBRARY LADY: Try again.

YOUNG TOMÁS: The big, tall, dino-sour—

LIBRARY LADY: Close. "Dinosaur."

YOUNG TOMÁS (singing):

    The big, tall, dinosaur!

LIBRARY LADY: Good! Read on!

YOUNG TOMÁS (singing):

    The big, tall, dinosaur
    Drank near the shiny shore

YOUNG TOMÁS: What's that say?

LIBRARY LADY (singing):

    Wild snakebirds fly so high

Now you.

YOUNG TOMÁS (singing):

    Wild snakebirds fly so high
    Up in the clear blue sky

LIBRARY LADY: Excellent! Go on!

YOUNG TOMÁS (singing):

    I saw smoke at an Indian camp
    Rode a horse I named Champ

YOUNG TOMÁS / LIBRARY LADY (singing):

    Across a hot and dusty plain
    Sheriff Earp was my name

FEMALE ACTOR: *Tomás* was swept away.

YOUNG TOMÁS (*singing*):

The baseball fans watched and sat
With Mighty Casey at the bat
Mudville down just four to two
What would Casey do?

FEMALE ACTOR: He forgot about Iowa and Texas.

YOUNG TOMÁS / LIBRARY LADY (*singing*):

A twister took Dorothy to Oz
She and Toto were scared and lost
Lions and tigers and bears, oh my
A big bad witch in the sky

(*The* LIBRARY LADY *exits.* PAPÁ GRANDE's *giant white mustache appears.*)

PAPÁ GRANDE: Tomasito, ¿qué haces?

YOUNG TOMÁS: I'm reading, *Papá Grande.*

PAPÁ GRANDE: Reading what?

YOUNG TOMÁS: *Cuentos,* stories.

(ENRIQUE *enters.*)

ENRIQUE: Can I see, *Tomás?*

PAPÁ GRANDE: *Tomasito,* why don't you read something to us!

YOUNG TOMÁS: I'm not very good yet.

PAPÁ GRANDE: The only way you'll get better is by practicing.

ENRIQUE: Yeah, practice on us!

YOUNG TOMÁS: Okay.

PAPÁ GRANDE: ¡Ándale, todos! Gather around! *Tomasito* is going to read *en inglés!*

YOUNG TOMÁS: The big, hun . . . gry tiger hun . . . ted in the migh . . . ty jungle. (*Confidently*) The big, hungry tiger hunted in the mighty jungle.

(*A tiger is heard prowling through a jungle. He growls loudly.*)

ENRIQUE: ¡Ay! What was that?

YOUNG TOMÁS: ¡Un tigre grande!

(*The tiger growls loudly again.*)

ENRIQUE: ¡Ay!

YOUNG TOMÁS: It hunted for its prey.

ENRIQUE: ¿Qué es eso?

YOUNG TOMÁS: I think *el tigre* is searching for something to eat.

ENRIQUE: I better "pray" it don't eat me!

YOUNG TOMÁS: He searched everywhere until he found a little monkey playing by himself.

ENRIQUE: Oh, no!

YOUNG TOMÁS: *El tigre* leaped to eat him but the little monkey got away.

ENRIQUE: Hurray!

YOUNG TOMÁS: But *el tigre grande* still searches for something else to eat!

(YOUNG TOMÁS *growls. Large tiger eyes appear on the screen.*)

ENRIQUE: *¡Mira, Tomás, es un tigre!*

YOUNG TOMÁS: *¡Yo soy el tigre grande!*

(*The library interior appears.*)

MALE ACTOR: All summer, whenever he could, *Tomás* went to the library.

YOUNG TOMÁS: How are you today?

LIBRARY LADY: Washington is dead. Lincoln too. And I'm not feeling so well myself.

YOUNG TOMÁS: Huh?

LIBRARY LADY: Never mind. First a drink of water and then some new books, *Tomás Rivera.*

(*Music. She hands him several books to read.*)

LIBRARY LADY (*whispering*):

We've got books on the tiger, dinosaurs, and spiders,
And anything that lives in a zoo
Elephants, cowboys, fishes, sports, sewing, and dishes,
And flags that are red, black, and blue

YOUNG TOMÁS (*singing*):

Libros, libros, libros I love to read
Libros, libros, libros, that's what I need
Libros, libros, libros carry me away
Libros, libros, libros, libros, libros

LIBRARY LADY (*whispering*):

Cooking and trampolines, newspapers, magazines,
So everyone can stay in touch
We've got so many books, Peter Pan, Captain Cook!
We've got books about Swedes, Finns, and Dutch

YOUNG TOMÁS (*singing*):

Libros, libros, libros I love to read
Libros, libros, libros, that's what I need
Libros, libros, libros carry me away
Libros, libros, libros, libros, libros

LIBRARY LADY: Shhh!

YOUNG TOMÁS (*singing quietly*):

Libros, libros, libros, libros, libros

(*A smiling moon appears through the window of the shack. Crickets are heard.*)

FEMALE ACTOR: During the summer nights *Tomás'* head filled up with new words in English.

MALE ACTOR: He was too excited to sleep.

FEMALE ACTOR: He read until his eyes could no longer stay open.

YOUNG TOMÁS: Space, aliens, Jupiter, moon . . .

FEMALE ACTOR: Young *Tomás* had almost forgotten about his nightmare intruder.

(*Sounds emerge from a suitcase.* YOUNG TOMÁS *opens the suitcase. The moon is replaced by the image of the* NIGHTMARE TEACHER.)

NIGHTMARE TEACHER: Say it, Tommy!

YOUNG TOMÁS: Aagghhh!

NIGHTMARE TEACHER: "I will not daydream, be lazy, or speak Spanish!" Say it!

YOUNG TOMÁS: *¡No entiendo!*

NIGHTMARE TEACHER: Say it!

YOUNG TOMÁS: *¡Déjame!*

NIGHTMARE TEACHER: I'm going to get you!

YOUNG TOMÁS: *¡No! ¡'Amá!*

(JOSEFA *enters, slamming the suitcase shut.*)

JOSEFA: Tomás, *¿qué te pasa?*

YOUNG TOMÁS: *'Amá,* I never want to go back to school. I want to stay and work with you, *'Apá,* and *Papá Grande* forever.

'AMÁ: I know that school isn't so easy. I wish that I had gone when I was your age.

YOUNG TOMÁS: You do?

'AMÁ: I would have made my parents so proud. It takes a very brave person to say "I'm going to finish." And you know what?

YOUNG TOMÁS: What?

'AMÁ: I think you're a very brave person.

(*She exits. The library appears.* YOUNG TOMÁS *holds up a stack of books. The* LIBRARY LADY *enters.*)

LIBRARY LADY: My, you are a voracious reader.

YOUNG TOMÁS: What's that mean?

LIBRARY LADY: It means that you read so much, like a hungry caterpillar who's just finished devouring a giant leaf.

YOUNG TOMÁS: Sometimes I'm a voracious dreamer too.

LIBRARY LADY: That's good.

YOUNG TOMÁS: Not when you have the same bad dream.

LIBRARY LADY: It probably means something is on your mind, eating away at you.

YOUNG TOMÁS: How can I stop it?

LIBRARY LADY: Well, the only way I know is to confront it. Face it head on, just like Dorothy did in *The Wonderful Wizard of Oz.*

MALE ACTOR: Young *Tomás* smiled.

FEMALE ACTOR: And so did the library lady.

(*She exits. A train whistle is heard. We see a train roll across the screen.*)

ENRIQUE (*entering*): ¡Tomás, mira el tren!

(ENRIQUE *waves. The train toots its horn.*)

YOUNG TOMÁS: Enrique, stop playing. We got work to do in the town dump.

ENRIQUE: It's so boring. Why do we have to collect *carbón*?

YOUNG TOMÁS: Because we have to.

ENRIQUE: Why?

YOUNG TOMÁS: 'Cause we need it to make fire to cook and stay warm.

ENRIQUE: But there's so much junk.

YOUNG TOMÁS: It's the dump.

ENRIQUE: Oh, there's one! How do you say it in English?

YOUNG TOMÁS: Coal.

ENRIQUE: Coal.

YOUNG TOMÁS: There's one.

ENRIQUE: *¡Carbón!*

YOUNG TOMÁS: Did you already forget the English?

ENRIQUE: No.

YOUNG TOMÁS: Coal!

ENRIQUE: Oh, yeah! Coal!

(YOUNG TOMÁS *opens a suitcase. He pulls out a scrap of paper, tossing it on the ground.*)

ENRIQUE: *Fuchi*, what an awful smell!

YOUNG TOMÁS: It's *el dompe.*

ENRIQUE: Look, *Tomás!* It's a toy car! Can I have it?

YOUNG TOMÁS: It's missing its back tires.

ENRIQUE: I don't care.

YOUNG TOMÁS: Maybe *Papá Grande* can fix it for you.

ENRIQUE: Okay.

YOUNG TOMÁS: Look, a book!

ENRIQUE: What's it called?

YOUNG TOMÁS: *In Darkest Africa.*

ENRIQUE: It looks real old.

YOUNG TOMÁS: It's probably older than *Papá Grande.*

ENRIQUE: Wow, that's old!

YOUNG TOMÁS: Look, a map of Africa!

ENRIQUE: Where's that?

YOUNG TOMÁS: Some place far away.

ENRIQUE: Like *Tejas?*

YOUNG TOMÁS: Who cares about *Tejas?*

ENRIQUE: I do.

(*African drums are heard.*)

YOUNG TOMÁS: Come on!

ENRIQUE: Where are we going?

YOUNG TOMÁS: To Africa!

(*They paddle as if they are in a canoe.*)

YOUNG TOMÁS: Be careful of the giant snakes!

ENRIQUE: Oh, no, will they eat me?

YOUNG TOMÁS: I'll protect you!

ENRIQUE: What's that over there?

YOUNG TOMÁS: A herd of wild elephants. *¡Ten cuidado!*

ENRIQUE: Oh, no, they're charging us!

YOUNG TOMÁS: Run for it!

ENRIQUE: I like playing Africa, *Tomás!* (*He finds another piece.*) Coal! When I grow up I'm going to have lots of coal and cars! *¡Carbón y carros!*

(YOUNG TOMÁS *picks up the scrap of paper he tossed earlier and begins writing on it.*)

ENRIQUE: Tomás, what are you doing?

YOUNG TOMÁS: I'm writing.

ENRIQUE: Why don't you just draw a picture?

YOUNG TOMÁS: 'Cause now I can describe a picture with words.

(*On the screen we see letters forming into words, "In darkest Africa there was a great explorer named Tomás." At the library.* FEMALE ACTOR *transforms into the* LIBRARY LADY. YOUNG TOMÁS *hands her several books.*)

LIBRARY LADY: You found these books at the town dump?

YOUNG TOMÁS: Yes. They're going to be the first ones in my own library!

LIBRARY LADY: The covers of these books are dirty, the pages are torn, and they have a bit of a smell to them.

YOUNG TOMÁS: It's not so bad. I put them out in the sun to dry.

LIBRARY LADY: Oh, my.

YOUNG TOMÁS: Aren't they the most beautiful things you've seen? *Don Quixote.*

LIBRARY LADY: But it's in Spanish.

(Music.)

YOUNG TOMÁS: *"Porque ves allí, amigo Sancho Panza, donde se descubren treinta, o pocos más, desaforados gigantes, con quien pienso hacer batalla y quitarles a todos las vidas . . ."*

LIBRARY LADY: What did you just say?

YOUNG TOMÁS: "Look over there, friend Sancho Panza, where more than thirty mon . . . strous . . . thirty monstrous giants appear. I intend to do battle with them and take all their lives."

LIBRARY LADY: *¡Muy bien!*

YOUNG TOMÁS: Look, I even made a book with my own stories, see?

LIBRARY LADY: Tomás, it's going to be a magnificent library!

MALE ACTOR: Tomás smiled.

FEMALE ACTOR: And so did the library lady.

MALE ACTOR: On quiet days the library lady would say—

LIBRARY LADY: Please teach me some new words in Spanish.

MALE ACTOR: Tomás liked being the teacher.

LIBRARY LADY: What is this called?

(*She holds up a pencil.*)

YOUNG TOMÁS: Lápiz. Pencil.

LIBRARY LADY: Lápiz.

YOUNG TOMÁS: Good.

(YOUNG TOMÁS *flaps his arms. She follows.*)

YOUNG TOMÁS: Pájaro.

LIBRARY LADY: Pájaro.

YOUNG TOMÁS: Bird.

LIBRARY LADY: And this?

(*She meows.*)

YOUNG TOMÁS: ¡Gato!

LIBRARY LADY: ¡Gato! And this?

(*She barks!*)

YOUNG TOMÁS: ¡Perro!

LIBRARY LADY: Perro!

YOUNG TOMÁS: ¡Muy bien!

LIBRARY LADY: Sehr gut!

YOUNG TOMÁS: Sehr gut?

LIBRARY LADY: It's German for "muy bien"!

YOUNG TOMÁS: Sehr gut!

(*'*AMÁ *and* 'APÁ's *silhouetted profiles appear outside the window of their shack.* YOUNG TOMÁS *and* ENRIQUE *overhear their conversation.*)

'APÁ: Josefa, ya nos podemos regresar a Tejas.

'AMÁ: ¿Cuándo?

'APÁ: Cuando quieras.

'AMÁ: ¿Y el trabajo?

'APÁ: *Pos, ya se acabó.*

ENRIQUE (*whispering*): What are they talking about, Tomás?

YOUNG TOMÁS (*whispering*): Shh, I can't hear, Enrique!

'AMÁ: *Nos vamos mañana.*

'APÁ: *Empacamos el carro y nos vamos.*

ENRIQUE: Well?

YOUNG TOMÁS: We're going back to Texas.

'AMÁ: *Cuando regresemos a Tejas, Tomás puede empezar la escuela.*

'APÁ: *Ándale.*

YOUNG TOMÁS: I'm going back to school, and my scary teacher.

ENRIQUE: When do we go?

'AMÁ: *Mañana.*

'APÁ: *Mañana.*

YOUNG TOMÁS: Tomorrow.

ENRIQUE: OH, BOY!

(ENRIQUE *does a crazy joy dance. The silhouettes of* 'AMÁ *and* 'APÁ *turn to look.*)

'APÁ/'AMÁ: *¡Duérmanse!*

(*Sounds from the suitcase emerge. On the screen the* NIGHTMARE TEACHER's *giant eye appears, looking through the shack window.* YOUNG TOMÁS *finally confronts her by opening the suitcase.*)

NIGHTMARE TEACHER: How many times have I told you to speak English, young man? I won't stand for this in my classroom!

YOUNG TOMÁS: I speak English!

(*He opens the suitcase, placing a book inside.*)

NIGHTMARE TEACHER: Hey, what are you doing?

YOUNG TOMÁS: And I can read too!

(*Another book.*)

NIGHTMARE TEACHER: Stop it!

YOUNG TOMÁS: I can understand you now!

(*Another book.*)

NIGHTMARE TEACHER: What's happening?

YOUNG TOMÁS: I'm not afraid anymore!

NIGHTMARE TEACHER: Nooo!

YOUNG TOMÁS: You don't exist! Go away!

(NIGHTMARE TEACHER *melts away.*)

NIGHTMARE TEACHER: I'm melting! Melting! Aaahhh!

(*He shuts the suitcase. He smiles.*)

MALE ACTOR: The next day *Tomás* brought *Papá Grande* to the library.

(PAPÁ GRANDE's *mustache appears on the screen.* FEMALE ACTOR *as the* LIBRARY LADY *enters.*)

LIBRARY LADY: Buenas tardes, señor.

PAPÁ GRANDE: Buenas tardes, señora. ¿Cómo está usted?

LIBRARY LADY: What did he say, Tomás?

YOUNG TOMÁS: He asks, "How are you?"

LIBRARY LADY: Washington is dead. Lincoln too. And I'm not feeling so well myself.

PAPÁ GRANDE: ¿Qué dice?

YOUNG TOMÁS: Dice que Washington está muerto, Lincoln también y que ella no se siente muy bien.

PAPÁ GRANDE: ¡Ah, sí! Mucho gusto.

LIBRARY LADY: Mucho gusto.

PAPÁ GRANDE: No tardes, Tomás.

(PAPÁ GRANDE's *mustache fades away.*)

LIBRARY LADY: Tomás, what are we going to do this afternoon?

YOUNG TOMÁS: Today, I have a sad word to teach you. The word is *adiós.*

LIBRARY LADY: Adios?

YOUNG TOMÁS: It means goodbye.

LIBRARY LADY: You're going back to Texas?

YOUNG TOMÁS: Yes. My 'apá says there's no more work for us here.

LIBRARY LADY: Oh.

YOUNG TOMÁS: My 'amá sent this to thank you. It's *pan dulce,* sweet bread. My 'amá makes the best *pan dulce* in Texas.

LIBRARY LADY: How nice. How very nice. Please make sure to thank her, Tomás.

YOUNG TOMÁS: I will.

LIBRARY LADY: I'm going to miss you reading to me. I'm going to miss you teaching me words in Spanish, but most of all —

YOUNG TOMÁS: I'm going to miss you too.

(LIBRARY LADY *gives* YOUNG TOMÁS *a brand new book.*)

YOUNG TOMÁS: What's this?

LIBRARY LADY: It's for you, for your library.

YOUNG TOMÁS: But there're no words in this book.

LIBRARY LADY: I know! This one is for your own stories. You're going to grow up to be something amazing, like a great writer with your very own books in the library! Or maybe even a librarian!

YOUNG TOMÁS: Thank you.

LIBRARY LADY: *Gracias, Tomás.*

(*They hug. On the screen the library begins to shrink farther and farther away.*)

MALE ACTOR/FEMALE ACTOR (*singing*):

Adios, adios, adios
Goodbye to you my friend
I wish it never end
So *adios, adios, adios*
Goodbye to you my friend
Adios

(*On the screen a shadow of a small car appears traveling back home while the moon follows.*)

'AMÁ (*voiceover*): More stories for the new storyteller.

YOUNG TOMÁS: Yes, 'Amá.

(YOUNG TOMÁS *opens the book and starts writing.*)

YOUNG TOMÁS: Once upon a time . . .

FEMALE ACTOR: The real *Tomás Rivera* was born in Crystal City, Texas, in 1935. He was a migrant worker who graduated from college and became a famous writer and professor. He created many magnificent stories in books.

(*Photographic images of the real Tomás Rivera appear during his speech. They begin with his childhood, his family, etc.* YOUNG TOMÁS *transforms into* ADULT TOMÁS. *He stands at a commencement.*)

ADULT TOMÁS: I accept this honorary degree on behalf of the many Chicano children who did not have the opportunity to get an education, through no fault of their own . . .

FEMALE ACTOR: *Tomás Rivera* became a national leader on education and the youngest person ever to run a major University of California campus, and the first Chicano to do so.

ADULT TOMÁS: On behalf of the many Chicano parents who have aspired for generations that their children be educated but who do not know what the education system is . . .

FEMALE ACTOR: He was a loving husband and a devoted father. He inspired a generation of young people to succeed.

(*An official image of Tomás Rivera as chancellor of UC Riverside.*)

ADULT TOMÁS: On behalf of the Chicano writer who hungers for community and justice . . .

(*The Tomás Rivera Library appears.*)

FEMALE ACTOR: And at the age of 48, *Tomás Rivera* died. At his memorial his friends and colleagues came from across the country to honor him. The campus library at the University of California Riverside now bears the name of the boy—

MALE ACTOR: —who was encouraged to read by a library lady in Iowa.

(*The final image is a photograph of Tomás Rivera as a nine-year old boy.* FEMALE ACTOR *and* MALE ACTOR *look at the image. They smile and exit.*)

CURTAIN

Designer's Response

This play provides another set of visual challenges: shadow imagery by puppets, actors, or video; use of variety in scale; and objects and digital projections that are manipulated by the actors. I like this script in particular because only two actors play all the characters and voices. Not only is having a small cast an advantage for companies that tour, but this convention also encourages greater engagement with children's imaginations as they see and hear the magic of the performance.

As for the playscript itself, it is imaginative, playful, and, again, filled with José's unique style and vision. The play has an important message of hope and inspiration for children—that with determination a person of any cultural background can succeed.

Elements and Images

Varying use of scale
Character-manipulated objects,
  including a toy theatre
Suitcases
Digital images
Shadow images
Pan dulce/los cochinitos
Crowing rooster
Big white mustache as visual
  metaphor for the larger-than-life
  figure of *Papá Grande*
Moustache becomes forest of trees

Actor running in place on gravel in
  open suitcase
Pop-up library revealed by opening
  lid of suitcase
Shack
Prowling tiger
Train whistle
In Darkest Africa, a book published
  in 1890
Photographic images of *Tomás
  Rivera* as a child and adult
Umbrella as metaphor for Library
  Lady

Resources

Internet images
Clip art

Plate A: Collage.

MUSTACHE BECOMES FOREST OF TREES

LOS COCHITOS

Plate B: Preliminary set design with two projections.

Watermelon Kisses

José Cruz González

Watermelon Kisses was originally published in
Dude! Stories and Stuff for Boys, edited by
Sandy Asher and David L. Harrison.

Characters

QUETZAL (ket-SAL): nine-year-old Latino boy. QUETZAL is an ancient
Aztec name that means "feather." He is the older brother of TLÁLOC.

TLÁLOC (TLA-loke): seven-year-old Latino boy. TLÁLOC is also an ancient
Aztec name that means "rain god."

Setting

The front porch steps of an old house.

Time

A summer's day.

Words In Spanish

Mamá (ma-MAH): Mom
Papá (pa-PAH): Dad
Tonto (TONE-toe): Dummy

AT RISE: QUETZAL and TLÁLOC *are seated, eating watermelon.*
Alongside them rest a rake and a hoe.
A lawnmower is heard in the background.

QUETZAL: Don't eat the watermelon seeds, Tláloc.

TLÁLOC: Why not?

QUETZAL: 'Cause they go into your tummy and get planted.

TLÁLOC: Huh?

QUETZAL: Yeah, they get planted in your stomach and then green vines start to rise up through your throat and ears and spill out everywhere.

TLÁLOC: Nah-uh!

QUETZAL: Ah huh! Pretty soon you can't hear 'cause you got vines growing out of your ears and you can't talk 'cause you got a watermelon growing on your chin.

TLÁLOC: For reals?

QUETZAL: For reals, little brother!

(TLÁLOC *accidentally swallows one, maybe even two watermelon seeds.*)

TLÁLOC: I think I ate a watermelon seed, Quetzal.

(*The lawnmower is heard shutting off.*)

QUETZAL: Why does *Papá* always wait until the grass is a foot high before cutting it?

TLÁLOC: Did you hear me? I think I ate a watermelon seed, maybe two.

QUETZAL: You're supposed to spit them out, *tonto.*

TLÁLOC: Hey, I didn't know! Nobody told me!

QUETZAL: You'll be okay. Just don't get kissed by a girl.

TLÁLOC: What?

(*The lawnmower is heard starting up.*)

QUETZAL: Nothing happens unless a girl kisses you.

TLÁLOC: I don't understand.

QUETZAL: Do I have to explain everything to you? Oh-oh, start raking!

TLÁLOC: Huh?

QUETZAL: *Papá* is giving us the eyebrow look. Get busy!

(QUETZAL *and* TLÁLOC *work in the yard.* TLÁLOC *turns to his brother.*)

TLÁLOC: What if *Mamá* kissed me?

QUETZAL: She kissed you?

TLÁLOC: Yeah, on my cheek before she went to the store.

QUETZAL: Oh, man.

TLÁLOC: What?

QUETZAL: She activated it.

TLÁLOC: Act-a-what?

QUETZAL: When a girl kisses you—

TLÁLOC: But *Mamá*'s not a girl.

QUETZAL: It doesn't matter. She used to be a girl. Now the seeds you ate are going to grow 'cause you got kissed.

TLÁLOC: You mean I'm going to have a watermelon growing on my chin?

QUETZAL: I told you not to eat the seeds.

(*The lawnmower is heard stopping again.*)

QUETZAL: *Papá*'s face is getting red again. He looks like a tomato.

(*A worried* TLÁLOC *drops his rake to the ground. He starts to hurry off as—*)

QUETZAL: What are you doing?

TLÁLOC: I'm telling *Papá* I got a watermelon growing out of my stomach!

QUETZAL: You better not!

TLÁLOC: Why?

QUETZAL: 'Cause he's going to be mad at you 'cause you got a kiss. Did you notice that *Mamá* didn't kiss him when she left?

TLÁLOC: No.

QUETZAL: Well, I did. *Papá*'s in the doghouse 'cause he didn't mow the lawn when he was supposed to.

TLÁLOC: Quetzal, I don't want a watermelon growing on my chin!

QUETZAL: Okay, pipe down! *Papá* will hear you.

TLÁLOC: Are you going to help me?

QUETZAL: Yeah, I'll think of something.

(*The lawnmower is heard starting up again.*)

TLÁLOC: Well?

QUETZAL: Okay. Stick your finger down your throat.

TLÁLOC: Why?

QUETZAL: You want those seeds out, right?

TLÁLOC: Yeah, but—

QUETZAL: There's no "buts," just do it.

TLÁLOC: ¡PAPÁ!

QUETZAL: Fine! You don't have to stick your finger down your throat.

TLÁLOC: Are you making this up?

QUETZAL: Why would I make this up?

TLÁLOC: I don't know.

QUETZAL: I'm your big brother. Big brothers never lie.

(QUETZAL sits on the porch steps.)

QUETZAL: Oh, man, it's so hot. I'm going to eat some more watermelon. Want some?

TLÁLOC: No way!

QUETZAL: Guess I'll have to eat it all myself.

TLÁLOC: Well?

QUETZAL: How much money you got?

TLÁLOC: I got a dollar.

QUETZAL: A whole dollar?

TLÁLOC: Yeah.

(TLÁLOC pulls a dollar from his pocket to show QUETZAL.)

QUETZAL: When did you get a whole dollar?

TLÁLOC: Mamá gave it to me 'cause I did my chores and yours all week.

QUETZAL: I was going to do it.

TLÁLOC: I'm going to save my dollar in my new piggy bank.

QUETZAL: Half of that dollar is mine, you know.

TLÁLOC: Mamá said you'd say that.

QUETZAL: She did?

TLÁLOC: Ah huh. (QUETZAL looks closely at TLÁLOC's face.) What?

QUETZAL: It's nothing. I thought I saw something green.

(The lawnmower is heard stopping again.)

QUETZAL: Don't look, but Papá's kicking the lawnmower.

TLÁLOC: Quetzal, tell me what I got to do.

QUETZAL: The only way to stop a watermelon seed from growing is to spend that dollar.

TLÁLOC: No.

QUETZAL: Yeah, you have to go to the corner store and buy ice cream.

TLÁLOC: Ice cream?

QUETZAL: Why do you always repeat everything I say?

TLÁLOC: 'Cause you mumble!

QUETZAL: No, I don't!

TLÁLOC: Yes, you do!

QUETZAL: Fine!

(QUETZAL *doesn't say a word.*)

TLÁLOC: Okay, you don't mumble.

(QUETZAL *still doesn't say a word.*)

TLÁLOC: Please!

QUETZAL: You buy an ice cream and eat it. The cold will freeze the seed and stop it from growing.

TLÁLOC: For reals?

QUETZAL: For reals. Why would I make this up? What would I have to gain?

TLÁLOC: I don't know.

(TLÁLOC *thinks for a moment.*)

TLÁLOC: Quetzal, Papá won't let me go to the store by myself.

QUETZAL: I'll go with you.

TLÁLOC: You will?

QUETZAL: Yeah, but—

TLÁLOC: What?

QUETZAL: You'll have to buy me an ice cream too.

TLÁLOC: For reals?

(QUETZAL *nods his head in agreement.* TLÁLOC *looks at his dollar. Then to his brother.*)

TLÁLOC: Okay.

QUETZAL: Great, let's go!

TLÁLOC: ¿Quetzal?

QUETZAL: Yeah?

TLÁLOC: If I ever find out you lied to me I'm going to climb up into your bunk when you're asleep and hit you real hard.

QUETZAL: You wouldn't do that, would you?

(TLÁLOC *just shrugs his shoulders.*)

QUETZAL: That's not right. You shouldn't say such a thing.

TLÁLOC: I didn't say anything.

QUETZAL: I look out for you. I'm taking you to the store.

TLÁLOC: I know you're scared of the night.

QUETZAL: No, I'm not.

TLÁLOC: Then why do you keep taking my teddy bear?

(TLÁLOC embraces the rake tightly.)

QUETZAL: 'Cause he makes a good pillow!

TLÁLOC: If I ever find out, you better learn to sleep with one eye open, big brother.

QUETZAL: You're joking, right? Right?

(TLÁLOC shrugs his shoulders once more. The lawnmower stops again.)

QUETZAL: ¡PAPÁ!

(QUETZAL runs off. TLÁLOC picks up a watermelon slice and eats it.)

CURTAIN

Designer's Response

Here again, I manipulated the scale of the scenery, regardless of whether the boys are played by adult actors or young performers. The stage floor is a representation of a slice of watermelon in combination with a sky filled with saturated color and a graphic representation of a hot summer sun. The grass, mentioned so prominently in the script, is represented in my interpretation as ground rows both in the foreground and upstage of the primary set piece. All scenic elements are influenced by the bold colors often found in Hispanic culture. Although comprised of colored paper, the collage shown here is reproduced in black and white along with clip art images from the Internet.

Resources

Construction paper
Clip art

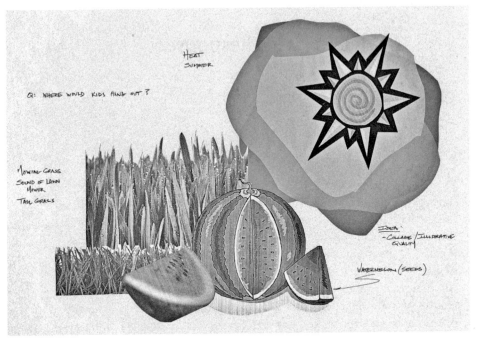

Plate A: Collage.

Plate B: Preliminary set design.

Old Jake's Skirts

Adapted for the stage by
José Cruz González

Based on the book Old Jake's Skirts by C. Anne Scott,
illustrated by David Slonim

Old Jake's Skirts premiered at Childsplay,
Tempe, Arizona

Characters

SARAH: a young woman. She is our storyteller. She also plays YOUNG SARAH, E. B. SWEENEY, and GOOD SAMARITAN LADY #3.

OLD JAKE: a tall, thin man with a beard. He wears overalls. His face is weathered from working the land. His clothes are loose on him. Old Jake is a pumpkin farmer and raises chickens for sale. His home is Stillwaters Farm, which is located on a hillside. He doesn't have much, but with the work he does it's enough to keep him going. Jake lives alone with his old hound dog, Shoestring. When he isn't working, Old Jake likes to carve little figurines. There is something sad and lonely about him.

SHOESTRING (ACTOR #3): Old Jake's hound dog. He likes to sleep inside Old Jake's farmhouse because it's quiet and warm, but during the planting season Old Jake's got Shoestring outside watching for hungry rabbits that like to eat the pumpkin sprouts. Shoestring is the closest companion Old Jake has. Will also play CLARENCE and GOOD SAMARITAN LADY #1.

OTIS BROWN: YOUNG SARAH's father. He is also the MUSICIAN, ELLIS, and GOOD SAMARITAN LADY #2.

Setting

Various locations, including Stillwaters Farm,
Old Jake's cabin, E. B.'s general store,
the countryside and church.

Note on Casting

Roles may be divided to increase the cast size
by assigning each actor a specific character.

List of Music
(sheet music included at end of script)

"Above the Plains"
"Jake's Skirts—Magic Skirts Opening"
"Rounder"
"Shoestring Blues"
"Truck-Drivin' Riff"
"Tin Lizzy"
"Jake's Skirts—Main Theme"
"Jimmy"
"Delbert Sweep—Fly"
"There's a Hole in the Bucket"
"Planting Crops with Plague Tag"
"Whistlin' & Whittlin'"
"Bill Cheatham"
"Opening the Trunk"
"Devil's Dream"
"Banks of the Ohio"
"Pre-Clean Music"
"Irish Washerwoman"
"Happy Planting"
"Soul of Man"
"This Train"
"Shall We Gather at the River"
"Beautiful Dreamer"
"Otis & Sarah Music"
"Jake's Skirts—Skirt Magic with Sarah Theme"
"Amazing Grace"
"Harmonies as Needed"
"This Train (alternate key of C)"
"Shall We Gather at the River (alternate key of C)"
"Amazing Grace (alternate key of E)"

AT RISE: *The stage is bare. A lone* MUSICIAN *enters, playing "Above the Plains."*
The ENSEMBLE *enters, joining the* MUSICIAN *in song*
as they begin setting up the stage.

ENSEMBLE (*singing*):

Above the plains
Of Gold and Green
A young boy's head
Is plainly seen
A-hoo-ya, hoo-ya, hoo-ya, ya!
Swiftly flowing river
A-hoo-ya, hoo-ya, hoo-ya, ya!
Swiftly flowing river
(Repeat.)

(*A backdrop of a painted landscape of hills and farmland is unrolled. An old trunk is placed onstage. The* ENSEMBLE *exits, except for the* MUSICIAN *and* SARAH.)

(MUSIC: *"Jake's Skirts — Magic Skirts Opening."*)

(SARAH *looks at the old trunk and smiles. She opens the trunk, delicately removing a calico skirt neatly bound with a beautiful ribbon. She closes the trunk and sits on it.* SARAH *discovers a colorful wood carving of a girl wrapped in the calico skirt.* OLD JAKE *enters. He is a hermit farmer.* OLD JAKE *does not see* SARAH *but* SARAH *remembers* OLD JAKE.)

OLD JAKE (*in a gravelly voice*): Take whichever one you want.

(*He introduces a miniature wooden cabin. We see the exterior of the cabin with a porch, door, and window.*)

SARAH: Old Jake wasn't much of a talker. It was his strong hands that did the talking by the hard work they would do. He was always up before the sunrise, working on his farm, feeding his chickens, milking old Sally, his cow, and repairing this or that.

(ACTOR #3 *enters.*)

ACTOR #3: Something always needed fixing.

SARAH: With each season he barely scraped by. But he didn't need much. He lived a simple life. His home was an old wooden shack, and his only source of light was a lantern. In the wintertime he would cover his windows with used burlap sacks to keep out the cold.

ACTOR #3: Old Jake didn't have a family and he liked to keep to himself. There was plenty to do on the farm and that suited him just fine.

SARAH: But when Old Jake wasn't planting, he was carving.

ACTOR #3: Uh-huh.

SARAH: He loved to whittle little wooden figurines.

ACTOR #3: That's right.

(MUSIC: "Rounder.")

ACTOR #3: Old Jake's only companion was his hound dog.

(ACTOR #3 places a wooden dog on the porch of the cabin.)

OLD JAKE (offstage): Shoestring!

(MUSIC: "Shoestring Blues.")

(ACTOR #3 transforms into SHOESTRING. He stretches, yawns, and scratches an itch. He lies on the trunk to sleep. OLD JAKE enters, whistling. OLD JAKE places an old toy truck in front of the miniature cabin.)

SARAH: It was still dawn when Old Jake rose. He was planning an early start into town to pick up supplies at the general store.

OLD JAKE: Come on, Shoestring.

SHOESTRING: Awu.

SARAH: Old Jake wanted to get his start before the morning regulars arrived for their morning round of coffee and chitchat.

OLD JAKE: Nuthin' worse than coffee and chitchat.

SHOESTRING (sleepy): Awu . . .

OLD JAKE: Clarence and Ellis will talk your ears off. 'Fore you know it the day's half gone.

SHOESTRING: Awu . . .

OLD JAKE: Let's go, you old hound dog.

SHOESTRING: Awu . . .

OLD JAKE (looks at his grocery list): Let's see, gonna get us a sack of flour.

SHOESTRING: Awu . . .

OLD JAKE: A can of lard.

SHOESTRING: Awu . . .

OLD JAKE: A new whetstone for my whittlin' knife.

SHOESTRING: Awu . . .

OLD JAKE: And a bone for you. That got you moving, didn't it?

SHOESTRING: Awu!

OLD JAKE: Get in the truck! (*The trunk becomes* OLD JAKE's *truck.*) Where are my keys?

SARAH: Old Jake and Shoestring had a peculiar way of starting into town. It always began with Shoestring sitting in the front seat of Old Jake's beat-up truck. And it was a routine as constant as the jackrabbits populating Old Jake's farm.

(OLD JAKE *crosses back to the cabin to get his keys while* SHOESTRING *sits in the front truck seat.* OLD JAKE *returns, unaware that* SHOESTRING *has climbed in.*)

OLD JAKE: How many times I gotta tell you, hound dogs belong in the back. People in front. Out you go.

(*He signals the hound dog to the back and opens the tailgate, helping* SHOESTRING *onto the bed of the truck.* SHOESTRING *goes to* OLD JAKE *and* OLD JAKE *scratches* SHOESTRING's *head.* OLD JAKE *sits in the truck and closes the imaginary door.*)

SARAH: Old Jake would use an unwired coat hanger to hold the truck door shut. And getting the truck started was always an adventure.

OLD JAKE: Come on now. You're gonna start real easy.

(MUSIC: *"Truck-Drivin' Riff."*)

(*He pumps the gas pedal several times. He turns the key but the engine doesn't start.* OLD JAKE *steps out of the truck, lifting the imaginary hood while* SHOESTRING *climbs back into the front seat.* SHOESTRING *presses on the horn.*)

OLD JAKE: Shoestring, you do that one more time! Get! (SHOESTRING *quickly jumps into the back of the truck.*) Didn't have any trouble getting in that time, did you? (OLD JAKE *pumps the gas pedal again.*) Finally, on the third try the truck starts.

(SARAH *picks up the toy truck and places the dog figurine in the back.*)

(MUSIC: *"Tin Lizzy."*)

ENSEMBLE (*singing*):

She's an old pile of tin,
Nobody know what shape she's in
Got four wheels and a running board
She's a pickup, she's a Ford
Honk, honk, rattle rattle rattle
Crash, beep-beep

Honk, honk, rattle rattle rattle
Crash, beep-beep

Honk, honk, rattle rattle rattle
Crash, beep-beep
(*Repeat.*)

(*While the* ENSEMBLE *sings,* SARAH *plays with the truck as if it is driving over a bumpy road.* OLD JAKE *and* SHOESTRING *transform into the road of hills, valleys, and curves. The little truck slowly climbs up a steep hill until it finally slides down the other side. Suddenly the truck stops before an old trunk in the middle of the road.* OLD JAKE *and* SHOESTRING *stand behind* SARAH, *who is holding the toy truck. The truck's tiny headlights shine on the trunk.*)

SARAH: Old Jake ground his truck to a stop. The headlights of his pickup had revealed the form of a trunk a few yards ahead.

MUSICIAN: Now, the trunk was in his way.

(MUSIC: "*Jake's Skirts—Main Theme.*")

(ACTOR #3 *transforms back into* SHOESTRING.)

OLD JAKE: Whatcha reckon it is, Shoestring?

(SHOESTRING *crosses to the trunk, sniffing it. He barks at it.*)

OLD JAKE: Be still, dog. A little ol' trunk can't hurt nuthin'.

(SHOESTRING *slinks away and sits down beside* OLD JAKE, *who scratches* SHOESTRING'S *ear.*)

OLD JAKE: How in the world did it get here? Musta fallen off some poor feller's pickup. Best we take it on to town. Hope it ain't heavy like books or somethin'.

SARAH: Old Jake slowly hunched over to lift the trunk. A bone popped in his back.

(OLD JAKE *and* SHOESTRING *lift the trunk up into the air.*)

OLD JAKE: 'Tain't books, Shoestring. Could be feathers.

(OLD JAKE *and* SHOESTRING *lift the trunk over their shoulders.* SARAH *slips herself and the toy truck through.*)

SARAH: Old Jake shoved the trunk into the back of his truck, slammed the tailgate shut, and off they went in a cloud of dust, traveling the last few miles to town.

(MUSIC: Resume "*Truck-Drivin' Riff.*")

(SARAH *places a wood carving of a trunk in the back of the toy truck.* SARAH *exits with the toy truck.*)

(MUSIC: "*Jimmy.*")

(SARAH *puts on an apron, transforming into* E. B. SWEENEY, *the storeowner.*)

ACTOR #3: In town, old E. B. Sweeney, the local storekeeper, was up early, preparing the general store for business.

E. B. SWEENEY: There's lots to do today.

(MUSIC: *"Jimmy" repeat.*)

ACTOR #3: Sure is. Items had to be stocked. Inventory had to be counted. Prices had to be marked.

E. B. SWEENEY: It's gonna be a hot one. I better get this floor swept. (*E. B. yawns.*)

(*E. B. SWEENEY rolls on a miniature grocery store. OLD JAKE and ACTOR #3 lift the trunk on its side, turning it into a store counter. They exit. E. B. flicks on a little light in the store.*)

(MUSIC: *"Delbert Sweep — Fly."*)

(*E. B. yawns as a fly buzzes about. She shoos it away. E. B. starts to sweep with the music. She yawns and the fly enters her mouth. She spits it out and the fly lands on the counter. She is about to smash it when it buzzes off. A music interlude of sweeping and fly squashing culminates with E. B. striking the countertop with her broom. OLD JAKE and SHOESTRING enter with the toy truck.*)

(MUSIC: *"Truck-Drivin' Riff" dies to "Jimmy," ending fast.*)

(*OLD JAKE leaves the toy truck parked in front of the general store. The door rings as OLD JAKE enters.*)

OLD JAKE: Stay in the truck, dog.

SHOESTRING: Awu.

OLD JAKE: I know! I know! I won't forget.

MUSICIAN: Old Jake was E. B. Sweeney's first customer that morning.

(MUSIC: *"There's a Hole in the Bucket" repeats under scene.*)

E. B. SWEENEY: Mornin' Jake.

OLD JAKE: E. B.

E. B. SWEENEY (*looks at SHOESTRING*): Mercy, what you been feedin' Shoe-string? That dog's grown near ten foot since I seen him last.

OLD JAKE: Ain't grown none. Standin' on a trunk.

E. B. SWEENEY: A trunk?

SHOESTRING (*slips off trunk*): Awu!

E. B. SWEENEY: Mercy. Whatcha gonna buy this mornin', Jake?

OLD JAKE: Same.

E. B. SWEENEY: Let me guess what you're gonna get.

OLD JAKE: Just the basics—

E. B. SWEENEY: —Nothing fancy, I know.

(OLD JAKE *removes a piece of paper from his pocket.* E. B. *crosses to the miniature general store, turning it around to reveal the interior filled with supplies, etc. She starts selecting* OLD JAKE's *groceries.*)

OLD JAKE: Gonna need a sack of flour.

E. B. SWEENEY: Sack of flour.

OLD JAKE: Can of lard.

E. B. SWEENEY: Can of lard.

OLD JAKE: A new whetstone for my whittlin' knife.

  (MUSIC: *"There's a Hole in the Bucket" stops.*)

E. B. SWEENEY: A new whetsone?

OLD JAKE: Yup.

E. B. SWEENEY: Well, what happened to the old one? Did Shoestring bury it again?

(E. B. SWEENEY *crosses to* SHOESTRING, *petting him.*)

  (MUSIC: *"Delbert Sweep—Fly," but stops suddenly.*)

E. B. SWEENEY: Oh, that darn fly!

(SHOESTRING *snaps at the imaginary fly, eating it in one gulp.*)

SHOESTRING: Awu.

E. B. SWEENEY: And a bone for Shoestring!

OLD JAKE: Yup. A bone for Shoestring.

SHOESTRING (*slips off the trunk again*): Awu!

(SHOESTRING *exits.*)

  (MUSIC: *"There's a Hole in the Bucket" repeat.*)

E. B. SWEENEY: You're always my first customer of the day, Jake. Now, why is that?

OLD JAKE (*gives money to* E. B.): Five dollars.

E. B. SWEENEY: Always a pleasure talking to you, Jake. Can I package it up and put it in the truck for you?

OLD JAKE: I'll manage. (E. B. SWEENEY *starts to exit.*) Pencil and paper?

  (MUSIC: *"There's a Hole in the Bucket" ends.*)

E. B. SWEENEY: Whatcha need that for?

OLD JAKE: For writin'.

E. B. SWEENEY: Writin' what?

OLD JAKE: A note.

E. B. SWEENEY: What kinda note?

OLD JAKE: Just a note.

E. B. SWEENEY (*hands pencil and paper.* OLD JAKE *writes.* E. B. *reads*): "Trunk lost. Old Miller . . . Toad"? (OLD JAKE *rewrites the letter "R" clearly.*) Ah, Old Miller Road! (*Reading.*) "Trunk lost. Old Miller Road. Found. Come to Stillwaters Farm." (OLD JAKE *hands the paper to* E. B.) Shall I post it up?

OLD JAKE: Yup.

E. B. SWEENEY: What's in the trunk?

OLD JAKE: Don't know.

E. B. SWEENEY: You don't know?

OLD JAKE: Nope.

E. B. SWEENEY: Ain't you interested in lookin'?

OLD JAKE: Nope.

E. B. SWEENEY: How can you not be interested? Why there could be all kinds of things in that trunk, like a dead body.

(*The doorbell is heard ringing.*)

OLD JAKE: Now listen, E. B. Oh, no!

MUSICIAN: Old Jake met the morning regulars coming in as he was going out.

(CLARENCE *enters. He is a town local. The* MUSICIAN *plays* ELLIS. *He is a town local too.*)

CLARENCE: Mornin', Ellis.

ELLIS: Mornin', Clarence.

CLARENCE: Mornin' E. B.

E. B. SWEENEY: Mornin', Clarence.

CLARENCE: Mornin', Jake.

ELLIS: Mornin', E. B.

E. B. SWEENEY: Mornin', Ellis.

ELLIS: Mornin', Jake.

(OLD JAKE *says nothing.*)

ELLIS/CLARENCE/E. B.: Sit with us a spell, Jake.

OLD JAKE: Cain't. (*To* E. B.) Mornin'.

E. B. SWEENEY: Mornin', Jake.

ELLIS: Mornin', Jake.

CLARENCE: Mornin', Jake.

ELLIS: He is quiet as ever.

CLARENCE: I bet he's shy too.

E. B. SWEENEY: Lonely is what he is.

SARAH (*puts her apron away*): Old Jake and Shoestring headed back home with the trunk and their supplies.

(MUSIC: *"Truck-Drivin' Riff" repeat.*)

(*The trunk is restored to how it was seen earlier.* OLD JAKE *picks up the toy truck and drives over the actor's arms and backs on his way to his cabin. He arrives at his farm, parking his toy truck out in front of his cabin.* OLD JAKE *opens the cabin door and slides the trunk inside. He turns the cabin around and the interior is revealed. It is a humble cabin.* OLD JAKE *places the trunk in the center of the cabin.*)

SARAH: Stillwaters Farm belonged to Old Jake.

ACTOR #3: The land had been in his family for generations.

(ACTOR #3 *transforms into* SHOESTRING *and lies in the middle of* OLD JAKE's *pumpkin field.*)

SARAH: It was a hardscrabble patch of earth that had produced very little over the years besides rocks and trouble. Year after year, Old Jake worked the land on his own. Come rain or shine, blazing summers and freezing winters, he never stopped to think about it much. It was planting season and he had to get started.

(MUSIC: *"Planting Crops with Plague Tag."*)

(OLD JAKE *enters with a hoe. He begins planting. He scrapes the earth and drops three seeds until he reaches* SHOESTRING. *He pokes him to move, which he does.* SHOESTRING *follows his tail in a circle. He lies back down a little farther away.*)

OLD JAKE: Rocks and trouble, trouble and rocks. (OLD JAKE *continues to plant. He reaches* SHOESTRING.) Move, dog.

SHOESTRING: Awu.

(OLD JAKE *plants around him. He stops to wipe his brow with his handkerchief.* SHOESTRING *gets up and exits.*)

OLD JAKE: Someday I'm gonna shoot that dog.

(OLD JAKE *just shrugs his shoulders. He sits and whittles.*)

MUSICIAN: Old Jake marked his years by the plagues that had visited him. There was—

(MUSIC: *"Planting Crops with Plague Tag"* — *a diminished chord.*)

OLD JAKE: —The Year of the Crows—

MUSICIAN: There was—

(MUSIC: *"Planting Crops with Plague Tag"* — B♭ *diminished chord.*)

OLD JAKE: —The Year of the Twisters—

MUSICIAN: There was—

(MUSIC: *"Planting Crops with Plague Tag"* — B *diminished chord.*)

OLD JAKE: —The Year of the First Baptist Church of Quail's Good Samaritan Ladies' Committee.

(MUSIC: *"Amen"* — *C chord to G chord.*)

OLD JAKE: I wonder which plague will visit me next? Is it gonna be the Year of the Locusts? Is it gonna be the Year of the Drought? Is it gonna be the Year of the Tax Collector?

SHOESTRING: AWU!

ACTOR #3: Old Jake quickly forgot the trunk.

(OLD JAKE *moves the trunk.* SHOESTRING *goes to rest on it.* SARAH *places a little dog carving on the miniature trunk inside the cabin.*)

SARAH: He shoved it into a corner of his cabin and it became a backrest for Shoestring—

(MUSIC: *"Whistlin' & Whittlin'."*)

MUSICIAN: —who, through the winter months, chose to curl up beside it rather than at the foot of Old Jake's bed. By spring, it had become a catch-all and was covered over with dirty long johns and overalls.

(OLD JAKE *throws a pile of clothes onto the trunk.* SARAH *adds a pumpkin patch in front of the cabin.*)

SARAH: By first planting, no one had yet claimed the trunk. Old Jake's pumpkins began to sprout, but hungry jackrabbits would keep things hopping.

(SARAH *adds woodcarvings of rabbits to the pumpkin patch.*)

(MUSIC: *"Bill Cheatham"* with pauses.)

(OLD JAKE *enters whittling. Imaginary rabbits appear. A stringed instrument is plucked to create them. He watches one as it bounces in and starts to eat pumpkin sprouts.*)

OLD JAKE: Shoo!

(*The rabbit leaps off quickly.* OLD JAKE *returns to whittling.*)

(MUSIC: *"Bill Cheatham"* resumes.)

(*Several more rabbits appear, eating pumpkin sprouts.*)

OLD JAKE: Shoo!

(*The rabbits leap off quickly.* OLD JAKE *returns to whittling.*)

   (MUSIC: *"Bill Cheatham" resumes.*)

(*Lots more rabbits appear, eating pumpkin sprouts.* OLD JAKE *starts chasing after them.*)

OLD JAKE: Shoo!

(*The rabbits leap off quickly.* OLD JAKE *returns to whittling.*)

   (MUSIC: *"Bill Cheatham" resumes.*)

OLD JAKE: Skedaddle! Come back here, rabbit! Gosh darn rabbits! (*The rabbits leap off quickly.*) Rocks, trouble. Rabbits and rocks.

(*Both* ACTOR #3 *and* SARAH *become rabbits.* OLD JAKE *chases after the rabbits.*)

OLD JAKE: Get! Come back here! Darn rabbits! (*He is unaware that* SHOESTRING *has already gone and laid down on the trunk. He's happy there.*) Shoestring! You gotta keep them rabbits from snacking on my crop.

SARAH: But Shoestring, for the first spring ever, whimpered each evening to stay in the house.

SHOESTRING: Awu.

OLD JAKE: What's got into you, dog? Them rabbits are gonna go plumb wild with you in here.

MUSICIAN: But Old Jake let Shoestring stay inside anyway, and the old hound dog happily curled up on the trunk.

(*The rabbits appear again.*)

OLD JAKE: Sic 'em!

(SHOESTRING *only barks at the imaginary rabbits. He lies back down on the trunk.*)

SARAH: By the third night of this, Jake had lost his patience.

OLD JAKE: There's one!

(SHOESTRING *barks at the rabbits. He lies back down again on the trunk.*)

SARAH: Shoestring was going to have to sleep outside, and it looked like the trunk was going to have to go with him.

(OLD JAKE *drags the trunk with* SHOESTRING *on it outside.* SHOESTRING *growls and then happily rests on the trunk.*)

OLD JAKE: Doggonit, Shoestring. You got to earn your keep. This ain't the Year of the Dog Sleepin' on the Trunk All Day!

SHOESTRING: Awu.

OLD JAKE: What is so important about this ol' trunk? 'Tain't books or feathers. 'Course we never looked inside to find out what's in it. Nobody's come to claim it. I reckon it wouldn't be too un-neighborly if we opened it.

(MUSIC: "Opening the Trunk.")

(OLD JAKE and SHOESTRING look at each other and then the trunk. OLD JAKE holds up the padlock.)

OLD JAKE: It's got a big padlock. Better use a hammer.

(SARAH holds out a hammer to OLD JAKE. He tries to move SHOESTRING but SHOESTRING is resting peacefully. OLD JAKE smashes the hammer down on the padlock. The sound of a hammer striking a padlock is heard. SHOESTRING quickly jumps off the trunk. OLD JAKE lifts up the trunk lid slightly and then closes it.)

OLD JAKE: What if it's gold?

SARAH: Old Jake lifted the lid slowly— (OLD JAKE opens it again.) Inside was no gold. (Beat.) Inside were—

OLD JAKE: I'll be!

(OLD JAKE reveals a beautiful, simple skirt.)

SARAH: Cotton calico—

OLD JAKE: Skirts! (SHOESTRING sniffs the skirt.) A trunk full of skirts? Just my luck I'd be the one who'd find a trunk full of useless skirts. I mean, what good are they for?

SARAH: Jake scratched his head so long he finally scratched up an unpleasant thought.

OLD JAKE: We shouldn't have opened this trunk, Shoestring!

(OLD JAKE throws the calico skirt into the trunk, slamming the lid quickly. He sits on the trunk.)

SARAH: A dark superstition had hatched inside of him.

OLD JAKE: Lord knows what mischievous spirits we let loose.

SARAH: You see, Old Jake was, after all, a believer in plagues.

OLD JAKE: It's gonna be the Year of the Skirts.

SHOESTRING: AWU!

(SHOESTRING yawns and stretches, snuggling up to the trunk.)

SARAH: For a fourth night Shoestring slept curled up against the trunk. The next morning, a soft spring rain came.

(MUSIC: A violin is plucked to create raindrops.)

SARAH: Old Jake remembered how soft the skirt had felt in his rough hands.

OLD JAKE: Rain as gentle as them skirts.

(OLD JAKE *notices the raindrops landing inside his cabin.*)

SARAH: Jake set up some buckets to catch the leaks.

OLD JAKE: Should've patched that roof.

SARAH: And he took up his whittling.

OLD JAKE: If it's gonna rain, let 'er rain.

SARAH: And he worked his knife to the beat of the bucket drops. But by noon, the rain had turned wicked and wild. Puddles grew into rivers. Lightning bolts crashed to earth. And once again Old Jake, alone, battled it out with the plague.

OLD JAKE: It's gonna be the Year of the Storms.

(*Thunder.*)

ACTOR #3: There was no point in getting excited at the thought of his pumpkin plants washing downstream.

(SARAH *removes the pumpkin patch from the cabin.*)

OLD JAKE: There they go.

SARAH: Old Jake didn't know he was licked. By nightfall the buckets had filled to overflowing.

(OLD JAKE *throws buckets of water outside his cabin. The leaks in the cabin are everywhere now.*)

ACTOR #3: Old Jake couldn't empty them fast enough.

OLD JAKE: Water is comin' in under the door!

SARAH: He feared that if he didn't stop this invasion, his cabin would wash downstream with his crop.

ACTOR #3: He gathered all he had—

OLD JAKE: Got to make a barricade!

SARAH: —in the way of cloth and jammed it under the door.

(OLD JAKE *places his old dirty clothes in front of the door entrance.*)

OLD JAKE: There!

ACTOR #3: But still the water came.

OLD JAKE: Oh, no!

(OLD JAKE *sits on the trunk as if it is floating in water.*)

SARAH: It began to swirl around the soles of his boots—

ACTOR #3: Old Jake suddenly remembered—

OLD JAKE: —them skirts!

(OLD JAKE *opens the trunk. The* ENSEMBLE *helps* OLD JAKE *to throw the skirts into the air.*)

(MUSIC: *"Devil's Dream."*)

SARAH: He flung the skirts out of the trunk, sending them flying in every direction—

ACTOR #3: —winging their way around the cabin like a flock of tropical birds.

SARAH: They landed on the floor and helped to drink up the water. And when the last skirt fluttered earthward, the rain stopped suddenly, as quickly as if someone had turned off a faucet. Old Jake, standing in water, stood still a moment and soaked up that silence. What a mess.

(OLD JAKE *surveys his cabin. He sits on the trunk.*)

(MUSIC: *"Banks of the Ohio."*)

OLD JAKE: I never asked nobody to give me nuthin'. I worked my whole life to build somethin', and for what? To watch it all washed downstream? I can't win for trying. What a fool I've been.

(SHOESTRING *crosses up to* OLD JAKE.)

OLD JAKE: Leave me be, Shoestring. I'm not in the mood.

SARAH: Old Jake sat there, too tired to move.

OLD JAKE: I give up. (SHOESTRING *returns to* OLD JAKE.) Go on now! Get! Don't you hear me? I don't want you! I don't need you! You're just a stupid old hound dog and what good are you? Go away!

SHOESTRING: Awu!

(SHOESTRING *crosses away from* OLD JAKE.)

OLD JAKE: Oh, Lord!

(OLD JAKE *sits alone.*)

SARAH: But Shoestring wouldn't go away; instead he came back to Old Jake with a muddied calico skirt.

OLD JAKE: What? I used them skirts to mop the water and dirt and they're used up just like me. It's hopeless, you know? They're in pitiful shape, all muddy and torn. They're ruined. It would take too much work to make them look pretty again.

SHOESTRING: Awu.

SARAH: But then Jake had a strange thought.

OLD JAKE: Why that storm stopped when we let them skirts out, Shoestring. What do you think about that?

SHOESTRING: Awu.

OLD JAKE: I guess there's no harm in tryin'. Better clean up.

(MUSIC: *"Pre-Clean Music."*)

(OLD JAKE *gathers up the skirts.*)

OLD JAKE: Move, dog.

MUSICIAN: Come daybreak, Old Jake was up to his elbows in soapsuds, bent over a washboard scrubbing skirts.

(MUSIC: *"Irish Washerwoman."*)

(OLD JAKE *starts washing the skirts with a washboard and bucket.* SARAH *pulls a clothesline across the stage.* ACTOR #3 *and* SARAH *dance a jig while hanging the skirts on the clothesline.*)

OLD JAKE: Ol' cabin's never looked cleaner. Shoestring, come look at your new doghouse. (OLD JAKE *turns the trunk on its side so* SHOESTRING *can lay in it.*) Shoestring!

SARAH: Shoestring lay curled up in his new doghouse. Now Old Jake felt superstitious about the skirts. It was the most color that Stillwaters Farm had seen since the Good Samaritan Ladies' Committee came with tea-cakes and Bibles the year before.

MUSICIAN (*singing*): Amen! (*Speaking.*) Later that day Old Jake surveyed his soggy pumpkin field.

SARAH: All was lost, even the scarecrow.

MUSICIAN: But a few days of sunshine dried out the field—

SARAH: —and Jake began to replant his pumpkins.

OLD JAKE: We'll give it one more go, Shoestring.

(OLD JAKE *works on his pumpkin field.*)

(MUSIC: *"Happy Planting."*)

OLD JAKE: Rocks, rabbits, storms, and mud.

(SHOESTRING *returns to the trunk.* SARAH *hands a sewing basket to* OLD JAKE.)

SARAH: The night after the last pumpkins were planted—

OLD JAKE: Now that we fixed everything outside we better start on the in-side, Shoestring.

SARAH: —Old Jake picked up scissors, needle, and thread.

OLD JAKE: Better patch things up.

(MUSIC: "*Soul of Man.*")

SARAH: Old Jake was beginning to become as handy with needle and thread as he was with a whittling knife. No more wind whistling through the holes in his overalls.

(OLD JAKE *patches up his overalls.*)

OLD JAKE: The skirts will take care of that.

(ACTOR #3 *takes a skirt down from the clothesline, handing it to* OLD JAKE *as he sews.*)

ACTOR #3: No more sun beating down on Old Sally's head as she pulled the plow across the pumpkin field.

OLD JAKE: The skirts will take care of that.

(SARAH *and* ACTOR #3 *take down skirts, handing them to* OLD JAKE *until only three remain on the clothesline.*)

SARAH: And no more sitting on the hard porch for Jake as he took turns whittling and sewing in the evenings.

(ACTOR #3 *and* SARAH *begin to dress up the farm using the skirts. Even the miniature cabin gets some color.*)

OLD JAKE: The skirts will take care of that.

ACTOR #3: He cut up a skirt, making it into a neckerchief, one for him and another for Shoestring.

OLD JAKE: The skirts will take care of that, too.

(OLD JAKE *places a neckerchief on* SHOESTRING *and then dresses up the trunk.*)

SARAH: His place began to look downright merry.

OLD JAKE: Shoestring, come and take a look at your fancy doghouse. Now go on and protect them pumpkins.

(MUSIC: "*Whistlin' & Whittlin'.*")

MUSICIAN: His spirits began to lift.

SARAH: And the days passed in sunshine and gentle rains.

(ACTOR #3 *places the pumpkin patch in front of the cabin.* OLD JAKE *whittles.*)

ACTOR #3: The pumpkin plants grew greener and fuller than ever, and it seemed that for this season at least, plagues would be held at bay.

(MUSIC: "*Whistlin' & Whittlin'*" *stops.*)

(*A convertible toy car with three small fancy hats appears.*)

SARAH: Old Jake didn't even grumble much when he saw the First Baptist Church of Quail's Good Samaritan Ladies' Committee bumping up his road.

(MUSIC: "This Train.")

OLD JAKE: Oh, Lord.

GOOD SAMARITAN LADY #2: Ready, ladies?

(They sing "Shall We Gather at the River" as they enter. Only fancy hats, white gloves, handkerchiefs, and fans appear behind the skirts on the clothesline.)

OLD JAKE: Be nice, Jake. Be nice.

GOOD SAMARITAN LADIES: Mornin', Mr. Jake.

OLD JAKE: Mornin'.

GOOD SAMARITAN LADY #3: How are you, Mr. Jake?

(GOOD SAMARITAN LADIES #1 and #2 agree with #3.)

GOOD SAMARITAN LADY #3: What a pleasant day, Mr. Jake! Fine crop you have growin' there.

GOOD SAMARITAN LADIES #1/#2: Why, yes he does!

GOOD SAMARITAN LADY #3: Why, I must say. Your farm is positively pretty this spring.

(The LADIES discover the calico dresses hanging on the clothesline. They instantly begin chattering to one another.)

GOOD SAMARITAN LADY #3: All right, Gertrude. Shh! Is there a Mrs. Jake now?

(GOOD SAMARITAN LADIES #1 and #2 agree with #3.)

GOOD SAMARITAN LADY #3: Well, we know you're busy with your farm and all so we'll say our piece and leave you be. We've come to invite you to our church picnic by the river on Sunday.

(GOOD SAMARITAN LADIES #1 and #2 agree with #3.)

GOOD SAMARITAN LADY #3: We'd be blessed to have you come.

(GOOD SAMARITAN LADIES #1 and #2 agree with #3.)

GOOD SAMARITAN LADIES #1/#2: 'Bye, Mr. Jake!

GOOD SAMARITAN LADY #3: That's enough, ladies.

(GOOD SAMARITAN LADIES #1 and #2 exit.)

GOOD SAMARITAN LADY #3: I brought you some teacakes.

(She passes a plate of teacakes to OLD JAKE. He takes them.)

OLD JAKE: Much obliged, ma'am.

ACTOR #3: Old Jake's fingertips brushed the soft white glove of the First Baptist Church of Quail's Good Samaritan.

GOOD SAMARITAN LADY #3: Oh, my . . .

(*She fans herself.*)

ACTOR #3: And Old Jake revealed an answer that surprised himself.

OLD JAKE: I'll think on the picnic.

GOOD SAMARITAN LADY #3: Oh, good. 'Bye, Mr. Jake!

MUSICIAN: A soft breeze—

  (MUSIC: *"Beautiful Dreamer."*)

MUSICIAN: —picked up, and the scent of rose perfume, heretofore swirling around the ladies, now settled into Jake's whiskers.

OLD JAKE: Oh, Lord.

ACTOR #3: That sweetness, the teacakes, the company of kind folks, the sunshine, the day, the greenness of his good fortune—all—

SARAH: —all for a moment unfolded in his heart as would a tender flower.

(*SARAH places a small colorful scarecrow in front of the miniature cabin while* OLD JAKE *removes several skirts, leaving only one on the clothesline.*)

SARAH: That night, under the moon's watch, Old Jake finished dressing his new scarecrow with a skirt, neckerchief, and hat.

(OLD JAKE *rolls out a scarecrow.*)

OLD JAKE: May I have this dance?

  (MUSIC: *"Beautiful Dreamer."*)

(OLD JAKE *dances with the scarecrow as* SHOESTRING *smiles.*)

OLD JAKE: What are you grinnin' at, you old hound dog? Well, I'm kickin', but not too high.

SARAH: After sewing and patching things up, Old Jake had but one skirt left.

MUSICIAN: This last one he left out as a good luck symbol of sorts.

SARAH: He liked to look up from his whittling from time to time to watch it flap in the autumn breeze.

OLD JAKE: Pretty, ain't it?

  (MUSIC: *"Otis & Sarah Music."*)

SARAH: And then one day a white pickup came rattling up his road—

MUSICIAN: —Old Jake stood with Shoestring beside him, absentmindedly scratching his faithful hound's head as a man and a young girl climbed out of the truck.

(MUSICIAN *places a small white pickup truck in front of the farmhouse. He becomes* OTIS BROWN.)

MUSICIAN: They approached the cabin, the girl following shyly behind the man.

(SARAH *has now transformed into* YOUNG SARAH. *She stands behind her father.* SHOE-STRING *barks.*)

OLD JAKE: Mornin'.

OTIS BROWN: Mornin'. My name's Otis Brown and this here's my daughter, Sarah.

OLD JAKE: What can I do for you, Mr. Brown?

OTIS BROWN: We saw a sign in town said you found a trunk in the road some time back.

OLD JAKE: That's right.

OTIS BROWN: E. B. Sweeney told us we might find it here.

OLD JAKE: Ah-huh.

OTIS BROWN: It was full of skirts. Them skirts belonged to my wife.

OLD JAKE: Oh, I see.

OTIS BROWN: She died this winter. I wanted to find the skirts if I could, for my daughter to have to remember her mama.

(YOUNG SARAH *comes out from behind her father. She sneaks a glance at* OLD JAKE *and then drops her gaze to the ground again.*)

OLD JAKE: Mighty sorry 'bout your missus. It was me and my dog Shoestring that found the trunk. After a while we didn't think no one was comin' for it.

(SHOESTRING *lies in the trunk.* OLD JAKE *snaps his fingers at* SHOESTRING *to get out.*)

OLD JAKE: I used them skirts to help out around the place. Mighty sorry. I do have one left.

(MUSIC: *"Jake's Skirts—Skirt Magic with Sarah Theme."*)

(OLD JAKE *goes to the clothesline, taking down the final skirt. He folds it gently. He crosses to give it to* OTIS BROWN, *but* OTIS *nods over to* YOUNG SARAH. OLD JAKE *crosses to* YOUNG SARAH. *He hands it to her. She takes it.*)

OLD JAKE: I'm mighty sorry 'bout your mama, Sarah.

SARAH: Thank you.

OLD JAKE: If it's all right with your pa there's something I'd like to give you.

(YOUNG SARAH *looks at her father.*)

OTIS BROWN: It's all right, sweetie. Go on.

(MUSICIAN *removes the white truck.* OLD JAKE *opens the trunk and* YOUNG SARAH *looks inside.*)

OLD JAKE: I want you to have a look at these. They're wood carvings. I made them myself.

SARAH: They're pretty.

OLD JAKE: Take whichever one you want.

ACTOR #3: Sarah gently fished through the oldest carvings, the ones of dogs, and guns, and long-bearded men. Her fingers began to play with the newer ones, roses and doves and dolls. Finally, she picked.

(YOUNG SARAH *smiles at him.* OLD JAKE *smiles back.* YOUNG SARAH *chooses a woodcarving of a doll wearing a calico skirt, the one first seen at the top of the play.*)

SARAH: I'd like this one, please.

OLD JAKE: I would've picked that one too.

(YOUNG SARAH *transforms back into a young woman.*)

SARAH: That year, Old Jake was blessed. He reaped a bountiful harvest. As it turned out, no plague visited him, and he remembered it as—

OLD JAKE: The Year of the Skirts.

   (MUSIC: "Happy Planting.")

(OLD JAKE *begins combing his hair.*)

MUSICIAN: With each passing year, nature smiled upon him more, treated him more kindly.

ACTOR #3: And he stored away memories of plagues, along with other unhappy memories.

(OLD JAKE *closes the trunk.*)

MUSICIAN: Old Jake never saw the little girl again, but sometimes wondered about her.

ACTOR #3: Wondered if she still had the doll and still liked it.

SARAH: How she was getting along without her mama or if by now she had a new one.

OLD JAKE: Shoestring! Time to go!

   (MUSIC: "Rounder.")

(OLD JAKE *drives his truck to* E. B. SWEENEY'S *store. His toy truck is filled with pumpkins.* SHOESTRING *follows.*)

MUSICIAN: And had the little girl paid Old Jake a visit in later days, she may not have found him holed up at Stillwaters Farm.

SARAH: She may instead have found him at E. B. Sweeney's store, sitting among the circle of morning regulars.

OLD JAKE: Mornin', Clarence. Mornin', Ellis.

CLARENCE: Mornin', Jake.

ELLIS: Mornin', Jake.

SARAH: Not talking much, mind you, but listening and whittling.

(OLD JAKE and ACTOR #3 place a miniature church on the trunk.)

SARAH: Or she may even have spotted him, on a rare Sunday, sitting in the back pew of the First Baptist Church of Quail—

(MUSIC: "Amazing Grace.")

SARAH: —his gravelly voice sending an occasional hymn to heaven.

(OLD JAKE sits on the trunk and sings. SHOESTRING howls along.)

OLD JAKE: Settle down, boy.

(The ENSEMBLE continues to sing. OLD JAKE and SHOESTRING exit. SARAH places the colorful woodcarving doll alongside the church. SARAH exits.)

(MUSIC: MUSICIAN closes with the tag as written at the end of "Amazing Grace," which is the first four notes of the "Jake's Skirts—Main Theme.")

CURTAIN

Above the Plains

traditional

A - bove the plains, of Gold and Green, A young boy's head, is Plain - ly seen, A - hoo - ya, hoo - ya, hoo - ya, ya! Swift - ly flow - ing ri - ver, A hoo - ya, hoo - ya, hoo - ya, ya! Swift - ly flow - ing ri - ver. A

Singers begin, first at A, then second begins at B, third at C, fourth at D
Ending harmonies found at end of music set.

Jake's Skirts - Magic Skirts Opening

Averill

Rounder

Adam Jacobson

Repeat as needed
Theme will be used multiple times

Shoestring Blues

Averill-Jacobson

Mandolin

Theme will be used multiple times

Truck-Drivin' Riff

too simple to say

Guitar

Theme will be used multiple times

Tin Lizzy

Traditional

Soprano

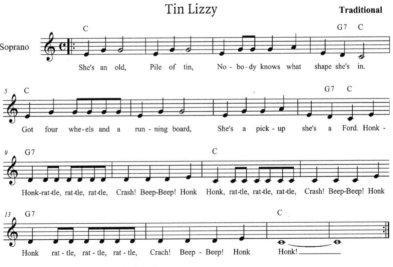

She's an old, Pile of tin, No - bo - dy knows what shape she's in.

Got four whe-els and a run - ning board, She's a pick - up she's a Ford. Honk -

Honk-rattle, rat-tle, rat-tle, Crash! Beep-Beep! Honk Honk, rat-tle, rat-tle, rat-tle, Crash! Beep-Beep! Honk

Honk rat - tle, rat - tle, rat - tle, Crach! Beep - Beep! Honk Honk!_____

Harmonies found at back of music

Jake's Skirts - Main Theme
Averill

Mandolin

Theme will be used multiple times

Jimmy
Adam Jacobson

Guitar

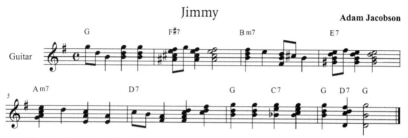

Theme will be used multiple times

Delbert Sweep - Fly
Averill/Traditional

Violin

There's a Hole in the Bucket

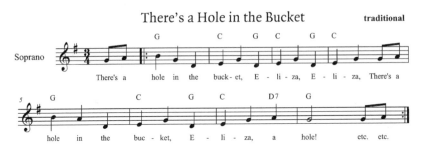

Theme will be used multiple times

Planting Crops with Plague Tag

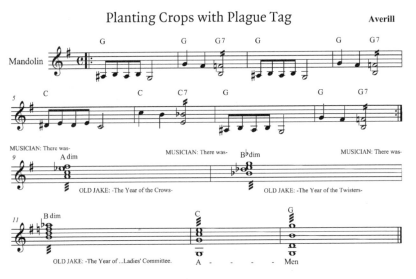

Music repeats during planting, then goes on to underscore plagues and 'amen.'

Whistlin' & Whittlin'

Theme may be used multiple times

Bill Cheatham

traditional

Opening the Trunk

Variation on Devil's Dream

Devil's Dream

Banks of the Ohio

Pre-Clean Music

Irish Washerwoman

Traditional
Mandolin

Happy Planting

Averill
Mandolin or Guitar

Theme may be used multiple times

Soul of Man

Traditional
Mandolin

This Train

traditional

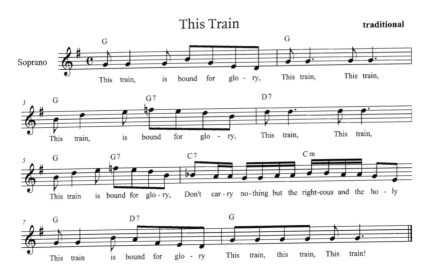

Shall We Gather at the River

traditional

Beautiful Dreamer

Stephen Foster

Repeat as needed for waltz
Add tremelo on all dotted quarters

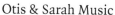

Harmonies As Needed

random

This Train

Shall We Gather at the River

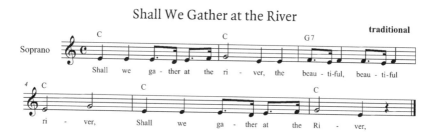

Amazing Grace

Designer's Response

This play, with its core of simplicity and quietude, calls for a small ensemble of actors. As in several of his other plays, the playwright uses actors who perform more than one role, and the setting, although rustic and realistic, includes the magic of toy theatre and puppets.

Although shown here in black and white (plate A), the collage is an exploration of color, textures, and images for a patterned wooden planking thrust stage. By metaphorically representing the farmland with wood, I have also indicated the era and social status of the characters. I discovered this approach in my study of photographs of farmland, the Depression era, and especially woodblock prints. The simplicity and solidity suggested in the stark contrast of the black lines on white in the prints seemed right for the play.

The larger scenic piece, of the General Store (plate B), can be repositioned by rotating it to reveal interior and exterior scenes. The crates and flour sacks downstage right provide a place for the more intimate moments of the scenes with the toy-theatre.

Images and Elements

Carved wooden images	Musical instruments
Wooden planking	Rabbits
Old trunk that becomes a truck	Dog
Miniature cabin	Calico fabric
Actors as landscape	Clothesline across stage
Folk melodies	Skirts

Resources

Garrett, Albert. A History of Wood Engraving. London: Bloomsbury, 1978.

Lange, Dorothea. Photographs of a Lifetime. Oakland: Aperture Foundation, 1982.

Lange, Dorothea, and Paul Taylor. An American Exodus. Paris: Jean-Michel Place, 1999.

Sander, David M. Wood Engraving: An Adventure in Printmaking. New York: Viking, 1978.

Plate A: Collage.

Plate B: Preliminary design for three-quarter thrust stage.

Lily Plants a Garden

José Cruz González

Originally commissioned by
Center Theatre Group at the Mark Taper Forum,
Los Angeles, California

Characters

YOUNG GIRL: our storyteller. She is a survivor in a war-torn era. She has a red wagon that contains all of her belongings.

ROSEY: a rose plant ballerina puppet. She speaks with a French accent. Played by the actor playing YOUNG GIRL.

LILY WULUMAN: a Zobeing child raised by Wulumans. She wears a bluzulu seed necklace. She has red, crooked hair and three fingers on each hand. Zobeings are vegetable-like creatures.

MAMA WULUMAN: a Wuluman. Wulumans are animal-like creatures. Mama Wuluman has long, hairy ears, a snout-a-puss, and tusks-a-wus. Mother to LILY, a tough but caring mother. Mama Wuluman will also be played as a puppet.

PAPA WULUMAN: a Wuluman. He has long, hairy ears, a snout-a-puss, and tusks-a-wus. Father to LILY.

SHADOW: a gentle Zobeing soul. Played by the actor playing PAPA WULUMAN.

MISS BEATRICE: a ladybug puppet. She speaks with an Irish accent. Rides an airship. A male actor should play MISS BEATRICE.

WULULANDER IN UNIFORM, ZOBEING IN UNIFORM: played by the actor playing MISS BEATRICE.

Setting

A room littered with the rubble of an abandoned dwelling,
as well as other locations from the imagination of our storyteller.

AT RISE: *Stars glow through the broken window of an abandoned dwelling. The room is littered with rubble. Several explosions are heard from nearby. Flashes of light flood the room, creating fragmentary shadows on the wall.*

(In the darkness a small figure scurries in with an old red wagon. She hides. Silence. The glow of a distant fire illuminates YOUNG GIRL. *She is not of our era. She sits very still, holding her torn teddy bear and ballerina slippers. She opens a music box and the sounds of war fade away. In the rubble she discovers a little package of sweets. She eats them. She finds a doll with a missing head and a plastic toy radish with lots of crooked roots that look like hair. She attaches it to the body of the doll. She begins playing with it.* YOUNG GIRL *unearths a toy castle with a door and windows.)*

YOUNG GIRL: Once upon a time, in a far distant land, on the doorsteps of a little wukastle with a little wukar, a baby named Lily Wuluman was found. *(YOUNG GIRL places the doll in a small basket, laying it in front of the castle door.)* Lily Wuluman had two eyes the color of chocolate, red, crooked hair, and a most beautiful milky smile. She had two hands and three fingers, two feet and five toes, and a tiny little nose that when she'd sneeze, went—

LILY *(from inside the castle)*: Wuchoo!

(A baby's laugh is heard.)

YOUNG GIRL: Lily Wuluman's laughter awoke a childless couple, who, upon seeing her, immediately took her into their wucastle.

(YOUNG GIRL opens the castle door, placing the basket inside. The castle door magically closes by itself. Footsteps are heard outside the abandoned bedroom. YOUNG GIRL *freezes until the footsteps are gone. The distant firelight creates shadowy figures on the wall.)*

YOUNG GIRL: No one knew how she got there. But some say they saw a mysterious figure sneaking about that very night in their neighborhood. No one ever spoke of it again. *(One of the shadows runs off.)* Lily Wuluman was just about the most perfect little baby ever, except for one slight, itsy-bitsy problem: around her neck dangled a bluzulu seed. You see, Lily was a Zobeing and her new mama and papa were Wulumans. Awooo!

(Three full moons of various sizes appear. YOUNG GIRL *plays with her teddy bear.* PAPA *and* MAMA WULUMAN *are heard offstage.)*

PAPA WULUMAN/YOUNG GIRL: Awoooooo!

(A baby's cry is heard coming from the castle.)

MAMA WULUMAN/YOUNG GIRL: Frank, keep it down! You're scaring baby Lily!

PAPA WULUMAN/YOUNG GIRL: Awoooooo!

MAMA WULUMAN/YOUNG GIRL: Frank!

YOUNG GIRL: You see, Wulumans were the mortal enemies of Zobeings. (*YOUNG GIRL adds another doll to her play.*) Long ago Zobeings and Wulumans shared the same lineage. They were one family. They traded bluzulu seeds and wusoil and they grew the most beautiful gardens in the whole world.

PAPA WULUMAN: Awoooooo!

(*In the distance, the imaginary sky becomes filled with plumes of fire and smoke. Fragmentary shadows on the wall come to life and depict her story.*)

YOUNG GIRL: But then a Zobeing and a Wuluman got into an argument, which led to a fight, which started the Great Endless Unforgotten War. They became so terrified of one another that Zobeings chose to exist by day, while the Wulumans chose the night. And their beautiful gardens vanished away forever. Centuries later the war still rages on but no one remembers why it started, nor do they remember how gardens came to be.

(*PAPA WULUMAN enters. Wulumans are tall creatures. PAPA WULUMAN is a security guard. He sees the moons and howls.*)

PAPA WULUMAN: Awooo!

(*MAMA WULUMAN enters, removing a baby bundle from the castle. At one end of the baby bundle red, crooked hair sticks out.*)

MAMA WULUMAN: Frank, you've awakened Lily again!

PAPA WULUMAN: Can't a Wuluman howl when he wants, Lois? It's a three full moon night, for gosh sakes.

MAMA WULUMAN: What has gotten into you lately? You've been in such a tizzy about things.

PAPA WULUMAN: Lois, you used to like my howling, riding with me on my wumotor hog and throwing caution to the wind. Now, every time I ride or howl, you shush me. "Don't, you'll wake the baby!"

MAMA WULUMAN: Things have changed. We have a little one now and your howling frightens her.

PAPA WULUMAN: How is it we have the only child on the entire block that cries when a Wuluman howls? Isn't she supposed to howl too?

MAMA WULUMAN: Lily's a special child.

PAPA WULUMAN: Lois, she's a Zobeing!

MAMA WULUMAN: Frank!

PAPA WULUMAN: There, I said it!

MAMA WULUMAN: She's our little baby!

PAPA WULUMAN: But she wears a bluzulu seed around her neck!

MAMA WULUMAN: Don't start!

PAPA WULUMAN: She doesn't look anything like us! She doesn't have big, hairy ears, a snout-a-puss, or even tusks-a-wus! Zobeings have wild, crooked hair, enjoy the sun, and have three fingers! They're scary looking! Maybe we shouldn't have taken her in!

MAMA WULUMAN: Don't say such an awful, monstrous thing!

PAPA WULUMAN: Why not? We're monsters! Good monsters! Fair monsters! Monsters who pay their taxes and give to the poor!

MAMA WULUMAN: No child should ever go unloved, no matter where it comes from or what it looks like.

PAPA WULUMAN: But how can a Zobeing ever live with a Wuluman? Is it possible?

MAMA WULUMAN: She's ours to raise.

PAPA WULUMAN: Our neighbors say we're cursed!

MAMA WULUMAN: They shouldn't stick their snout-a-pusses where they don't belong!

PAPA WULUMAN: But she's so soft and tiny!

MAMA WULUMAN: Not another word, Francis Spencer Wuluman!

PAPA WULUMAN: Oh, what's the use! (Sadly.) Awooooooo!

YOUNG GIRL: Mama and Papa Wuluman tried protecting Lily as best they could, but it kept getting more and more difficult.

PAPA WULUMAN: The neighbors want us to hand her over to them.

MAMA WULUMAN: They're not talking about eating her, are they?

PAPA WULUMAN: They want to sauté her in butter.

MAMA WULUMAN: They're wucrazy!

PAPA WULUMAN: Or have her for dessert with a little ice cream, chocolate sauce, and sprinkles!

MAMA WULUMAN: Frank, the moons are out. They're talking wunonsense. It's fear that has them spreading wildfires of gossip about her! You've just got to ignore them.

PAPA WULUMAN: I've tried, Lois, but it isn't so easy. No one in our neighborhood likes us. They've started throwing wuchuckeggs at me.

MAMA WULUMAN: If we hadn't taken Lily in there's no telling what might have happened to her. This child arrived on our doorstep for a reason, Frank.

PAPA WULUMAN: I just wish I knew why.

MAMA WULUMAN: Go on now, you'll be late for work.

(*She hands him a lunch pail.*)

PAPA WULUMAN (*sadly*): Awoooo!

(*He exits.*)

MAMA WULUMAN (*to* LILY): Give me a smile. That's my sweet angel. Woo . . .

YOUNG GIRL: To Mama Wuluman, Lily was the most beautiful thing she had ever seen, even with her small ears, tiny nose, and soft skin.

MAMA WULUMAN: What am I going to do with this wild, crazy hair of yours? Hmmm . . .

(*MAMA WULUMAN exits as* LILY *appears. She is now a little girl. She wears a bluzulu seed necklace and her red, crooked hair is in the shape of Wuluman ears. She carries a Wuluman teddy bear and hums to herself.* PAPA WULUMAN *enters, watching* LILY *play.*)

YOUNG GIRL: As Lily grew, Papa Wuluman came to love her even though she didn't look like a Wuluman or sound like one, even though her voice was soft and quiet, not loud and gruff. Papa Wuluman tried everything to make Lily fit in so the neighbors wouldn't say hurtful things.

PAPA WULUMAN: Lily, come here.

LILY: Yes, Papa?

PAPA WULUMAN: I have something for you.

LILY: Is it a surprise, Papa?

PAPA WULUMAN: Tah-dah! Look what I made you!

LILY: What is it?

PAPA WULUMAN: It's a Wuluman mask, with ears, tusks-a-wus, and a snout-a-puss! Here try it on! You look marvelous!

(*LILY scoops up some wuludirt.*)

LILY: Papa wuludirt! Papa wuludirt!

(*PAPA WULUMAN smears the wuludirt over* LILY.)

PAPA WULUMAN: Lily wuludirt! Lily wuludirt! (*PAPA WULUMAN and* LILY *roll on the ground.*) Now, Lily, sniff and growl for Papa!

LILY: Errr . . . Errr . . .

PAPA WULUMAN: Louder.

LILY: Errr . . . Errr . . .

MAMA WULUMAN (*entering*): Frank, what in the name of Theodore Roozabelt Wuluman are you doing?

PAPA WULUMAN: I made Lily a mask.

MAMA WULUMAN: Why?

PAPA WULUMAN: So she can look like a Wuluman and fit in!

LILY: Mama, look! Errr . . .

MAMA WULUMAN: Lily, take that awful thing off this instant!

LILY: Yes, Mama.

(LILY *takes off the mask.*)

PAPA WULUMAN: Lois, I'm only trying to make things better—

MAMA WULUMAN: Lily doesn't need to be made better! What matters is what's inside.

PAPA WULUMAN: I know that, but try telling it to our neighbors with their wunasty words and wuhate looks.

MAMA WULUMAN: Lily, cover your ears and hum!

LILY: Yes, Mama!

(LILY *takes off her mask. She cowers underneath her little wukastle. A Wuluman in silhouette appears, looking through their window.* PAPA WULUMAN *waves at him. The Wuluman in silhouette quickly disappears.*)

PAPA WULUMAN: They believe that her bluzulu seed is a curse.

MAMA WULUMAN: Frank, I won't stand for this!

(LILY *uncovers her ears.*)

PAPA WULUMAN: Lois, you can't ignore what's happening around us!

MAMA WULUMAN: I know exactly what is going on!

PAPA WULUMAN: Sooner or later Lily will be taken from us and we'll be arrested!

MAMA WULUMAN: No one is taking her away from us!

PAPA WULUMAN: Lois, she'll never be normal! She'll never fit in! She'll never be accepted!

(LILY *rips off her necklace.*)

LILY: Bad bluzulu!

MAMA WULUMAN: Lily?

LILY: All your fault!

MAMA WULUMAN: Look what we've done!

PAPA WULUMAN: Lois, let her be.

(LILY *digs a hole in the earth.*)

LILY: Cursed bluzulu!

PAPA WULUMAN: It's for the best.

MAMA WULUMAN: How can you say that?

PAPA WULUMAN: Because if she doesn't bury it we're all in danger!

LILY: Go away!

(LILY *buries the bluzulu seed, covering it with wuludirt. She cries over it. A musical note is heard for each tear. An* ANGRY MOB OF WULUMAN WITH FISTS *appears in silhouette. They carry torches.*)

ANGRY MOB OF WULUMAN WITH FISTS: She's not wanted! Send her away! Zobeing, leave us! Zobeing, leave us!

LILY: Mama?

MAMA WULUMAN: It's all right, Lily.

PAPA WULUMAN: My fellow Wululanders, I have great news! Her bluzulu seed is gone!

(*The* ANGRY MOB OF WULUMAN WITH FISTS *shakes their fists at the family.*)

ANGRY MOB OF WULUMAN WITH FISTS: She's not wanted! Send her away! Zobeing, leave us! Zobeing, leave us!

PAPA WULUMAN: You needn't be afraid! It's buried away forever! See!

(PAPA WULUMAN *stomps on the ground where* LILY *buried her bluzulu seed.* YOUNG GIRL *makes the mound glow while springing up a single blue sprout.*)

LILY (*frightened*): Mama!

PAPA WULUMAN: Oh, no!

MAMA WULUMAN: Oh, my!

ANGRY MOB OF WULUMAN WITH FISTS: Aagghhh!

YOUNG GIRL: The Angry Mob of Wuluman attacked their home, smashing it to bits! Kaboom!

(YOUNG GIRL *smashes the castle with her fist. The* ANGRY MOB OF WULUMAN WITH FISTS *fades away.*)

YOUNG GIRL: Oh, no!

LILY: Mama! Papa!

PAPA WULUMAN: Is anyone hurt?

LILY: What was that, Mama?

MAMA WULUMAN: That was a kaboom, baby.

PAPA WULUMAN (*sadly*): Awooooo!

YOUNG GIRL: Lily didn't know what to make of this.

MAMA WULUMAN (*sadly*): Awooooo!

YOUNG GIRL: She had never seen a wukastle go—

LILY: Kaboom.

PAPA WULUMAN: They're gone.

MAMA WULUMAN: Frank, what are we going to do?

PAPA WULUMAN: How could they do this to us, to their own family? (*Sadly.*) Awooo!

YOUNG GIRL: Poor Lily. Poor Mama and Papa Wuluman. Papa began getting sadder and sadder. He started drinking wulujuice. He drank so much of it that his stomach ballooned until he started floating into the sky.

(PAPA WULUMAN *picks up a bottle of wulujuice and gulps it. He exits.*)

MAMA WULUMAN: Frank? Frank?

(MAMA WULUMAN *follows.* LILY *stomps on the bluzulu seedling until it fades away.* MAMA WULUMAN *enters, carrying* PAPA WULUMAN *as a balloon.*)

YOUNG GIRL: Mama Wuluman had to attach a rope to Papa so he wouldn't float away. But he kept getting larger and larger and floating further and further away until Papa Wuluman was just a little dot in the sky.

MAMA WULUMAN: Frank, you come down this instant!

PAPA WULUMAN (*offstage*): Send up another bottle of wulujuice!

LILY (*waving*): Hello, Papa!

YOUNG GIRL: Then one day Papa Wuluman's rope snapped—

PAPA WULUMAN (*offstage*): Awooooo!

YOUNG GIRL: —and he floated far away, never to been seen again!

(YOUNG GIRL *carries* PAPA WULUMAN'*s balloon away.*)

LILY: Papa! Papa, come back!

MAMA WULUMAN: Oh, Frank . . . (LILY *hides under her wukastle.*) Lily!

LILY: Mama, why did Papa float away?

MAMA WULUMAN: Sad Papa went kaboom, baby.

LILY: Kaboom?

MAMA WULUMAN: Sometimes kabooms can happen to us, too.

LILY: It's all my fault!

MAMA WULUMAN: You're not to blame for our mistakes.

LILY: Why was I ever born a Zobeing?

(*LILY cries over the mound of dirt. A musical note is heard for each tear.*)

MAMA WULUMAN: Lily, you came to our doorstep and changed our life. Changed it in so many wonderful and unexpected ways. The world that we live in doesn't see your special beauty yet. It can't see much of anything right now. And changing it takes time. But we first have to start with ourselves, okay?

(*LILY hugs MAMA WULUMAN. YOUNG GIRL makes the mound glow and a single blue sprout springs back up.*)

LILY (*frightened*): Mama! Mama, it's come back!

MAMA WULUMAN: Lily, you know what you've done?

LILY: I'm sorry, Mama!

MAMA WULUMAN: No, baby, you did nothing wrong. You buried your bluzulu seed into our wusoil and watered it with your tears. Lily, you started a garden!

LILY: I did?

MAMA WULUMAN: Yes, I'm sure of it! My grandmother Wulumeana said that gardens were the center of their lives. I remember seeing pictures of them in books. But I thought it would be much bigger.

LILY: What am I supposed to do with it, Mama?

MAMA WULUMAN: Baby, I don't know. I've never raised a garden before. I guess we'll have to learn together, won't we?

LILY: Okay, Mama!

(*ANGRY MOB OF WULUMAN WITH FISTS appears.*)

YOUNG GIRL: Soon after the bluzulu seed sprouted, a bigger problem blossomed for Mama Wuluman and Lily.

(*Windows are heard shattering.*)

ANGRY MOB OF WULUMAN WITH FISTS: She's not wanted! Send her away! Zobeing, leave us! Zobeing, leave us!

(*The ANGRY MOB OF WULUMAN WITH FISTS is replaced by an image of barbed wire.*)

MAMA WULUMAN: We've been uprooted, Lily. Replant your garden.

(*LILY uses her lunch pail to replant her bluzulu seedling. She carries her lunch-pail garden and her Wuluman teddy bear. LILY takes MAMA WULUMAN's hand. The abandoned dwelling becomes fragmented, shifting into a borderline checkpoint. WULULANDER IN UNIFORM appears. MAMA WULUMAN and LILY cross to the WULULANDER IN UNIFORM.*)

WULULANDER IN UNIFORM: Papers!

MAMA WULUMAN: Here you go.

WULULANDER IN UNIFORM: What is your relationship to this Zobeing?

MAMA WULUMAN: She's my daughter.

WULULANDER IN UNFORM: Hah, impossible! Wulumans do not raise Zobeings!

MAMA WULUMAN: Well, I have!

WULULANDER IN UNIFORM: Mind your wulutongue! I could make you stay and send her out there alone!

LILY: Mama?

MAMA WULUMAN: Please! No.

WULULANDER IN UNIFORM (to LILY): We don't need her kind living among us! Or Zobeing sympathizers!

MAMA WULUMAN: May we go now, sir?

(He stamps their papers loudly.)

WULULANDER IN UNIFORM: Lift the gate! (YOUNG GIRL lifts the checkpoint rail.) Don't ever come back! Go on now! Shuwulu!

MAMA WULUMAN: We're going to Zobeelanda.

LILY: But aren't Zobeings our mortal enemy?

MAMA WULUMAN: Yes, they are, but I won't wuhate Zobeings, especially one as brave and strong as you! I refuse!

LILY: Then me too, Mama!

(The borderline checkpoint shifts and transforms into another borderline checkpoint as WULULANDER IN UNIFORM is now transformed into ZOBEING IN UNIFORM. MAMA WULUMAN and LILY cross to him.)

ZOBEING IN UNIFORM: Papers!

MAMA WULUMAN: Here you go.

ZOBEING IN UNIFORM: Why have you come to Zobeelanda?

MAMA WULUMAN: I've brought my daughter to live here among her kind.

ZOBEING IN UNIFORM: Hah! Zobeings are not raised by Wulumans!

MAMA WULUMAN: But I did raise her!

ZOBEING IN UNIFORM: Impossible! The child may stay, but you must go! Come, child!

LILY: Mama!

ZOBEING IN UNIFORM: Prepare the dewululizer! She must be bathed, sprayed, and X-rayed!

MAMA WULUMAN: Please, sir, I beg you, don't take her from me!

ZOBEING IN UNIFORM: Go away!

LILY: Mama!

MAMA WULUMAN: I can prove she's my child!

ZOBEING IN UNIFORM: Impossible!

MAMA WULUMAN: Lily, I want you to howl! Do it like Papa showed you!

LILY (*softly*): Awoo!

MAMA WULUMAN: Louder, baby!

LILY (*a little louder*): Awooo!

ZOBEING IN UNIFORM: Arrest the beast!

MAMA WULUMAN: That's it, Lily! Awooo!

LILY (*loudly*): Awooooo!

(*YOUNG GIRL joins in. Howls are heard off in the distance.*)

ZOBEING IN UNIFORM (*frightened*): What was that?

MAMA WULUMAN: That's a wuluhowl!

ZOBEING IN UNIFORM: What a strange and scary child! She appears to be a Zobeing but she howls like a Wuluman! She must be cursed!

LILY: No, I'm not! Mama says!

ZOBEING IN UNIFORM: You cannot live in Zobeelanda!

MAMA WULUMAN: But we must! We have nowhere else to go!

ZOBEING IN UNIFORM: You can stay—

YOUNG GIRL: In the Land of Rubble!

ZOBEING IN UNIFORM: In the Land of Rubble! That's where the unwanted and unloved go!

MAMA WULUMAN: No!

(*He stamps their papers loudly.*)

ZOBEING IN UNIFORM: Close the gate! Shuzulu! (*YOUNG GIRL closes the checkpoint rail. The sky becomes filled with plumes of fire and smoke.*) Oh-oh!

(*ZOBEING IN UNIFORM exits as bombs are heard exploding everywhere. The borderline checkpoint shifts and transforms into the Land of Rubble. MAMA WULUMAN and LILY run toward a lopsided chimney shelter for cover. YOUNG GIRL opens an umbrella over them and the explosions cease.*)

MAMA WULUMAN: Are you hurt?

LILY: Mama, I want to go back!

MAMA WULUMAN: Chin up. We're going to handle ourselves as Wulumans. Proud Wulumans never feel sorry for themselves. I know it doesn't look like much but we've got to make the best of it. This is our new home.

LILY: I miss my home! I miss my papa! I want things the way they were!

(LILY *starts to cry. She cries over her lunch pail.* MAMA WULUMAN *sits by her.*)

MAMA WULUMAN: Lily, do you know how we make ourselves feel better?

LILY: No!

MAMA WULUMAN: It starts when you want to play and laugh again.

LILY: I don't feel that yet.

MAMA WULUMAN: Or maybe when you want to smile.

LILY: Or make up stories?

MAMA WULUMAN: Or play hide and seek!

LILY: Or draw pictures?

MAMA WULUMAN: Or bake cookies!

LILY/MAMA WULUMAN: Or walk a dog!

(LILY *laughs and her lunch pail springs open, revealing lots of bluzulu grass.*)

LILY: Mama, look!

MAMA WULUMAN: Oh, my, it's grown!

LILY: Wulot!

MAMA WULUMAN: If only there was something bigger to place it in.

(YOUNG GIRL *produces her red wagon.*)

LILY: Like a red box with four black rings, Mama?

MAMA WULUMAN: A red box with four black rings?

LILY: Tah-dah-dah!

(LILY *runs to it.*)

MAMA WULUMAN: Lily, that's a little red wagon! Lily Wuluman, you are the most resourceful young lady I know!

LILY: Awooo!

MAMA WULUMAN: Awooo!

YOUNG GIRL: Awooo! (LILY *and* MAMA WULUMAN *replant the garden in the little red wagon. The bluzulu garden glows. Three moons appear in the night sky. Music is heard as they replant the bluzulu seedling into the red wagon and fix up their new* home.) Lily and Mama Wuluman made a new home for themselves in the Land of Rubble.

MAMA WULUMAN: Lily, I want you to promise me that you'll care for this little garden with all your wuheart no matter what happens.

LILY: I will, Mama.

MAMA WULUMAN: It's just like I care for you. You're my little bluzulu seed and I will always watch over you. I'll never let anything bad happen to you and I will always love you.

LILY: Okay.

MAMA WULUMAN: You're the boss now!

LILY: The big wucheese!

(*LILY yawns. MAMA WULUMAN wraps LILY in her blanket.*)

MAMA WULUMAN: Time for bed.

LILY: Aren't you going to sleep, Mama?

MAMA WULUMAN: In a little while. I want to keep watch tonight. Now, close your eyes. (*Singing*)

Sleep, sleep, Lily, sleep
Sleep sweet dreams
Sleep, sleep, Lily, sleep
Sleep sweet dreams

When you wake
You'll get wucake
And all the hugs and kisses

(*LILY falls asleep. MAMA WULUMAN struggles to stay awake and then soon joins LILY. Night passes into dawn as a shadowy figure in silhouette appears. He stops to catch his breath, hears something, and scampers off. SHADOW quickly enters, looking for his shadow. He wears a long, old military trench coat that reveals only his bare feet. He also wears a tall, cone-shaped hat, and a bluzulu seed necklace around his neck. He looks through his spyglass. No sight of his shadow. SHADOW sees the wagon garden. He crosses to it and rests his bare feet on the grass.*)

SHADOW: Ooohhh . . . Uuuhhhh . . . Aaahhh . . .

(*He hears crying. From his coat pocket he brings out something small and gently places it in the wagon garden. LILY suddenly sits up. SHADOW sees LILY. LILY sees SHADOW. They share a silent scream while their hands shake. Then—*)

LILY: Awooo!

(*SHADOW runs off.*)

MAMA WULUMAN (*awakening*): Awooo!

LILY: Mama, I saw a . . . a . . . a—

MAMA WULUMAN: What?

LILY: He was standing right there!

MAMA WULUMAN: Who?

LILY: A big giant!

MAMA WULUMAN: What did he look like?

LILY: He had a tall hat, long coat, and no shoes!

MAMA WULUMAN: Was he a Zobeing?

LILY: Ah-huh! Maybe? I don't know!

MAMA WULUMAN (*sniffs the air*): Well, he's gone now, baby. You scared him away with your wuluhowl. He's probably just some harmless wanderer looking for shelter and food, just like us.

LILY: Food, Mama?

MAMA WULUMAN: Look what I have for you!

LILY: Wulufood! Wulufood! But, Mama, you got to eat too. Grow big and strong, remember?

MAMA WULUMAN: I know dear, but Mama saved this for you. Go on now. Eat. (YOUNG GIRL *turns on a flashlight, pointing it at* MAMA WULUMAN.) Oh, my, it's so hot!

LILY: I like how it feels!

(MAMA WULUMAN *opens up a tattered umbrella.*)

MAMA WULUMAN: Lily, I've got to find us some food.

LILY: Can I come, Mama?

MAMA WULUMAN: No, baby. I want you to stay here. There's no telling what I'll find out there.

LILY: But I don't want to stay by my—

MAMA WULUMAN: You'll be safe here. Look after your garden. Just wuluholler if you need me. Give me a smile. (LILY *reluctantly smiles.*) That's my girl.

(MAMA WULUMAN *exits.* LILY *starts to cry.* YOUNG GIRL *holds her teddy bear and pretends to make it giggle.* LILY *turns, looking at the teddy bear.* YOUNG GIRL *stops giggling. Then she starts to giggle again.* LILY *crosses to the teddy bear, picking it up. It giggles again. It frightens her. She tosses it to the ground.* LILY *hears someone crying. She crosses to her wagon garden.* MISS BEATRICE, *a small ladybug puppet, appears. She speaks with an Irish-like accent.*)

LILY: It's a ladybug!

MISS BEATRICE: Where am I? How did I get here?

LILY: I don't know? What happened to your wings?

MISS BEATRICE: All I remember was this big ball of noise and when I woke up my wings were gone. (*Suddenly frightened.*) Are you going to tear off my head?

LILY: No.

MISS BEATRICE: Are you going to crush me to smithereens?

LILY: No, that would be cruel.

MISS BEATRICE (*crying*): I'll never be the same again.

LILY: I think ladybugs are beautiful.

MISS BEATRICE: You do?

LILY: Ah-huh. (MISS BEATRICE *bursts out crying.*) Why are you crying now?

MISS BEATRICE: That's the nicest thing anyone has ever said to me.

LILY: You can stay here in my garden with Mama and me, but you'll have to do what I say because I'm the boss, the big wucheese, okay?

MISS BEATRICE: Okay.

LILY: My name is Lily Wuluman!

MISS BEATRICE: I'm Miss Beatrice Ladybug!

LILY: Miss Beatrice, I'm building a safe place for us. You want to help?

MISS BEATRICE: I wish I could, dear, but I can't get about without some mode of transportation.

LILY: Mode of transportation?

MISS BEATRICE: A ladybug is always on the move. Buzz, buzz, you know?

LILY: Maybe I can help!

(LILY *and* MISS BEATRICE *exit.* YOUNG GIRL *removes a pinwheel from her wagon and plays with it.*)

YOUNG GIRL: Lily was growing into an excellent gardener and a magnificent fixer-upper of things! Why, she even had time to invent a "mode of transportation" for Miss Beatrice!

MISS BEATRICE (*offstage*): Oh, my, Lily, it's so beautiful!

LILY (*offstage*): Awooo!

YOUNG GIRL: But in the Land of Rubble, fear and danger are also constant companions. Something strange was happening to Mama Wuluman. She kept getting smaller and smaller.

(MAMA WULUMAN *enters.* YOUNG GIRL *turns on her flashlight and* MAMA WULUMAN *instantly gets smaller. She becomes a puppet.* LILY *enters.* YOUNG GIRL *manipulates the* MAMA WULUMAN *puppet.*)

MAMA WULUMAN: It's so hot!

LILY: Mama, what happened?

MAMA WULUMAN: It's so hot! Wulumans don't do well in the sunlight.

YOUNG GIRL: This weighed heavily on Lily.

(LILY *picks up* MAMA WULUMAN, *holding her.*)

LILY: How do I make it all better, Mama?

MAMA WULUMAN: You mustn't worry. I'll be fine. This is all the food I could gather. I'll try again tomorrow.

LILY: No, Mama. You rest. Get all better.

(MAMA WULUMAN *coughs.* LILY *places her in an old picnic basket and then into the chimney, where it is safe.* LILY *eats alone while* MAMA WULUMAN *sleeps.*)

YOUNG GIRL: Lily soon realized that the only way to help Mama Wuluman was by searching for food herself.

LILY: Just wuholler if you need me, Mama!

YOUNG GIRL: So Lily summoned up the courage to leave her garden. She ordered Miss Beatrice to keep guard over it and her mama while she was away.

(LILY *exits. Dusk. A shadowy figure appears. He stops to catch his breath. He runs off as* SHADOW *quickly enters, looking for him. He hangs his head and shoulders in disappointment.* SHADOW *sees the wagon garden. He crosses to it to rest his bare feet on the bluzulu grass.*)

SHADOW: Ooohhh . . . Uuuhhhh . . . Aaahhh . . .

(SHADOW *removes a rose flower puppet from his coat. He places it in the wagon garden.* LILY *enters, seeing* SHADOW.)

LILY: It's you again! (SHADOW *screams silently and his hands shake again.*) Awooo!

(SHADOW *exits as a small airship appears.* MISS BEATRICE *sits on a tiny bicycle. Her legs turn the propeller.*)

MISS BEATRICE: Lily, what is it?

LILY: Miss Beatrice, you're supposed to keep watch on Mama and the garden!

MISS BEATRICE: I'm sorry, Lily, I was dreaming of the most delicious meal of fried lice!

LILY: I don't like that nasty Zobeing sneaking up on us!

MISS BEATRICE: I won't let you down again, dear. I'll stand watch! The scoundrel shall not pass! Which way did he go?

(LILY *points.* MISS BEATRICE *flies off.*)

LILY: Next time I'll be ready for you! Whoever you are!

(YOUNG GIRL *picks up* ROSEY. ROSEY *is a small rose plant puppet.* YOUNG GIRL *manipulates her.* ROSEY *coughs.* LILY *imitates her cough.* ROSEY *coughs again.* LILY *coughs too.*)

LILY: Ehlo!

ROSEY (*French-like accent*): Who are you?

LILY: Lily Wuluman.

ROSEY: Please don't hurt me!

LILY: I won't. I promise. What's your name?

ROSEY: *Le Rose du Rosey.*

LILY: Ehlo, Rosey! You talk funny.

MISS BEATRICE (*offstage*): Lily! Lily Wuluman, he's nowhere to be found!

LILY: I'm over here, Miss Beatrice!

(MISS BEATRICE *enters.*)

MISS BEATRICE: Lily, all this flying has made me famished. We've got to find some tasty aphids for me to eat now! (ROSEY *coughs. Gruff.*) Who's she?

LILY: This is Rosey.

MISS BEATRICE: She's one skinny-looking plant. You got a problem with eating, dearie?

ROSEY: No.

LILY: Now, Miss Beatrice, be nice to our guest.

MISS BEATRICE: Who does she think she is, a prima ballerina or something?

ROSEY: I am a prima ballerina!

MISS BEATRICE: Huh! You're a ballerina, a rose plant ballerina?

ROSEY: Oui!

LILY: Oui?

MISS BEATRICE: Let's see!

ROSEY: All right. I'll show you! (ROSEY *manages to stand and then slumps over.*) Oh, no!

MISS BEATRICE: Hah! I knew it! You're no ballerina. You can't even stand up straight!

LILY: Are you all right, Rosey?

ROSEY: *Oui.* I mean, "yes."

LILY: *Oui.*

MISS BEATRICE: You're not very graceful, are you?

LILY: Miss Beatrice, you're not being very nice today.

MISS BEATRICE: I don't trust exotic plants. They're very high-maintenance. And stuck-up too!

LILY: Stop it, Miss Beatrice!

ROSEY: You're not good enough to kiss my roots!

MISS BEATRICE: Not "good enough," am I?

ROSEY: Hah, I refuse to speak to you!

LILY: See what you've done?

MISS BEATRICE: Well, I won't talk to you either! Hah!

LILY: You have to get along with Rosey.

MISS BEATRICE: Why?

LILY: Because I say!

MISS BEATRICE: Why?

LILY: Because I'm the boss! The big wucheese! (*Nicely.*) Would you like to stay with us, Rosey?

ROSEY: Yes, *merci.*

LILY: *Merci!* Miss Beatrice?

MISS BEATRICE: Oh, all right, but I won't like it! (*To herself.*) I still don't believe she's a ballerina.

ROSEY: I am too!

MISS BEATRICE: No, you're not!

ROSEY: Yes, I am!

MISS BEATRICE: Baloney!

ROSEY: Baloney! Maloney!

MISS BEATRICE: Come, Lily, I'm in the mood for some scrumptious aphids!

(*Off in the distance kabooms are heard and the sky becomes illuminated with plumes of fire and smoke.*)

LILY: Not tonight, Miss Beatrice. We have to stay in our safe place. Mama's got to eat.

YOUNG GIRL: Mama Wuluman kept getting weaker and weaker. And it was now up to Lily to care for her.

(LILY *brings out the picnic basket from the chimney. She feeds* MAMA WULUMAN *some food.*)

LILY: Mama, this is my new friend, Rosey.

ROSEY: Bonjour, madame!

MAMA WULUMAN: Awoo.

LILY: She's a ballerina.

ROSEY: One day, madame, when my roots are stronger I will dance for you.

MISS BEATRICE: That'll be the day.

LILY: Miss Beatrice, be nice. (*To* MAMA WULUMAN.) Mama, you eat now. Grow big and strong. (MAMA WULUMAN *starts to cry.*) Don't cry, Mama.

MAMA WULUMAN: I can't help it. I'm supposed to take care of you and I can't.

LILY: It's okay, Mama.

(ROSEY *coughs.*)

MAMA WULUMAN: Lily, take the last of my wuludirt and pour it into your garden so it'll help Rosey grow.

LILY: But, Mama—

MAMA WULUMAN: Please, baby.

LILY: Okay.

(LILY *takes* MAMA WULUMAN's *pouch of wuludirt and pours it into the garden.*)

ROSEY: Oh, that feels so magnifique!

(LILY *kisses* MAMA WULUMAN, *placing her back into the picnic basket and inside the chimney again. Three crescent-shaped moons appear. A kaboom is occasionally heard off in the distance.*)

LILY: You rest now. (*She sings.*)

Sleep, sleep, Mama, sleep
Sleep sweet dreams
Sleep, sleep, Mama, sleep
Sleep sweet dreams

When you wake
You'll get wucake
And all the hugs and kisses

(ROSEY *and* MISS BEATRICE *fall asleep.* LILY *yawns and soon falls asleep too.* YOUNG GIRL *turns the flashlight on* LILY *and she instantly wakes up.*)

LILY: Wake up, Miss Beatrice!

MISS BEATRICE: Lily, I was feasting on the most delicious meal of barbecue aphids!

LILY: *Bonjour,* Rosey! How are you feeling now?

ROSEY: Standing in the garden has made me very itchy. I'm so thirsty.

LILY: Miss Beatrice, it's time we watered the garden!

MISS BEATRICE: But I'm famished!

LILY: Miss Beatrice.

MISS BEATRICE: Do we have to?

LILY: *Oui.*

(*MISS BEATRICE hands a small cup to LILY, who in turn gives it to ROSEY.*)

MISS BEATRICE: Take it!

ROSEY: Hah! What am I supposed to do with it?

MISS BEATRICE: You'll find out!

LILY: It's a surprise, Rosey!

MISS BEATRICE: Yes, an ingenious discovery by my best friend, Lily Wuluman!

ROSEY: What is it?

LILY: Wutickle bugs!

ROSEY: Wutickle bugs?

MISS BEATRICE: They're small five-legged creatures with three eyes and a nose that loves to wutickle you! They live in the garden.

ROSEY: This garden? The one I'm planted in?

LILY: There's one!

MISS BEATRICE: There's two! I'm going to enjoy this!

ROSEY: Oh, no!

(*Music. LILY stands on the bluzulu grass as imaginary WUTICKLE BUGS tickle her. She laughs hysterically. ROSEY soon follows, laughing hysterically. LILY laughs so hard she begins crying tears.*)

MISS BEATRICE: It's working! Keep it up!

(*ROSEY captures LILY's tears in the small cup.*)

LILY: Oh my! Oh my!

(*LILY steps off the wagon.*)

MISS BEATRICE: I haven't had this much fun since I learned to fly my airship!

LILY: How much water we got, Rosey?

ROSEY: Wulot.

LILY: Good! Drink up!

(LILY *smiles proudly. The bluzulu grass instantly grows.*)

MISS BEATRICE: Lily, look! Your garden's gotten taller!

ROSEY: Where did everyone go?

(LILY *grabs an old eggbeater from the wagon.*)

LILY: Miss Beatrice, I think it's time we trim the grass!

MISS BEATRICE: Oh, yes, mow the lawn!

ROSEY: Mow the lawn?

LILY: Don't move, Rosey!

(MISS BEATRICE *begins making lawnmower noises as she spins the eggbeater. She flies back and forth, cutting the bluzulu grass.* ROSEY *reappears. They all laugh wildly.*)

MISS BEATRICE: Cutting the lawn is hard work! Let's eat!

ROSEY: I can see! What's this?

LILY: It's that teddy bear again! (LILY *picks up a teddy bear with a missing eye and arm.* YOUNG GIRL *can't stop laughing.* LILY *laughs.*) What's so funny? Stop giggling! Stop it! There!

(LILY *buries the teddy bear in the rubble, pouring some wuludirt over it and watering it with her tears of laughter.* YOUNG GIRL *instantly produces a beautiful fruit tree with little fruit teddy bears hanging from it.*)

YOUNG GIRL: In the Land of Rubble the unusual and the odd occurs but sometimes it turns into the puzzling and fantastical!

LILY: Look, it's a tree! It's got fruit teddy bears!

MISS BEATRICE: Uh, Lily, let me taste one! Oh, oh!

LILY: Well?

MISS BEATRICE: Oh, it's so sweet!

(ROSEY *eats a fruit teddy bear.*)

ROSEY: Oh, yummy!

(LILY *takes one to* MAMA WULUMAN.)

LILY: Mama! Mama, wulufood! Wulufood!

(MAMA WULUMAN *eats it. She instantly grows a little taller.*)

MAMA WULUMAN: Oh, my! Lily, where did you get this?

LILY: I planted a teddy bear in my garden.

MAMA WULUMAN: You've done something remarkable, baby.

LILY: I did?

MAMA WULUMAN: You started with a bluzulu seed and now look!

LILY: What do you mean, Mama?

MAMA WULUMAN: We Wulumans believe that everything has a soul.

LILY: Do teddy bears and broken toys have souls?

MAMA WULUMAN: If someone thought to create it, shaped it by their loving hands, then it must have a part of their soul too, don't you think?

LILY: I think, Mama. Now, you eat.

MAMA WULUMAN: I can't finish it. I'm so tired.

(MAMA WULUMAN coughs.)

LILY: Then you rest, Mama. Get all better. (Night begins to fall.) I have to go now, Miss Beatrice. Keep watch over Mama and Rosey.

MISS BEATRICE: Where are you going, dear?

LILY: Just wuholler if you need me.

MISS BEATRICE: Don't forget to find me some tasty aphids.

LILY: I won't, Miss Beatrice.

(LILY exits.)

ROSEY: Where is she going?

MISS BEATRICE: I don't know, dear, but sometimes she likes to play alone in the quiet of the night.

(MISS BEATRICE opens the music box. Music. Three smiling full moons appear in the night sky. YOUNG GIRL introduces a piece of fabric that becomes the sea as LILY enters, wearing a scuba mask and snorkel. LILY dives into the water as the kabooms fade away. LILY surfaces and the kabooms are still there. She dives back in and the kabooms vanish. YOUNG GIRL imagines herself swimming too. Under the water it is peaceful. Back on shore, LILY falls asleep. SHADOW enters, picking LILY up and placing her near the garden. Dawn.)

MISS BEATRICE (awakening): It's him!

ROSEY: He's back!

LILY: Grab him!

(LILY jumps onto SHADOW's back. ROSEY hangs on to his leg. MISS BEATRICE buzzes his face.)

SHADOW: Please don't hurt me!

LILY: Why do you keep scaring us?

SHADOW: I don't mean to. I've been trying to catch my own shadow, he's s-s-so scared of kabooms.

MISS BEATRICE: Why stand on Lily's garden?

ROSEY: Answer us!

SHADOW: I do it to cool off my feet; they get terribly hot when I run!

MISS BEATRICE: I don't trust him, Lily!

ROSEY: Nor I!

SHADOW: I keep lo-lo-looking for my shadow, but all I ever find are his foot-steps, or lost and damaged souls like you.

(*MAMA WULUMAN's voice is heard coming from the chimney. She sniffs the air.*)

MAMA WULUMAN: Lily, let him go.

LILY: No, Mama, he's a bad Zobeing!

(*An air-raid siren is heard.*)

MAMA WULUMAN: Come inside now! All of you!

LILY: What is it, Mama?

MAMA WULUMAN: Hurry!

(*Suddenly, explosions happen everywhere and the chimney crumbles. MAMA WULUMAN is buried. LILY searches for MAMA WULUMAN.*)

LILY: Mama? Mama? Where are you? Mama? (*LILY finds the MAMA WULUMAN puppet. LILY plants her in the garden wagon.*) No, Mama, you come back to me! I know you can! Everything's got a soul! You said! Mama, come back to me! Please come back! (*Nothing happens.*) Awoooo!

YOUNG GIRL: No!

(*LILY begins to destroy her garden. She runs off.*)

LILY: Awoooo!

(*YOUNG GIRL sits alone as her shadow appears on the wall. It looks like a giant mountain. A small LILY figure in silhouette appears and begins walking up YOUNG GIRL's back. A crescent-shaped moon with the face of the man in the moon rises into the sky and the LILY figure reaches up, climbing onto it using her umbrella. LILY enters, walking on the moon surface with her umbrella. YOUNG GIRL sits alone crying. LILY crosses to her.*)

LILY: Ehlo. (*YOUNG GIRL remains very still.*) I see you.

YOUNG GIRL: You do?

LILY: Ah-huh. Why are you hiding?

YOUNG GIRL: My mommy told me to wait here. She said I would be safe. She promised she'd be right back.

LILY: Are you a Zobeing?

YOUNG GIRL: No.

LILY: Are you a Wuluman?

YOUNG GIRL: No.

LILY: What are you?

YOUNG GIRL: I don't know.

LILY: What's your teddy bear's name?

YOUNG GIRL: Snow Flake.

LILY: Ehlo, Snow Flake!

YOUNG GIRL: "Ehlo!"

LILY: Why's he missing an eye and foot?

YOUNG GIRL: I don't want to talk about it.

LILY: Are you hurt?

YOUNG GIRL: No.

LILY: Are you hungry?

YOUNG GIRL: Ah-huh.

LILY: Here. They're from my garden. (LILY *hands her a fruit teddy bear.* YOUNG GIRL *eats.*) One day you won't hurt as much.

YOUNG GIRL: How will I know?

LILY: When you want to laugh and play again.

YOUNG GIRL: I feel that sometimes.

LILY: Or maybe you'll want to make up stories.

YOUNG GIRL: Or maybe play hopscotch?

LILY: Or skip all the way to school!

YOUNG GIRL: Or ride a bike!

LILY/YOUNG GIRL: Or eat ice cream!

(*Explosions are heard close by.*)

YOUNG GIRL: Oh, no, they're back!

LILY: Don't be scared, little one. (LILY *opens up the old, tattered umbrella and the kabooms fade away.*) All better?

YOUNG GIRL: Are you an angel?

LILY: No. I'm a gardener and good fixer-upper of things.

YOUNG GIRL: Look.

(YOUNG GIRL *brings out* PAPA WULUMAN *as a balloon. Only* PAPA WULUMAN'S *voice is heard.*)

LILY: Papa? Papa, is it really you?

PAPA WULUMAN: Lily?

LILY: Oh, Papa, I've missed you so much!

PAPA WULUMAN: Oh, look how you've grown!

LILY: Where have you been, Papa?

PAPA WULUMAN: I got lost, but I'm back now. Let's go home to Mama.

LILY: I can't go back there, Papa.

PAPA WULUMAN: Why not?

LILY: Because everything I love goes kaboom.

PAPA WULUMAN: From up here I can see your garden. It shouldn't exist but it does. You took your kaboom and turned it into something beautiful.

LILY: But, Papa, all I see are children hiding in rubble afraid to play and laugh.

PAPA WULUMAN: Your garden is a beginning, and isn't that what hope is?

LILY: Hope, Papa?

PAPA WULUMAN: Yes, Lily, hope.

LILY: Okay, Papa.

("Awooos" are heard off in the distance.)

PAPA WULUMAN: Someone's calling for you.

LILY: It's Miss Beatrice and Rosey.

PAPA WULUMAN: Well?

LILY: Okay, Papa.

(LILY floats down from the moon, using her umbrella.)

MISS BEATRICE: Lily! Lily, you're back!

ROSEY: Oh, we missed you!

LILY: I'm sorry I left you. I never will again.

(SHADOW enters.)

LILY: You!

MISS BEATRICE: Lily, Shadow's become our friend.

ROSEY: We couldn't have done it without him.

LILY: Done what?

(SHADOW introduces MAMA WULUMAN. She is back to her normal size.)

LILY: Mama!

MAMA WULUMAN: Lily!

(LILY *hugs her.*)

LILY: But how?

MAMA WULUMAN: Shadow and your friends never gave up looking for me. Your garden helped me to grow.

LILY (*to* SHADOW, MISS BEATRICE, *and* ROSEY): Thank you. Mama, I found Papa.

MAMA WULUMAN: Oh, Lily! Frank!

(MAMA WULUMAN *kisses the* PAPA WULUMAN *balloon.* SHADOW *begins to leave.*)

LILY: Shadow, wait. (LILY *whispers into* YOUNG GIRL's *ear. She nods to* LILY.) There's someone waiting for you.

(*The shadowy figure appears on the wall.* SHADOW *is joined with his shadow.*)

SHADOW: Th-th-thank you.

LILY: Shadow, bring all the broken toys and souls you can find to my garden.

SHADOW: I will.

(SHADOW *waves goodbye and he and his shadow exit.*)

LILY: We've got lots of work and so much planting to do!

ROSEY: But, Lily, there's no room in the wagon.

MISS BEATRICE: The spiders have been arguing and the bees are making too much noise.

ROSEY: And the caterpillars won't come out of their cocoons.

LILY: Well, then, we'll make the garden bigger!

ROSEY (*tries to scratch her back*): Oh-oh!

MISS BEATRICE: What is it, Rosey?

ROSEY: I'm itching again, Miss Beatrice.

MISS BEATRICE: Here, let me help. Oh, my! You've got aphids!

ROSEY: I do?

MISS BEATRICE: Shall I remove them for you, dear?

ROSEY: *Oui!*

MISS BEATRICE: It'll be my pleasure!

MAMA WULUMAN: Listen.

(*Silence.*)

LILY: Are the kabooms gone?

MISS BEATRICE: Could they?

ROSEY: Is it possible?

(*Beat. Music.* ROSEY *dances like a ballerina as the Land of Rubble transforms back into the abandoned dwelling.*)

YOUNG GIRL: So it came to pass that a little seed grew into the most magnificent garden ever. And the Great Endless Unforgotten War ended, and gardens once again bloomed everywhere. And so the little girl who "would never be normal, who would never fit in," did. And everyone cheered!

EVERYONE: Awoooo!

YOUNG GIRL: And they lived happily ever after.

(YOUNG GIRL *smiles. And somewhere off in the distance another kaboom rattles her world. She looks out. Then she exits.*)

CURTAIN

Designer's Response

For *Lily Plants a Garden* I returned to the quick sketch images that I created during the Bonderman Playwriting Workshop when the script was being developed (plate A). The doodles and sketches evoke the isolation faced by Lily when she is exiled from her own society and rejected by a neighboring one. Since the plot takes place on a planet with three moons, spherical shapes and curves became important in the design.

Resources

Bonderman images
Space calendar

Plate C: Final design.

Plate A: Original sketch from Bonderman Workshop.

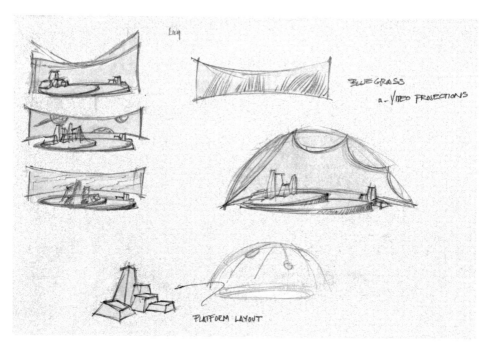

Plate B: Preliminary drawings using plate A as inspiration.

Salt & Pepper

José Cruz González

Salt & Pepper premiered at Childsplay,
Tempe, Arizona.

Characters

SALT: a ten-year-old boy. Loves his grandpa and brother.

PEPPER: a ten-year-old Latina girl. She dresses like a boy. She likes to read books.

OLD MAN: Salt and Andy's grandfather. Hannah's father. In his fifties. He is a hard man to live with.

ANDY: a seventeen-year-old boy. Salt's older brother. Very protective of Salt.

HANNAH: appears as a memory. She has a beautiful singing voice. She is Salt and Andy's mother.

Setting

A small agricultural town, somewhere near a desert. 1952.

A Note about Music

To the best of our knowledge, the children's songs used in this play are considered public domain. They are: "Hush 'n' Bye"; "Johnny Get Your Hair Cut (Hey Betty Martin)"; "Built My Lady a Fine Brick House"; "Go to Sleep"; and "The Juniper Tree." Sheet music appears at the end of the script.

Scene One

SETTING: *On stage letters of the alphabet are scattered about.*
They come in all different shapes and sizes. The letter characters are not
in any recognizable order. They may be used to create settings as well as words.

AT RISE: HANNAH appears. There's a glow about her. HANNAH is a memory.
She throws small paper letters up into the air. She is a young woman.
She wears a plain cotton dress and no shoes.

HANNAH (*singing*):

Hush 'n' Bye
Don't you cry
Oh, you pretty little babies

When you wake
You'll get sweet cake
And all the pretty little ponies

A brown and a gray
And a black and a bay
All the pretty little ponies

OLD MAN (*offstage*): Hannah?

(HANNAH *runs and hides. The* OLD MAN, *Hannah's father, enters. He is half-dressed in overalls and carries a lantern. He wears no shoes.*)

OLD MAN: Hannah, where are you?

HANNAH: Hidin', Daddy! You gotta find me!

OLD MAN: Hannah, it's the middle of the night.

HANNAH: Where am I?

OLD MAN: You gonna catch yourself a cold.

HANNAH: It's been rainin' letters again.

OLD MAN: Letters?

HANNAH: In all shapes and sizes mixed together.

(HANNAH *throws some letters into the air. She runs and hides again. The* OLD MAN *searches for her.*)

OLD MAN: Where are you?

HANNAH: I've collected a bunch of 'em, see? Ain't it beautiful, Daddy?

(HANNAH *throws some more letters into the air. She runs off again. The* OLD MAN *searches for her.*)

OLD MAN: Honey, come inside where it's safe.

HANNAH: I can't, Daddy.

OLD MAN: Why not?

HANNAH: 'Cause I'm writin' you a postcard.

OLD MAN: A postcard?

HANNAH: Give up?

OLD MAN: No.

HANNAH: I found me the most pretty one you ever seen. Look!

(Her hand appears. She holds up a small postcard.)

OLD MAN: There you are!

HANNAH: It's a picture of the Grand Ole Opry. Ain't it the most beautiful buildin' you ever seen? It's where I'm gonna make my professional debut.

OLD MAN: Debut? What's that?

HANNAH: It means I'm gonna sing in front of the whole world, Daddy. And you gonna be proud of me. People will want my autograph and want me to star in their Hollywood pictures!

OLD MAN: Let me see your forehead.

HANNAH: I ain't got a fever!

(She crosses away from him.)

OLD MAN: You ain't makin' any sense, Hannah.

HANNAH: That's 'cause it's a dream, Daddy.

OLD MAN: A dream?

HANNAH: And it's yours.

OLD MAN: Mine?

HANNAH: Yes, sir. Rememberin' how things were. Good and bad. But there isn't much time.

OLD MAN: Time for what?

HANNAH: Before I go away.

OLD MAN: Why you wanna do that?

HANNAH: It's in the postcard, Daddy. All you gotta do is read it.

OLD MAN: Hannah, you can't leave.

HANNAH: Daddy, I gotta go and find my future.

OLD MAN: But it's here with your boys and me.

HANNAH: It's in the wind, callin' to me.

OLD MAN: What wind?

HANNAH: The same one that brings the rain and the dust storms. It's callin' my name . . . wantin' to sweep me up and take me far away.

OLD MAN: To where?

HANNAH: Anywhere my little songs will he heard, Daddy.

OLD MAN: There's nothin' but heartache out there. I seen it. Felt it.

HANNAH: That's all I've ever known, but not no more. I'm gonna let that wind carry me and my babies into the future and take us wherever it wants.

OLD MAN: But them boys are too little to go anywhere.

HANNAH: That's why I need your help, Daddy. You gotta come with me.

OLD MAN: I ain't goin' nowhere, and neither are you.

HANNAH: If I don't go now I'll just wither away and die. Can't you understand?

OLD MAN: No, I can't. You got a place here. Ain't that enough?

HANNAH: I made up my mind.

OLD MAN: I forbid you to go!

HANNAH: I'm takin' my babies with me.

OLD MAN: No, you ain't. You wanna go chase after some stupid dream then go, but them boys are stayin' here with me.

HANNAH: No.

OLD MAN: You made your choice. So get!

HANNAH: Please, Daddy . . .

OLD MAN: Get off my place! Get! (HANNAH *rushes away, dropping the postcard.*) Hannah?! Hannah?!

HANNAH (*singing*):
Hush 'n' Bye
Don't you cry . . .

OLD MAN: Don't you leave!

HANNAH (*singing*):
Oh, you pretty little babies . . .

OLD MAN: Hannah!

(*The* OLD MAN *stands there for a moment, alone. He sees the postcard lying on the ground. He picks it up, crumpling it and throwing it to the ground. A moment later he picks it up and places it in his pocket.*)

Scene Two

(*A country song is heard.* ANDY, *a seventeen-year-old boy, enters, flipping a large blue pancake from a frying pan high into the air. He grabs a plate of multicolored pancakes stacked atop one another.* SALT, *Andy's younger brother, rushes in, wearing a metal pot on his head and carrying a broom as weapon. He falls to the floor, shooting everything in sight.*)

SALT: Pa-pow! Pa-pow! Pa-pow! Pa-pa-pa-pa-pow! (*Enemy fire is returned at* SALT.) Ughhh!!! Pow! Ughhh! (SALT's *death is dramatic. He falls onto one of the letters. Beat. Opening his eyes.*) You wanna play war, Andy?

ANDY: No.

SALT: Come on! I'll be the enemy.

ANDY: Go away, Salt. Can't you see I'm busy?

SALT: Whatcha doin'?

ANDY: Makin' breakfast.

SALT: Pancakes?

ANDY: Yup.

SALT: Colored ones?

ANDY: Yup.

SALT: Which colors you makin'?

ANDY: I got green, yellow, and blue.

(*He flips the blue pancake high into the air and catches it with the plate of colored pancakes.*)

SALT: Wo! Can I help?

ANDY: Take that stupid pot off your head.

SALT: Andy, I can't do that.

ANDY: Why not?

SALT: 'Cause it's my helmet! It's my only protection.

ANDY: Against what?

SALT: The enemy. They're all around. Hidin'. Waitin' to strike me dead.

ANDY: Well, you look real stupid, Salt.

SALT: I ain't stupid!

ANDY: Fine, then you can't help!

SALT: Okay, there, see!

(*He drops his helmet to the floor.*)

ANDY: Too late.

SALT: Andy!

ANDY: I guess there's nothin' to save you now!

SALT: Huh?

ANDY: From the hounds of war!

(*He howls loudly and then sticks his arms out and flies by* SALT *making airplane noises.*)

SALT: Air raid!

(SALT *grabs the pot and puts it back on his head.* ANDY *returns, strafing* SALT. SALT *uses his broom as an anti-aircraft gun.*)

ANDY: I'm hit!

SALT: Yeah!

ANDY: But now I'm a kamikaze!

SALT: Oh, no, duck for cover!

ANDY: Too late!

(ANDY *crashes into* SALT. SALT *and* ANDY *lie there dead. Beat.*)

SALT (*jumping up*): I won!

ANDY: No, you didn't! You're dead!

SALT: No, I'm not, see?! It was my general!

ANDY: What?!

SALT: You killed my general, but I still lived!

ANDY: Salt, nobody survives a kamikaze attack.

SALT: But I did! You lost! I won! Victory dance!

(*He pounds out a beat on his helmet using wooden spoons. He dances a victory dance.*)

ANDY: Will you be quiet!

SALT: Sore loser.

ANDY: Salt, eat your pancakes!

SALT: They're gonna need more salt.

ANDY: I already added some. Eat.

(SALT *grabs a blue pancake. He rolls it up and eats it.*)

SALT: Um . . . blue one's real good!

ANDY: It don't taste any different from the others.

SALT: It do too. Blues taste different from yellows. Yellows taste different from greens. Greens taste real different from blues.

ANDY: Whatever you say, Salt . . .

SALT: Andy, who taught you how to make colored pancakes? Was it Ma?

ANDY: No.

SALT: Then who?

ANDY: I can't tell you that.

SALT: Why not?

ANDY: 'Cause it's a big fat secret.

SALT: But you can tell me. We're brothers. Right?

ANDY: Nope. We ain't brothers. Somebody left you on the porch step. The old man took you in 'cause all you did was cry.

SALT: That ain't true!

ANDY: Sure is!

SALT: Well, I don't care 'bout your big fat secret! I don't wanna know!

ANDY: Fine. Suit yourself. But you better hurry before the old man gets here. It's your turn to wash them plates.

SALT: I can't—my arms got broke.

ANDY: Salt!

SALT: They are. See? They won't move.

(*He wiggles his body and his arms flap side to side.*)

ANDY: You ain't weaselin' outta this again. It's your turn.

SALT: No, I'm not gonna do 'em.

ANDY: Yes, you are!

(*He grabs* SALT *in a headlock.*)

SALT: Ow! Let me go!

ANDY: Not until you say "I give."

SALT: Why do I always gotta wash 'em?

ANDY: When you learn how to cook then you won't have to do 'em! Now say it!

SALT: No!

ANDY: Say it!

SALT: I give!

(ANDY *releases* SALT. SALT *places his helmet back on.*)

ANDY: When the old man catches you wearin' that pot on your head, you're gonna be sorry.

SALT: No, I won't.

ANDY: Why's that?

SALT: 'Cause he loves me more than you.

ANDY: Oh, really?

SALT: Yup. So you better watch out.

ANDY: He's been in a foul mood all week.

SALT: That's 'cause he wrecked his truck and hurt his arm.

ANDY: And he's takin' it out on me. It ain't no picnic.

OLD MAN (*offstage*): Andy?

ANDY: See?

SALT: It's Grandpa!

(*The* OLD MAN *enters. He wears overalls, boots, a soiled baseball cap, and gloves. His arm is in a sling.*)

OLD MAN: Salt, go get ready for school.

SALT: Yes, sir.

OLD MAN: And take that stupid pot off your head. (*To* ANDY.) Don't you hear me callin' you?

ANDY: No, sir.

OLD MAN: Well, we got a truck to fix. It ain't gonna fix itself.

ANDY: I was gonna eat first.

OLD MAN: The day already started.

ANDY: I'm hurryin'.

OLD MAN: You stayin' out nights don't help any.

ANDY: I got my reasons.

OLD MAN: Well, your reasons ain't helpin' me fix my truck. All that schoolin' you're so proud of, where's it got you? It can't fix my truck engine. And you know even less about produce. I got a business to run. Them bills ain't gonna pay themselves.

ANDY: All you ever do is complain.

OLD MAN: 'Cause you give reason.

ANDY: I'm gonna leave one day and then you'll be sorry.

OLD MAN: You'll never leave.

ANDY: I might. I got plans.

OLD MAN: Plans?

ANDY: I wanna see the world. Travel to faraway places. Learn to speak different languages, even.

OLD MAN: How are you gonna do that?

ANDY: I'm gonna join the Marines.

OLD MAN: The Marines? They won't take you. You just like your ma. Head in the clouds. And look where it got her.

ANDY: I'm gonna show you.

OLD MAN: Well, you show me how to fix my truck first, 'cause while you're under my roof you'll do as I say! There ain't no room for fools or dreamers in this house.

ANDY: Fine, I'm goin'!

(ANDY *storms out. The* OLD MAN *eats one of the colored pancakes.*)

OLD MAN: Blue one's good. At least he learned how to cook.

(SALT *enters, combing his hair and dressed for school. He hums "Go to Sleep."*)

OLD MAN: What's that song you hummin', Salt?

SALT: I don't know.

OLD MAN: I heard it before.

SALT: Where?

OLD MAN: That was one of the songs your mama liked to sing.

SALT: Really?

OLD MAN: She had the prettiest voice you ever heard.

SALT: I don't remember her too good.

OLD MAN: She was always singin' and playin' her guitar for you boys. Wrote her own songs and even made records too. Just about everybody in Nashville knew her.

SALT: Andy says she had her own bus with her name written on it.

OLD MAN: Oh, that's right. She was a big radio star, too. She was always singin' at the Grand Ole Opry, and she even went to make a Hollywood picture once.

SALT: My ma was a movie star?

OLD MAN: I think she even won one of them actin' awards.

SALT: How come Ma didn't ever take us with her?

OLD MAN: Well, that's 'cause she was always on the road. Them entertainers have got a lot of travelin' to do and it ain't no place for little ones. That's why you two come to live with me.

SALT: Was Ma rich?

OLD MAN: She had so much money she had to put it in two banks.

SALT: No.

OLD MAN: Yup, but she gave it all away to needy people.

SALT: My ma was somethin' else, wasn't she?

OLD MAN: She loved you a whole lot.

SALT: Grandpa, did my ma go to school?

OLD MAN: For a little while, 'til Andy was born.

SALT: She did real good for herself and she didn't need no school.

OLD MAN: That's right.

SALT: You know more about things than my teachers do.

OLD MAN: Well . . .

SALT: Why do I gotta go to school, Grandpa? Everythin' I need to know is right here with you. One day, I wanna drive a truck just like you.

OLD MAN: You do?

SALT: Ah huh.

OLD MAN: Well, maybe missin' one day won't hurt.

SALT: You mean I don't have to go?

OLD MAN: Nope.

SALT: I'll work real hard and I won't complain like Andy.

OLD MAN: Then go get changed. We got us a truck to fix and produce to deliver!

Scene Three

(A bus is heard driving away. HANNAH enters, carrying her guitar and suitcase. An image of a postcard appears behind her.)

HANNAH: Dear Daddy, I've ridden the wind and it's carried me as far as Hope, Texas. I ain't got a cent to my name but it don't matter. I'm writin' this postcard to tell you I'm doin' fine. I'm gonna send you a picture postcard from every place I go, so you'll know where I've been. I hope you'll show them to my babies and explain what I am doin'. I know you're still mad and I don't expect you'll write me, but that's okay. Well, I gotta go for now, Daddy. Yours truly, HANNAH.

Scene Four

(The OLD MAN and ANDY enter, carrying crates of produce. SALT drags one in.)

OLD MAN: We ain't got all day, Andy!

ANDY: I'm workin' as fast as I can!

OLD MAN: A snail is faster than you!

ANDY: Well, I don't see one liftin' these heavy crates!

OLD MAN: If we don't get this produce off to market today, we ain't gettin' paid. We need the money. You see this?!

(He holds out a stack of bills.)

SALT: What are they, Grandpa?

OLD MAN: They're bills. Lots of 'em.

ANDY: I didn't wreck the truck. You did.

OLD MAN: How was I suppose to know they was fixin' a road? There were no road signs.

ANDY: Yes, there were.

OLD MAN: You weren't even there to help. That's my point.

ANDY: Well, what do you want me do?

OLD MAN: Tell me what they say. I ain't got my glasses.

SALT: I'll help you, Grandpa.

OLD MAN: No, I need Andy to do it, Salt. It's his job. He goes into town and pays the bills. 'Cept lately his head's been somewhere else and he ain't been no good for nothin'. Well, how much do I owe?

(He removes a roll of dollar bills held together by a rubber band.)

ANDY: This one's five dollars!

OLD MAN (counting): One, two, three—

ANDY: This one's seven!

OLD MAN: Four, five—

ANDY: This one's six!

OLD MAN: Slow down! One, two, three—

ANDY: Six!

OLD MAN: Four, five—

ANDY: Two twenty-five.

OLD MAN: One, two—

ANDY: Eight.

OLD MAN: You're confusin' me! One, two, three—

ANDY: Oh, what's the use? They're past due!

OLD MAN: All of them? But how can that be? I always pay my bills on time. I send you into town to . . . you ain't been payin' them?

ANDY: No.

OLD MAN: Why not?

ANDY: Because I hate doin' it. People are always laughin' and whisperin' behind my back! So from now on you do it. I quit!

(He crumples up the bill and throws it on the ground.)

OLD MAN: Pick it up!

ANDY: No, you pick it up!

SALT: Andy?

OLD MAN: You march yourself to town and pay them bills right now!

ANDY: No! I told you I quit!

OLD MAN: You wanna go?

ANDY: Why is everythin' I do not good enough for you?

OLD MAN: Don't you talk to me that way! You ain't any better than me!

ANDY: You make everythin' so difficult!

OLD MAN: Garbage is garbage. That's where we come from but you wanna pretend you somethin' better?!

ANDY: What's wrong with that?

OLD MAN: You forget who you are!

ANDY: How can I when you remind me of it every day? "You just an Okie. Never amount to much."

SALT (picking up the delivery form): I can fix this letter!

ANDY: You always sayin', "You ain't got a lick of horse sense! You ain't good for nothin'!"

OLD MAN: I done it to make you strong!

ANDY: How? By tellin' me I'm no good?

SALT: I'll make it all better!

OLD MAN: People walk all over you if you let them.

ANDY: What are you so afraid of?

SALT: No more wrinkles!

OLD MAN: I ain't afraid of nothin'! You hear me? I kept you both here with me when your ma left!

ANDY: She was gonna take us with her but you wouldn't let her.

OLD MAN: I did it to protect you!

ANDY: Protect us from what? From the big bad world? Or were you just protectin' yourself?!

OLD MAN: You ain't got no right to say that!

ANDY: You're just an ignorant old fool holdin' on to nothin'!

SALT: It's gonna be as good as new!

OLD MAN: Don't you say another word!

ANDY: Made up lies and secrets! I'm sick of it!

SALT: See?

ANDY: And I ain't comin' back!

OLD MAN: Just like your ma!

ANDY: One day he's gonna leave you too!

OLD MAN: Get off my place!

ANDY: What are you gonna do then?

SALT: Andy?

ANDY: 'Cause you won't have nobody!

SALT: Grandpa?

ANDY: Nobody!

(*Andy exits.*)

OLD MAN: He thinks he's so smart! That I'm stupid! Ignorant!

SALT: No, you're not, Grandpa.

OLD MAN: Spit on everythin' I done.

SALT: I don't like spittin'.

OLD MAN: He don't care nothin' 'bout us.

SALT: I do.

OLD MAN (*yelling*): Don't you be here when I get back!

SALT: I'll help you, Grandpa. You can trust me.

OLD MAN: It's just I can't find my glasses.

SALT (*reading with difficulty*): It says you gotta take twenty crates of lettuce to Hadley's. Ten crates of carrots to Friendly—

OLD MAN: —Corners.

SALT: Six crates to . . .

(*They exit.*)

Scene Five

(*A car is heard passing by.* HANNAH *enters, sticking out her thumb to catch a ride, but the car just passes her by. She climbs onto one of the letters and sits playing her guitar.* ANDY *rushes in with a pile of clothes and comic books. He drops them onto the floor.*)

HANNAH (*singing*):

I built my lady a fine brick house
I built it in a garden
I put her in but she jumped out
So fare ye well my darlin'

Oh, swing a lady,
Ump-tum
Swing a lady,
Round
Swing a lady,
Ump-tum
And promenade around

(SALT *enters.*)

SALT: Andy, Grandpa didn't mean none of those things!

ANDY: Of course he did.

SALT: He just a little mad 'cause he's got so much work to do. I can help from now on.

ANDY: It's all right, Salt.

SALT: I'll even wash them plates! You'll never have to ask me again!

ANDY: It's too late for that now.

SALT: Andy, please don't go!

(HANNAH *begins writing a postcard.*)

ANDY: I want you to have my favorite comic books.

SALT: No, I don't want 'em. I want you!

ANDY: I can't stay here no more. I gotta go.

SALT: No, please?!

ANDY: Look, Salt, you gonna have to grow up.

SALT: I will!

ANDY: You can't behave like a kid no more. I ain't gonna be around. All the old man ever does is put me down. Don't you let him tell you you're nothin', 'cause you're not.

SALT: But he loves us.

ANDY: He's got a funny way of showin' it. It's like he's built walls around himself. And they just keep gettin' higher and higher.

SALT: What walls?

ANDY: You gonna have to ask him yourself.

SALT: Ask him what?

ANDY: About his big fat secret.

SALT: Was I left on the porch step?

ANDY: What?

SALT: You said Grandpa found me on the porch step. Is that the big fat secret?

ANDY: Ain't you been listenin'?

SALT: Ugghhh!

(*He pushes* ANDY *as hard as he can.*)

ANDY: What are you doin'?

SALT: You don't care nothin' about us!

ANDY: I care a lot.

SALT: Then why are you sayin' mean things?!

ANDY: 'Cause they're true!

SALT: No they're not! All you wanna to do is leave us! So go!

ANDY: If I don't I'll end up just like him. A broken-down old man, just like his stupid truck. My future's out there and I ain't afraid to go after it.

SALT: What about me?

ANDY: You gonna be okay.

SALT: Why don't you take me with you?

ANDY: I can't.

SALT: That's 'cause you're selfish!

ANDY: I gotta do this alone, Salt.

SALT: You ain't my brother! "Family don't leave," that's what Grandpa says!
   I ain't ever leavin' him!

(SALT sits on the ground and covers his face. ANDY stops packing and brings over his comic books to SALT.)

SALT (crying): I don't want your stupid stuff!

(SALT pushes him away. ANDY thinks for a moment. He removes a postcard from his pocket. HANNAH begins playing her guitar.)

HANNAH (singing):

   Go to sleepy baby, bye
   Go to sleepy baby, bye

ANDY: Salt, what do you remember 'bout Ma?

HANNAH (singing):

   Mama's goin' to the mailboat

SALT: Lots of things.

HANNAH (singing):

   Mama's goin' to the mailboat, bye

ANDY: How could you? You were just a baby.

HANNAH (singing):

   Bye ole baby, bye

SALT: So?

HANNAH (singing):

   Bye ole baby, bye

ANDY: She liked to sing.

SALT: No, she didn't.

HANNAH (singing):

   Papa's goin' to the mailboat
   Papa's goin' to the mailboat, bye

ANDY: How would you know? All you did was eat, sleep, and poop.

SALT: Be quiet.

ANDY: She'd hold you in her arms and rock you to sleep every night. Her hair was long and messy. She liked suckin' on red popsicles and givin' us butterfly kisses. She could skip rocks on the water, climb trees, and make funny animal noises.

SALT: What kind?

ANDY: She could do a duck.

(ANDY and HANNAH imitate a duck sound.)

ANDY: A dog.

(ANDY and HANNAH imitate a dog barking.)

ANDY: And a cow.

(ANDY and HANNAH imitate a cow.)

ANDY: But most of all she loved singing and playin' on her guitar.

(HANNAH sticks her thumb out hoping to hitch a ride. The car just passes by. HANNAH plays softly.)

SALT: I remember sunlight.

ANDY: Sunlight?

SALT: She made me feel safe and sleepy.

ANDY: That's 'cause we all slept in the same bed.

SALT: Grandpa says she sang at the Grand Ole Opry.

ANDY: I got a postcard from there. You wanna see it?

SALT: Okay.

HANNAH: Dear Daddy, this here is where I'm gonna make my professional debut.

ANDY: The old man used to tell us all the places she'd been to by the post-cards she sent us.

HANNAH: I get nervous just thinkin' about it.

(The OLD MAN enters, holding a postcard. He is a memory.)

OLD MAN: Your ma sent you boys another postcard. Now, hold on. I reckon she must be playin' her music there. Yup, that's what it must be. You can see it's a rich people's place. How? Well, that's easy. Look at them lawns. They're nice and straight. And they got fancy flowers growin' all over.

SALT: Andy, how did Ma die?

ANDY: In a car accident. A state trooper told the old man and me she was headin' back home to us.

OLD MAN: Them rich people places ain't no place for us, but your mama knows how to talk real nice. I bet you she's got a dress for every day of the year and suitcases bigger than this house! And one day, she's gonna come ridin' back here in a big ol' bus with her name written all over it.

HANNAH: "Hannah Holcomb"!

(The OLD MAN exits.)

HANNAH: I've been workin' at all sort of jobs.

ANDY: I want you to keep this for me.

HANNAH: I'll send money as soon as I can.

ANDY: This is all I got of her. I don't know what ever happened to them other postcards. So you gotta take care of it.

SALT: Okay.

HANNAH: Tell my babies I love them.

ANDY: Salt? I gotta go now.

SALT (crying): Who's gonna make me colored pancakes?

ANDY: You're gonna have to learn yourself. And one day you'll leave too. Just like me and Ma.

SALT: No. He needs me.

ANDY: I don't wanna end up like him. Can you understand that?

SALT: No.

ANDY: I'm goin'.

SALT (grabs ANDY's leg tightly): No . . .

ANDY: Let go!

SALT: No!

(ANDY tears SALT away from him. He grabs his grocery bag of clothes and exits.)

ANDY: I'll write you!

SALT: Andy, don't go!

HANNAH (singing):

Bye ole baby, bye
Bye ole baby, bye
Papa's goin' to the mailboat
Papa's goin' to the mailboat, bye

SALT: Andy!

(SALT stands there alone, holding the postcard.)

Scene Six

(Blue sky and white clouds. It's a beautiful day. PEPPER, *a young Latina girl dressed like a boy, appears. She wears a hat. She carries a stack of books. She chooses her place. She picks her most favorite book, and kicks her shoes off. She lies on one of the large letters, wiggles her toes, and starts to read.* SALT *enters, carrying a fishing pole. He's in a foul mood. He stops in shock, seeing the two feet. He picks up a shoe and throws it back.)*

PEPPER *(sitting up)*: Ow!

SALT: This is my spot!

PEPPER: . . .

SALT: My spot!

PEPPER: . . .

SALT: Hello, you talk English?!

PEPPER: . . .

SALT: Go! Get outta of here! Vamoose!

PEPPER: You vamoose! I don't see a sign anywhere with your name on it.

SALT: I don't need a sign! This is my secret spot!

PEPPER: Says who?

SALT: Says me!

PEPPER: I'm not leavin'.

SALT: I ain't warnin' you again!

PEPPER: I was here first! *(*SALT *grabs* PEPPER's *book.)* Give me back my book!

SALT: Not until you go!

PEPPER: I was here first!

SALT: "To my best pupil, Pepper . . ."

PEPPER: That's private!

SALT: "Best wishes, Mrs. Federico."

PEPPER: Give it back to me!

SALT: What kinda stupid name is that?

PEPPER: You're asking for it!

SALT: No, you are!

*(*SALT *throws* PEPPER's *book offstage into the creek.)*

PEPPER: Agghhh!

*(*PEPPER *charges* SALT. *They start wrestling. In the melee* PEPPER's *hat is torn off and her hair falls onto her shoulders.* SALT *stops.)*

SALT: You're a girl!

PEPPER: That's right, you moron!

(PEPPER *decks* SALT. *He falls to the ground.*)

SALT: Ow!

PEPPER (*upset*): Why did you throw my book into the creek?

SALT: You wouldn't leave.

PEPPER: It's gone!

SALT: Serves you right. I warned you.

PEPPER (*crying*): That was my most favorite book.

SALT: Stop whinin'. It's just a stupid book.

(PEPPER *decks* SALT *again.*)

SALT: Ow!

PEPPER: It's not a "stupid" book. It's one of a kind. It can't be replaced!

SALT: So what?

PEPPER: My teacher gave it to me as a going away present. And now it's lost forever! You are so mean.

SALT: I told you this was my spot!

PEPPER: How was I supposed to know?

SALT: What are you, a pecan picker?

PEPPER: I am not a pecan picker!

SALT: Bet your dad is.

PEPPER: No, he isn't!

SALT: Bet you live in those old barracks on Castro Hill?

PEPPER: No, we don't!

SALT: Bet your dad don't even speak English!

PEPPER: I hate this place and I hate you!

SALT: I hate you too, Pecan Picker!

(PEPPER *picks up her stack of books and exits, crying.*)

SALT: Dumb girl! Stupid book! My spot!

Scene Seven

(HANNAH *enters. She wears a waitress dress and pours a cup of coffee to an imaginary customer. Simultaneously the* OLD MAN *enters carrying several wooden crates of produce. He stops to wipe his forehead. He no longer wears his arm sling.*)

HANNAH (*singing*):

> Johnny get your hair cut
> hair cut, hair cut
> Johnny get your hair cut
> Just like me
>
> Johnny get your hair cut
> hair cut, hair cut
> Johnny get your hair cut
> Just like me

(ANDY *enters marching, wearing Marine fatigues.* HANNAH *takes an order. The* OLD MAN *removes a delivery form from his pocket and tries to make sense of it, but can't. In frustration he crumples it, throwing it away.*)

HANNAH (*singing*):

> Johnny get your gun
> And your sword
> And your pistol
> Johnny get your gun
> And come with me
>
> Johnny get your gun
> And your sword
> And your pistol
> Johnny get your gun
> And come with me

(HANNAH *pours another cup of coffee while* ANDY *continues marching.* SALT *runs in to help the* OLD MAN *carry away the crates.*)

HANNAH/ANDY (*singing*):

> Hey, ya Betty Martin tiptoe, tiptoe
> Hey, ya Betty Martin tiptoe, tiptoe-fy
> Hey, ya Betty Martin tiptoe, tiptoe-fy
>
> Hey, ya Betty Martin tiptoe, tiptoe
> Hey, ya Betty Martin tiptoe, tiptoe-fy
> Hey, ya Betty Martin tiptoe, tiptoe-fy

(SALT, *the* OLD MAN, *and* HANNAH *exit.* ANDY *sits on his helmet and begins writing a postcard.* SALT *enters looking at a postcard. He climbs onto one of the letters to read.*)

ANDY: February 17th, 1952. Dear Salt—I told you I'd write.

SALT: "This is a postcard from San Die . . . go."

ANDY: It's a pretty place with lots of blue ocean and sandy beaches.

SALT: "You must be won . . . der . . . in' what I'm doin' out here."

ANDY: Well, surprise, I joined the U.S. Marine Corps!

SALT: Why'd you do that?

ANDY: To show the old man he's wrong. They did take me. Besides, I like it. The food's great. The sarge reminds me of the old man 'cause he's always yellin' at me. Grandpa woulda made a good Marine.

SALT: Of course he would.

ANDY: I never thought I'd miss him and home so much. Can you believe that?

SALT: No.

ANDY: I'll be in boot camp for a few more months, and then I'll get stationed somewhere I hope is—

SALT: "Ex . . . o . . . tic"?

ANDY: Somewhere there's sandy beaches and plenty of—

SALT/ANDY (together): —girls? / —girls!

SALT: Ughh . . .

ANDY: Yup! You made any friends yet?

SALT: No.

ANDY: You ain't still mad at me, are you?

SALT: . . .

ANDY: Will you write me?

(SALT tears up the postcard. He begins to leave but returns, picking it up.)

Scene Eight

(PEPPER enters, taking off her shoes. She rolls up her pant legs. She searches for her book. SALT enters, carrying a fishing pole.)

SALT: Not you again!

PEPPER: I ain't standin' near your stupid "spot"!

SALT: I can see that.

PEPPER: Did you come to laugh at me?

SALT: No. What you lookin' for?

PEPPER: I'm looking for my book! You remember my book, don't you? My most favorite one!

(SALT *pulls out* PEPPER's *book and looks at it.*)

SALT: Yes, I do. Them rocks are slippery. You better be careful.

PEPPER: It's gotta be here somewhere.

SALT: You ain't gonna find it.

PEPPER: Yes, I will!

SALT: It mighta floated all the way out to sea.

PEPPER: Go away.

SALT: Maybe all them words slipped off them book pages and now they're fish food.

PEPPER: That ain't funny.

SALT: Or maybe some hobo's used your book to make himself a warm toasty fire.

PEPPER (*sarcastically*): Ha, ha! (*She falls into the creek.*) Aaghhh!

SALT: Told you them rocks were slippery.

PEPPER: Oh, darn it! I give up!

SALT: Here.

(*Hands* PEPPER *her book.*)

PEPPER: You found my book?

SALT: I didn't throw it that far.

PEPPER: It's dry.

SALT: My brother Andy and me once had all our comic books get rained on and we hung them up on a clothesline and they were almost good as new.

PEPPER: Almost as good?

SALT: Your book was too heavy so I put it near the stove and it dried real fast. 'Cept the outside got a little crispy.

PEPPER: Oh, no.

SALT: But the pages aren't stickin' together. I'm sorry I threw your book into the creek.

PEPPER: Why are you bein' nice? Did you get into trouble or somethin'?

SALT: No.

PEPPER: This ain't a stupid boy trick, is it?

SALT: No.

PEPPER: 'Cause if you're tryin' to make fun of me—

SALT: I ain't.

PEPPER: I'll hit you even harder.

SALT: I'm really sorry. Honest.

PEPPER: You go to church or somethin'?

SALT: No.

PEPPER: I don't understand why you're bein' so friendly.

SALT: There's nobody else to play with around here.

PEPPER: I noticed.

SALT: All everybody does is work. Work before the sun comes up. Work 'til the sun goes down. They might as well work while they sleep too.

PEPPER: My daddy's got me cookin' meals every day. Cook and wash. Cook and wash. Sometimes I wish someone would make me somethin'.

SALT: Like what?

PEPPER: Somethin' fancy. Somethin' sweet!

SALT: Like pancakes?

PEPPER: Yeah, pancakes!

SALT: I can show you how.

PEPPER: Okay.

SALT: I'm sorry I called your daddy a pecan picker.

PEPPER: You wanna know somethin'?

SALT: What?

PEPPER: My daddy is a pecan picker. And a lettuce picker. And an apple picker.

SALT: All three?

PEPPER: Sometimes a strawberry picker too.

SALT: I like strawberries.

PEPPER: I don't. They turn your fingers all red and sticky and you can only eat so many before you feel sick.

SALT: My grandpa used to pick pecans but now he drives a produce truck. I get to go with him lots of places. Where'd you learn to fight?

PEPPER: I have four big brothers. I'm the only girl.

SALT: You hit like a boy.

PEPPER: My father taught me how to box. You wanna learn?

SALT: No, thanks.

PEPPER: My name's Pepper.

SALT: Mine's Salt.

(*They burst out laughing.*)

SALT: That's funny!

PEPPER: We're named after spices!

SALT: Pepper ought to be a boy's name.

PEPPER (*holding up her fist at* SALT): You got a problem with it?

SALT: Not no more.

PEPPER: Good. So how'd you get stuck with the name Salt?

SALT: I like eatin' it on everythin'. Lots of it. What about you?

PEPPER: I'm named after my grandma on my father's side. Her name was Josefina, but they called her *Pepita*.

SALT: That's a funny sorta name.

PEPPER: That's why I changed it to Pepper. 'Cause pepper has got a kick to it.

SALT: So what do you like to do?

PEPPER: I like to climb trees. Swap for things. Skip rocks on water, and watch clouds pass by. But most of all I like readin' books.

SALT: I hate reading.

PEPPER: When I was little, I used to love chewin' on paper. My daddy says I chewed so much that I got all them letters and words floatin' in my head now. That's why I like piecin' them together. Easy as pie.

SALT: Well, it ain't so easy for me. Every time I try puttin' them letters together they just seem to float away. Nothin' makes sense. I feel stupid and the kids at school know it. That's why I hate school.

PEPPER: I don't. I miss it.

SALT: Why?

PEPPER: 'Cause I miss my teachers and friends. Just when I feel happy in one place, my daddy picks up and goes.

SALT: Goes where?

PEPPER: Anywhere there's a crop to pick. I hate movin'. That's why I pretend I'm in school, 'cause I can visit my friends and teachers and feel normal. One day, when I grow up, I wanna be a school librarian, 'cause they sit and read all day and sip tea like the English.

SALT: I wanna be just like my grandpa. He's pretty smart. Can fix anythin'.

PEPPER: My daddy too.

SALT: So what's your book about?

PEPPER: It's about a princess, a shoemaker's apprentice, a castle, and a green-colored dragon. I even got me a collection of books. I got happy books. Sad books. Adventure books. And even fairy tale books.

SALT: I like comic books better.

PEPPER: I like 'em too. Maybe we could swap some time. (*She opens her book. Torn pieces of a postcard fall out.*) What's this?

SALT: Oh, that's mine.

PEPPER: What is it?

SALT: It's a postcard.

PEPPER: It's all in pieces.

(SALT *pieces the postcard together.*)

SALT: That's 'cause I tore it up.

PEPPER: Why'd you do that?

SALT: 'Cause I'm mad at my brother.

PEPPER: Does he know you're mad at him?

SALT: I don't know.

PEPPER: You should write to him.

SALT: What for?

PEPPER: So you can tell him how you feel. Besides, when somebody writes to you, you're supposed to write back. It's polite.

SALT: I don't know what to say. Besides, I can't write too good.

PEPPER: All you need is an address, some paper, an envelope, and a little bitty stamp. I can show you, if you want.

SALT: I don't know.

PEPPER: I like the picture of the palm trees and sandy beach. Can I keep it?

SALT: No.

PEPPER: But you tore it up.

SALT: I'm gonna glue it back together.

PEPPER: I'll swap you for it.

SALT: Nah. (*He puts the postcard pieces in his pocket.*) Pepper, you like fishin'?

PEPPER: Ah huh.

SALT: You wanna fish?

PEPPER: Okay.

SALT: Do you like catchin' fish?

PEPPER: Nope.

SALT: Do you like cookin' fish?

PEPPER: Nope.

SALT: Well, what do you like about fishin' then?

PEPPER: Eatin' 'em!

Scene Nine

(HANNAH *enters. She throws small paper letters into the air.*)

HANNAH (*singing*):

Hush 'n' Bye
Don't you cry
Oh, you pretty little babies

OLD MAN (*offstage*): Hannah?

HANNAH (*singing*):

When you wake
You'll get sweet cake
And all the pretty little ponies

OLD MAN (*offstage*): Hannah?

HANNAH (*singing*):

A brown and a gray
And a black and a bay
All the pretty little ponies

(*The* OLD MAN *appears. He is half-dressed in overalls and carries a lantern.*)

HANNAH: Ain't it beautiful, Daddy?

OLD MAN: Honey, it's the middle of the night.

HANNAH: And it's rainin' letters again.

OLD MAN: Letters?

HANNAH: In all shapes and sizes mixed together.

OLD MAN: You gonna catch yourself a cold.

(ANDY *appears. He is also a memory. Dressed in his civilian clothes, he carries a crate of envelopes.*)

ANDY: I've packed these for you, see?

OLD MAN: Andy, what are you doin'?

ANDY: Truckloads full of 'em.

HANNAH: Ain't it the most beautiful thing you ever seen?

OLD MAN: Let me see your forehead.

HANNAH/ANDY: I ain't got a fever!

(HANNAH *rushes away from him, throwing letters into the air.* ANDY *throws the envelopes onto the ground.*)

OLD MAN: Why are you here?

ANDY: I'm unloadin' crates of made-up lies and secrets.

HANNAH: Daddy, there isn't much time.

ANDY: You got so many.

OLD MAN: Take 'em back.

HANNAH: You ain't makin' sense, Daddy.

ANDY: They're gonna bury you alive.

OLD MAN: Andy, I need your help.

ANDY: You ain't good for nothin'.

ANDY/HANNAH: Garbage is garbage. Don't you remember?

OLD MAN: I was wrong.

HANNAH: It's a dream, Daddy.

ANDY: Ignorant old fool!

HANNAH: Ignorant old fool!

OLD MAN: Andy, please don't go!

HANNAH: It's in the postcards, Daddy.

OLD MAN: Hannah, bring him back!

HANNAH: All you gotta do is read them.

(ANDY *and* HANNAH *laugh at him. They exit.*)

OLD MAN: Hannah! Andy!

(SALT *enters.*)

SALT: Grandpa?

OLD MAN: Did you see your brother?

SALT: Andy?

OLD MAN: He was just here, and so was your ma.

SALT: Ma? Grandpa, you got a fever?

OLD MAN: They was just here. Go find 'em.

SALT: What are all these bills doin' on the floor?

OLD MAN: Never mind.

SALT: Why haven't you opened them?

OLD MAN: I ain't had time.

SALT: This one's from the bank. And this one's from the feed store.

OLD MAN: Them little bitty letters are hard to read. You know, I can never find my glasses!

SALT: I found 'em. I found 'em yesterday under the truck seat. Here.

(*He gives the* OLD MAN *his glasses.* SALT *tears open an envelope.*)

OLD MAN: I wonder how they got there?

SALT: Ain't you gonna read it?

OLD MAN: This one is from the . . . the . . .

SALT (*unsure*): Feed store?

OLD MAN: That's right. And they want me to pay my bill.

SALT: How much is it?

OLD MAN: I owe 'em three dollars and twenty-five cents.

SALT: That doesn't sound like the feed store.

OLD MAN: No?

SALT: Let me see, Grandpa. It's from the bank, and it ain't three dollars and twenty-five cents.

OLD MAN: It's not?

SALT: It's three hundred and twenty-five dollars! It says you're "past due."

OLD MAN: What? That ain't my fault! Andy should be here! He sorts the bills. I count the money! That's the way it's always been.

SALT: Grandpa, what's goin' on?

OLD MAN: Nothin'. Everythin's all right. Go to sleep.

SALT: What does this one say?

OLD MAN: It ain't your business! Now, go to bed!

SALT: You can't read, can you?!

OLD MAN: No, that ain't true!

SALT: Yes, it is! You can't read and they're gonna take everythin' away from us!

OLD MAN: That's not how it is!

SALT: Grandpa, why didn't you tell me?

OLD MAN: You gotta help me sort this out, Salt.

SALT: Andy knew all along, didn't he? That's your big fat secret.

OLD MAN: You tell me what them bills say and I'll count the—

SALT: Andy loved you and so did Ma. But you drove them away!

OLD MAN: No.

SALT: You lied to me. I hate you, Grandpa!

OLD MAN: You don't mean that!

SALT: Andy was right about you. You're just an ignorant old fool!

OLD MAN: Salt!

(SALT exits.)

OLD MAN: Salt, you don't know what it's like goin' around not knowin' what things say! Scared of what people think. Makin' excuses all the time. Pretendin' you know what things mean but don't. Salt?

(The OLD MAN exits.)

Scene Ten

(Blue sky and white clouds. SALT and PEPPER enter. They carry a fishing pole and are walking barefoot.)

SALT: Pepper, it ain't workin'!

PEPPER: You gotta wiggle your nose more.

SALT: I don't feel any better.

PEPPER: You just gotta give it time. Try wigglin' your ears.

SALT: No.

PEPPER: Well, it always works for me. Try wigglin' your toes.

SALT: I don't wanna.

PEPPER: You gotta let the air circulate around them.

SALT: Why?

PEPPER: To cool off. That way you'll feel better. I do this whenever I get upset.

SALT: I thought my grandpa was the smartest man in the whole world.

PEPPER: You can't be mad at him forever, you know?

SALT: Why not?

PEPPER: 'Cause you live in the same house.

SALT: He's a big fat liar. Pretendin' he knows everythin' but he don't know nothin'. He can't even read a road sign. That's why he wrecked his truck.

PEPPER: It don't mean he's stupid. Maybe he never learned how to read. My daddy never did, but he knows now.

SALT: How'd he do that?

PEPPER: I taught him one letter at a time.

SALT: One letter at a time?

PEPPER: Ah huh. Then that letter turned into a word, then that word turned into a sentence, which added up to a paragraph, which turned into a page, and then a whole book. Here, I got somethin' for you.

(*She hands* SALT *a small wrapped package.*)

SALT: What is it?

PEPPER: Just say "thank you" and open it.

SALT: Thank you.

(*He opens it, finding paper, a pencil, some envelopes, and some stamps.*)

PEPPER: It's so you can write to Andy and anybody else that you want to.

SALT: Who else would I want to write to?

PEPPER: Me.

SALT: You?

PEPPER: My daddy's fixin' to leave soon.

SALT: You too?

PEPPER: Pecan season is almost finished. I thought, if I showed you how to write a letter, maybe you'd want to write back.

SALT: We ain't boyfriend and girlfriend, are we?

PEPPER: No!

SALT: 'Cause I hate girls.

PEPPER: And I hate boys.

SALT: We're just friends.

PEPPER: Friends.

SALT: Okay, I'll write you. But you gotta show me how.

PEPPER: Let's start by writin' to Andy.

SALT: I don't know what to say to him.

PEPPER: Tell him how you feel.

SALT: All I got to say is awful things about my grandpa.

PEPPER: That's a start.

SALT: What is?

PEPPER: "Dear Andy, Grandpa is an idiot! Love, Salt."

SALT: Are you makin' fun of me?!

PEPPER: No. It helps to write out what you feel.

SALT: I can't spell too good.

PEPPER: It don't matter. I'll help.

SALT: I don't know how to start.

PEPPER: Start with "Dear Andy."

SALT: That's stupid!

PEPPER: Then you do it!

(Pause.)

SALT: I'm sorry.

PEPPER: I'll write. You just talk.

SALT: "Dear Andy . . ."

PEPPER: "Dear Andy . . ."

SALT: "How are you?"

PEPPER: "How are you?" Now tell him how you feel.

SALT: "I am fine."

PEPPER: Now, tell him . . .

SALT: Who's writin' this letter?

PEPPER: You are.

SALT: Then let me say what I gotta say!

PEPPER: Okay!

SALT: "I wish I could see you. Nothin' has been the same since you left."

PEPPER (overlapping): "Nothin' has been the same."

SALT: "Why didn't you . . ."

PEPPER: ". . . didn't you . . ."

SALT: ". . . tell me . . ."

PEPPER: ". . . tell me . . ." Slow down!

SALT: ". . . about Grandpa?"

PEPPER: ". . . about Grandpa?"

SALT: "Your brother, Salt."

PEPPER: That's it?

SALT: Yup.

PEPPER: Don't you want ask him what he's doin'? Where he's been?

SALT: Nope.

PEPPER: You got a lot more room still left, you know?

SALT: That's all I wanna say. It's my letter, right?

PEPPER: Right. Don't you wanna draw a picture of somethin'?

SALT: Pepper!

PEPPER: Okay!

SALT (*leans back and wiggles his toes*): My toes feel better.

(HANNAH *appears, playing her guitar. A moment later,* ANDY *enters, carrying his duffel bag. He reads a postcard.*)

SALT: I got another postcard from Andy.

ANDY: May 6th, 1952. Dear Salt—

(*The* OLD MAN *enters, carrying a small shoebox. He opens it. It is filled with dozens of postcards.*)

HANNAH: Daddy, where do I begin? How do I explain my life to you? The choices I've made?

ANDY: I should've told you about the old man, but I couldn't. You're always lookin' up to him. I'm sorry I didn't.

HANNAH: My life has been a sorry state of affairs. And I know how it's saddened you.

ANDY: He carries a big hurt inside. It's shaped the way he is and the way he's treated us.

HANNAH: I'm sorry for causin' you so much heartache. And I'm sorry for the mean things I said.

ANDY: I wish I could help him, but I've never known what to do.

HANNAH: I'm so thankful that my boys are with you. I was pretty mad at you for the longest time.

ANDY: But don't be too angry at him.

HANNAH: God, how I miss their smiles and their little warm bodies sleepin' next to me.

ANDY: He loves you, you know?

HANNAH: I think Andy took my leavin' the hardest. I know he cried when I left. I could feel him in my heart.

ANDY: I'm shippin' out soon. Thought I was gonna see sandy beaches and girls. Just my luck. I'm goin' to Korea.

HANNAH: A child shouldn't have to grow up so quickly in this world.

ANDY: You ever heard of Korea?

SALT: No.

PEPPER: Me either.

HANNAH: Daddy, I hope you can get somebody to read this for you. And if you're not too mad at me, would you mind lettin' me come back home?

ANDY: Your brother—

HANNAH: Your little girl—

ANDY/HANNAH (*together*): —ANDY. /—HANNAH.

(HANNAH *and* ANDY *exit. The* OLD MAN *continues to look at the postcards.*)

PEPPER: You miss him, don't you?

SALT: A whole lot. I keep thinkin' if maybe I could've done somethin' more Andy would still be here. Things would be just the way they used to be.

PEPPER: Salt, it ain't your fault Andy left.

SALT: Why didn't I wash them dishes!

PEPPER: You really think it would've mattered?

SALT: Maybe. I don't know. No.

PEPPER: It was just his time to go, Salt. I bet your grandpa misses him too.

SALT: Why would he?

PEPPER: Maybe he thinks it's his fault Andy left 'cause, you know—

SALT: You really think so?

PEPPER: Maybe if you showed him how, you could write to Andy together.

SALT: I can hardly read and write myself. How am I gonna teach him?

PEPPER: One letter at a time. Remember? All you gotta do is ask.

SALT: Okay.

(*They begin to exit.*)

SALT: Pepper?

PEPPER: Yeah?

SALT: Thanks for the present.

(*They run off.* HANNAH's *voice is heard, singing. The* OLD MAN *enters with a shoebox. He* looks at the postcards. SALT enters. The OLD MAN hides the shoebox. SALT holds out the postcard he had torn up earlier. It has been glued back together.)

SALT: Andy sent this.

OLD MAN: Andy?

SALT: He wrote to me.

OLD MAN: It's all tore up.

SALT: That's 'cause I did it.

OLD MAN: You still mad at him?

SALT: Not no more. Are you?

(Beat.)

OLD MAN: What's it say?

SALT: He joined the Marine Corps.

OLD MAN: He did?

SALT: He misses us. I've been thinkin', maybe if we write to him he'll wanna come back home and live with us again. You think?

OLD MAN: That's up to him, Salt.

SALT: If he wanted to, would it be all right with you?

OLD MAN: Family is family.

SALT: You really mean that?

OLD MAN: Yup.

SALT: Grandpa, who taught Andy to make colored pancakes? Was it Ma?

OLD MAN: No.

SALT: Was it you?

OLD MAN: . . .

SALT: You gonna teach me?

OLD MAN: Maybe.

SALT: You wanna help me write Andy a letter?

OLD MAN: I got lots of things to do.

SALT: It won't take long. I know how.

OLD MAN: I got all them bills to pay and produce to deliver.

SALT: I'll help you after we write Andy.

OLD MAN: I'm behind already. The day's begun and—

SALT: Okay.

OLD MAN: Go on now. Get yourself to school.

(SALT *begins to exit.*)

OLD MAN: Salt?

SALT: Yeah, Grandpa?

OLD MAN: You study hard. Learn them books.

(SALT *exits.*)

Scene Eleven

(SALT *enters, flipping a blue pancake high into the air.*)

SALT: Hurry up, Pepper. The pancake's ready!

(PEPPER *enters, carrying a plate filled with colored pancakes. They both wear pots on their heads.*)

PEPPER: It's my turn to flip!

SALT: Okay, I'll catch!

(*They switch.* PEPPER *flips the blue pancake high into the air . . .*)

SALT: Wo!

PEPPER: Wo!

(*. . . as* SALT *catches it on the plate.* PEPPER *pounds a beat on her frying pan as* SALT *and* PEPPER *do a victory dance.*)

PEPPER: Salt, how many postcards you got from Andy now?

SALT: Ten.

PEPPER: You wanna swap for 'em? I got thirty Lincoln pennies I found on Stevens Road. My daddy says it'll bring a whole lot of luck. You can make wishes and they'll come true.

SALT: How do you know that?

PEPPER: 'Cause I made thirty of 'em and they all came true.

SALT: No, they didn't!

PEPPER: Yes, they did!

SALT: What'd you wish for?

PEPPER: I can't tell you that. Wishes are supposed to be secrets. They don't come true if you tell. Everythin' gets undone. So you wanna trade or not?

SALT: Okay, but just for a little while.

(*They swap.*)

PEPPER: Good trade.

SALT: Even trade.

PEPPER: Now, make a wish.

(SALT *makes a wish.*)

PEPPER: I know what your wish is!

SALT: I'm not sayin'.

PEPPER: You wished for—

SALT: Air raid!

PEPPER: Oh, no!

SALT/PEPPER (*ducking for cover*): Pa-pow! Pa-pow! Pa-pow! Pa-pa-pa-pa-pow!

SALT: We ain't gonna make it, Pepper!

PEPPER: This is our last stand!

SALT/PEPPER: Pa-pow! Pa-pow! Pa-pow! Pa-pa-pa-pa-pow!

(ANDY *enters, wearing battle fatigues, backpack, and helmet.*)

ANDY: Dear Salt, Last night I was eatin' my dinner out of a can, and it was good!

SALT/PEPPER: Pa-pow! Pa-pow! Pa-pow! Pa-pa-pa-papow!

ANDY: But I wish I had some salt and pepper. Like you and your friend.

SALT: Ughhh!!! I'm hit!

PEPPER: Me too!

ANDY: Salt and Pepper: You can't have one without the other.

(*An explosion occurs nearby.* ANDY *exits.* SALT *does a horrible death scene.* PEPPER *does an even more horrible and dramatic death scene. She knocks something over and the* OLD MAN's *shoebox is revealed.*)

PEPPER: What's this?

SALT: It's a shoebox.

PEPPER: What's inside?

SALT (*picks it up and shakes it*). It don't sound like shoes.

PEPPER: Do you think we should open it?

SALT: Could be dangerous.

PEPPER: Real dangerous, huh?

SALT/PEPPER: Let's open it!

(*They open the box.*)

SALT: They're postcards.

PEPPER: There's a whole lot of them. Who's "Daddy"?

SALT: Let me see.

PEPPER: Who they from?

SALT: From my ma.

PEPPER: Your ma?

(They look at the postcards as HANNAH enters. She holds a mop. She looks around cautiously.)

HANNAH: Hello, is anybody here?

SALT: This one's from the Grand Ole Opry.

HANNAH: Hello?

PEPPER: Where's that?

SALT: Nashville.

(HANNAH curtsies to an imaginary audience. She holds the mop as if it's a microphone.)

HANNAH: It's a great honor to be here with you tonight. I wanna say hello to my little ones back home and to my daddy. I made it! I wanna sing this little song I'm dedicatin' to them.

(She holds her mop like a guitar. Sings:)

Oh, sister Phoebe
How merry were we
The night we sat
Under the Juniper Tree
The Juniper Tree
Hi-ho, hi-ho
The Juniper Tree
Hi-ho . . .

(The OLD MAN enters.)

OLD MAN: Salt, what are you doin' with that?

SALT: We found it.

PEPPER: It was an accident, Mr. Holcomb.

OLD MAN: That belongs to me.

SALT: These postcards are from my ma, aren't they?

OLD MAN: Yup.

SALT: Why are you hidin' them?

OLD MAN: 'Cause it's all I got left of your ma. I don't know what they say.

You see, her life wasn't easy. She was just a girl when she had Andy. Then you come along. I wasn't the most understandin' daddy. My little Hannah tried to set her life straight, but she never could. One day she just packed off and left. Maybe she tried to sing, maybe she didn't.

SALT: All them stories about my ma, are they lies?

OLD MAN: I made them up so you would be proud of her. So you wouldn't be ashamed. She was always singin' and laughin' with you boys. Your ma did have the prettiest voice you ever heard. I ain't lyin' about that.

SALT: So my ma was never a famous singer?

OLD MAN: No.

HANNAH: Hello, is anybody out there?

(*She takes her mop and exits.*)

SALT: And she never sang at the Grand Ole Opry either?

OLD MAN: I'm not really sure. All I got left are these postcards from your ma. And I don't even know what they say. I'm sorry I lied to you and Andy. Once you tell a lie it only gets bigger and bigger until it buries you.

(*Another explosion is heard. Then "Taps" is heard played on an acoustic guitar.* ANDY *enters in a Marine uniform, holding an American flag under his arm. He stands at attention.*)

OLD MAN: I got this today. Looks important. Tell me what it says.

SALT: "Dear Mr. Holcomb, it is with my deepest regret I have to inform you that your grandson—"

ANDY: Corporal Andrew Holcomb was killed in action—

OLD MAN: Andy.

ANDY: In Korea, on December 12th, 1952.

SALT: "Your grandson was under my command. And I am proud to say I knew him well. He spoke highly of both you and his little brother."

(SALT *hands the letter to* PEPPER.)

ANDY: He talked of going home, learning the family business, and cooking colored pancakes for his little brother and best friend.

PEPPER: "Andrew was a brave young man, and a proud Marine. Signed, Thomas R. Murrow, Captain, United States Marine Corps."

(ANDY *places the folded American flag on the shoebox. He steps back and salutes. He exits. The* OLD MAN *sits quietly.*)

PEPPER (*reaches for* SALT's *hand*): I'm sorry, Salt.

SALT: I know.

PEPPER: You want to go to the creek or somethin'?

SALT: No.

PEPPER: Maybe we could go fishin', huh?

SALT: No thanks.

(The OLD MAN removes the flag and opens the shoebox.)

OLD MAN: Times were hard when I was a boy. My daddy didn't believe schoolin' was important. So he took me to work. And that's all I've ever known. But he was wrong. I've been ashamed all my life because I couldn't read. And I've ruined everythin' I've ever loved because of it.

SALT: Not everythin', Grandpa.

OLD MAN: Will you teach me to read?

(He hands SALT a postcard. A guitar is heard playing softly.)

SALT: Okay. But I'm gonna need Pepper's help.

OLD MAN: What do you say, Pepper?

PEPPER: It would be my honor.

OLD MAN: I wanna learn to read my little Hannah's postcards. Can you teach me that?

SALT/PEPPER: One letter at a time.

(HANNAH appears.)

HANNAH (singing):
    Hush 'n' Bye
    Don't you cry
    Oh, you pretty little babies

OLD MAN: Where do we start?

SALT: That's the letter "D."

OLD MAN: "D."

HANNAH (singing):
    When you wake
    You'll get sweet cake
    And all the pretty little ponies

PEPPER: That's the letter "a."

OLD MAN: . . . a . . .

HANNAH (singing):

A brown and a gray
And a black and a bay
All the pretty little ponies

SALT: . . . "d."

OLD MAN: . . . d . . .

(ANDY *appears in his uniform.*)

HANNAH/ANDY (*singing*):

Hush 'n' Bye
Don't you cry
Oh, you pretty little babies

OLD MAN: There's another "d."

PEPPER: Ah huh.

HANNAH/ANDY (*singing*):

When you wake
You'll have sweet cake
And all the pretty little ponies

SALT: . . . "y."

OLD MAN: . . . y . . .

HANNAH/ANDY (*singing*):

And a black and a bay
A brown and a gray
All the pretty little ponies

SALT: That word means "Daddy."

OLD MAN: "Daddy." So that's what that little word looks like? Imagine that.
(*The* OLD MAN *smiles.*)

CURTAIN

Hush 'n' Bye

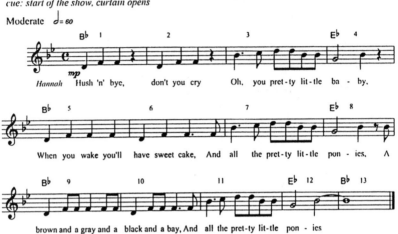

Built My Lady a Fine Brick House

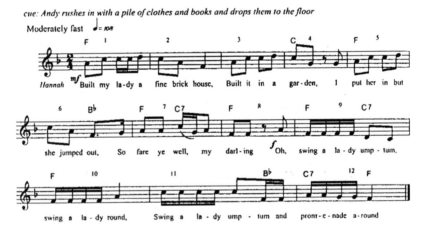

Go to Sleep

cue: Salt - "I don't want your stupid stuff!"
Andy - Thinks for a moment and removes a card from his pocket

Hannah: Go to sleep-y ba - by, bye. Go to sleep-y
bye - ole - ba - by bye, bye - ole -

ba - by bye, Ma - ma's go-in' to the mail - boat
by - by bye, Pa - pa's go-in' to the mail - boat

Ma - ma's go-in' to the mail - boat, bye.
Pa - pa's go-in' to the mail - boat, bye.

Johnny Get Your Hair Cut

cue: Old man enters carrying produce. He stops to wipe his forehead.

Hannah: John-ny get your hair cut - hair cut - hair cut, John-ny get your hair cut
John-ny get your gun and your sword and your pis - tol, John-ny get your gun and
Hey, ya Bet-ty Mar - tin - tip - toe - tip-toe, Hey, ya Bet - ty Mar - tin

just like me. John-ny get your hair cut - hair cut - hair cut,
come with me. John-ny get your gun and your sword and your pis - tol,
tip - toe - fy. Hey, ya Bet - ty Mar - tin - tip - toe - tip - toe,

John - ny get your hair cut just like me.
John - ny get your gun and come with me.
Hey, ya Bet - ty Mar - tin tip - toe - fy.

The Juniper Tree

cue: Hannah - "I made it! I wanna sing this little song I'm dedicatin" to them."

Hannah O sis - ter Phoe - be, how mer - ry were we, The night we sat

un - der the jun - i - per tree, The jun - i - per tree, Hi - o, hi -

o, The jun - i - per tree, Hi - o

Designer's Response

For *Salt & Pepper* I began by making notes about images, important events, and themes, something I always do—whether as designer, director, or actor:

Images

Letters from the alphabet and postal correspondence
Farm
Mother as dream image
Automobile
Postcards
Colored pancakes
The Grand Ole Opry

Themes

Loss of parent, lullaby
Child as parent
Friendship from adversity
Adult literacy

In thinking about the play and its setting I gathered source material for a collage (plate A) from the early forties through the mid-1950s: photographs of farms, farm workers, and the Great Depression by Dorothea Lange and other photographers of that era in America. I found images of the Korean War; a variety of fonts for alphabet letters; sheet music of lullabies; and photographs of the Ryman Auditorium, which houses the Grand Ole Opry.

From this collage I created a design for the proscenium stage that was inspired by a photograph by Wright Morris. My drawing (plate B) captures the moment from scene 6 in which the character of Pepper is introduced at the stream, reading her book.

The set is designed to indicate rolling farmland. The windmill and house are on tracks to move left and right to change the perspective of the audience in relationship to the position of the characters in each scene. The tree in this particular scene would be either tracked in from the side or flown in along with a gripped fence section. Letters are expressed visually in the large rock at the edge of the stream and in the two X's as the uprights of the fence. Leaves of the tree are also letter shapes. The sky is a painted scrim of sheet music of the lullaby heard within the action of the plot. Overlaid with soft clouds, the sheet music appears along with Hannah in flashback scenes, then dissolves as she exits.

Resources

Jacobs, Martin S. *Homefront Collectibles*. Iola: Krause, 2000.

Lange, Dorothea. *Photographs of a Lifetime*. Oakland: Aperture Foundation, 1982.

Menchine, Ron. *Propaganda Postcards of World War II*. Iola: Krause, 2000.

Mora, Gilles, and Beverly W. Brannan. *FSA: The American Vision*. New York: Abrams, 2006.

Reed, Robert. *Paper Collectibles: The Essential Buyers Guide*. Radnor: Wallace-Homestead, 1995.

Trachtenberg, Alan, and Ralph Lieberman. *Distinctly American: The Photography of Wright Morris*. London: Merrell, 1998.

Plate A: Collage.

Plate B: Scene 6: The meeting of Salt and Pepper.

The Highest Heaven

José Cruz González

The Highest Heaven premiered at Childsplay,
Tempe, Arizona, in association with
Borderlands Theatre, Tucson, Arizona.

When we are really honest with ourselves we must admit that our lives are all that really belong to us. So, it is how we use our lives that determines what kind of men we are. It is my deepest belief that only by giving our lives do we find life.

—César Chávez

La necesidad desconoce fronteras.
(Necessity knows no borders.)

—Mexican American proverb

Butterflies
Flying Like the Breeze
Sucking Nectar Quietly
Colors Everywhere

—Kelsey Miguel González, age nine

If you haven't forgiven yourself something,
how can you forgive others?

—Dolores Huerta

Characters

HURACÁN: A twelve-year-old Latino boy.

EL NEGRO: A Black man in his fifties. Worn like the earth, he is troubled by his past. Caretaker of the monarch butterflies.

KIKA: HURACÁN'S mother. A memory. (May also play the WIFE)

DOÑA ELENA: A dark-skinned Mexican widow. Old, possessive, petty, and disturbed.

MOISÉS: A fool. Related to DOÑA ELENA. (MOISÉS, the POLICE OFFICIAL, the ADDICT, the UNDERTAKER-BARBER, and the HUSBAND may be played by one actor.)

Time and Setting

1930s, various locales in America and Mexico.

Music

The Negro spirituals used in the play are believed to be public domain. They are: "O, Sit Down Servant"; "Somebody's Calling My Name"; "Couldn't Hear Nobody Pray"; and "Roll, Jordan, Roll."

A Note on Scene Titles

Scene numbers are followed by a [title], which is indicated in brackets. This is not necessarily intended for use within a production, but rather for the reader's information.

Scene 1

[The Great Depression. October, 1931.
The monarch butterfly begins his journey.
—*La Gran Depresión. Octubre, 1931.*
La mariposa monarca comienza su viaje venturoso.]

SETTING: *The 1930s, when America was in the middle of the Depression.*
During that period thousands of Mexican nationals, as well as Americans
of Mexican descent, were "repatriated" to Mexico with or without their consent. The
setting represents various locales and should only be suggestive. Title projections
are optional. A Negro spiritual is heard. Several monarch butterflies appear,
fluttering over the stage. Their wings glow, revealing deep vibrant colors.

AT RISE: *A train station. It is chaotic. Noisy. Dusty. Lights rise on a young*
Latino boy named HURACÁN, *who is holding a suitcase. He is scared and alone.*
KIKA, *Huracán's mother, appears.*

KIKA: ¡Huracán!

HURACÁN: What is it, 'Amá?

KIKA: Grab your things.

HURACÁN: But why?

KIKA: They're taking us away.

HURACÁN: Who is?

KIKA: Men with guns and badges!

HURACÁN: Where are we going?

KIKA: They're taking us away on a train to Mexico!

HURACÁN: But why?

KIKA: I don't know! Where's your father?

HURACÁN: 'Apá was right behind us.

KIKA: I've got to find him. Stay here.

HURACÁN: Can't I go with you?

KIKA: I'll be right back. Everything is going to be fine.

HURACÁN: How do you know?

KIKA: I just do.

(*Another train whistle blast is heard.* HURACÁN *sits on a suitcase.*)

KIKA: Remember, when you're scared God's watching.

(KIKA *exits.* EL NEGRO, *an old black man, appears.*)

EL NEGRO (*to* HURÁCAN): Boy?

HURACÁN: Huh?

EL NEGRO: That suitcase belongs to me.

HURACÁN: My 'amá told me to wait here.

EL NEGRO: You're sittin' on it.

HURACÁN: That's what she said.

EL NEGRO: What are you lookin' at?

HURACÁN: You must be *San Martín de Porres.*

EL NEGRO: Who?

HURACÁN: The patron saint of the defenseless. Have you come to answer my prayer?

EL NEGRO: I ain't *San Martín.*

HURACÁN: But he's black like you. Am I in heaven?

EL NEGRO: You ain't dead and I ain't no saint! This is *Misas*, Mexico, boy. Don't you know where you at?

HURACÁN: No, my 'amá said to stay here.

EL NEGRO: They all gone, boy. You're on your own. *Ándale*, I got a train to catch.

(HURACÁN *watches as* EL NEGRO *picks up his suitcase and waits for the train. Then . . .*)

EL NEGRO: I can't do it. I can't get on.

(EL NEGRO *exits as the train leaves.*)

HURACÁN (*yelling*): 'Amá!

Scene 2

[Far from home a small caterpillar searches for food.
—*Lejos de su casa una pequeña oruga busca comida.*]

(*November. El Día de los Muertos—The Day of the Dead. A cemetery. A remembrance for the dead. Like a Diego Rivera painting, shawled women kneel whispering prayers before the graves of their dead. Candles burn, fresh cempasúchil flowers [marigolds] adorn the graves, and candy skulls and bread lie out on plates inviting the lost souls to partake. A wealthy woman,* DOÑA ELENA, *dressed in black, and her servant,* MOISÉS, *enter.* DOÑA ELENA *stands before her husband's tomb.*)

DOÑA ELENA: Help me down, Moisés.

MOISÉS: Sí, Doña Elena.

DOÑA ELENA: Bring me his basket.

MOISÉS: Here it is, Doña Elena.

DOÑA ELENA (*kneels at a grave*): Porfirio, my dear sweet dead husband, I bring you wine from your vineyard, bread from your bakery, and meat from your rancho. (*To Moisés.*) What are you looking at, *indio*?

MOISÉS: Nothing, Doña Elena.

DOÑA ELENA: Turn your back and cover your ears. This conversation doesn't concern you.

MOISÉS: Sí, Doña Elena.

(*He turns his back and covers his ears.*)

DOÑA ELENA: I'm afraid I don't trust your unwanted son, Porfirio. You created him, but he's nothing like you. None of those "cousins" are. There's the banker, the bread maker, the harlot, the nun, the police official, the addict, and this *indio* half-breed. Your infidelities have cost me dearly, *querido*. I spit on you. (*She spits and then crosses herself.*) But I remember you, husband, as a faithful wife should on the Day of the Dead. I want all of those "cousins" to know how loyal I am. (*Pause.*) It gets me things.

(HURACÁN *enters and crosses to* DOÑA ELENA.)

HURACÁN: *Señora*, may I have a piece of sweet bread?

DOÑA ELENA: No, you may not. This food belongs to me and my dead husband.

HURACÁN: But I'm hungry.

DOÑA ELENA: Begging won't do you any good. I gave at church. *¿iMoisés?!*

HURACÁN: Please, I haven't eaten all day.

DOÑA ELENA: I don't care! *¿iMoisés?!*

(*She hits* MOISÉS *with her cane. He uncovers his ears.*)

MOISÉS: ¡Ay! ¿Doña Elena?

DOÑA ELENA: What are you doing?

MOISÉS: Talking to the spirits, Doña.

DOÑA ELENA: Crazy *indio*. Help me up. Go away, you wretched boy.

MOISÉS: You heard the *señora*. Go!

HURACÁN: But I'm dizzy from hunger.

DOÑA ELENA (*tempting him*): Then take the bread.

MOISÉS: ¿Doña?

DOÑA ELENA: Be my guest.

HURACÁN: Thank you, *señora*. (HURACÁN *reaches for the sweet bread and* DOÑA ELENA *hits him with her cane.*) Ouch!

DOÑA ELENA: Stupid boy. I said "no" the first time. Now do you understand? My possessions are not to be touched. Not! Not! Not! (HURACÁN *hides.*) Moisés, you should be more attentive.

MOISÉS: Sí, Doña Elena.

DOÑA ELENA: I tire of this country's filth, its lack of culture, and mostly of its poor. My dead husband and I started with nothing. We became quite successful and respected. Why must we carry the poor on our backs?

MOISÉS: I don't know . . .

(DOÑA ELENA *hits* MOISÉS *with her cane.*)

DOÑA ELENA: I wasn't speaking to you. If only you had lived, *querido*. We would have been rid of El *Negro* by now. Taken what's ours. Everyone would fear us. But you died too soon. Once again, leaving me to clean up your mess. El *Negro* is like a cancer. How I hate him. But I'll find a way. Find his weakness. Then strike. (*To Moisés.*) Why hasn't Don Porfirio's tomb been cleaned? I'm ashamed at how dirty it looks. There's dust everywhere. One can never be clean in this godforsaken country. Take me home!

(DOÑA ELENA *and* MOISÉS *exit.* HURACÁN *begins to eat as incense burns and prayers are whispered.* MOISÉS *reenters.*)

MOISÉS: The dead must be respected, *muchacho*. Leave an offering.

HURACÁN: Huh?

(MOISÉS *places some coins on the tombstone.*)

MOISÉS: If Doña Elena catches you we'll both be in trouble. Serious trouble. (MOISÉS *begins collecting food from other tombs and placing it on Don Porfirio's tomb.*) She's going to tell my cousin, the police official, and he'll come looking for you. You better leave now. You can't stay here. She does hateful things to people, especially children.

HURACÁN: Have you seen my 'amá? I lost her at the train station.

MOISÉS: No, I'm sorry, I haven't. But what do you expect? The whole station was a disaster. It's been like that all month. People everywhere. Screaming and crying. It makes no sense. And now everyone's gone.

HURACÁN: Do you know where the train went?

MOISÉS: Maybe south. I'm not sure.

HURACÁN: But I have to find my 'amá.

MOISÉS: You can't go back there. Not even into town. *Doña Elena* has spies everywhere.

HURACÁN: Please help me.

MOISÉS: There's nothing I can do. If *Doña Elena* knew I was talking to you . . .

HURACÁN: I want my 'amá.

(*A coyote's howl is heard off in the distance.*)

MOISÉS: Perhaps you can go into the forest.

HURACÁN: Forest?

MOISÉS: That's where *El Negro* lives. Nobody ever goes there. Everyone's afraid of him, but not me. I'll go find him for you. But if *Doña Elena* finds out I helped you . . .

HURACÁN: I won't say a word.

MOISÉS: Good. Here, take this blanket. It'll be cold tonight. It's all I can give you. And remember my cousin will be looking for you.

HURACÁN: Who?

MOISÉS: The police official.

(*MOISÉS exits. HURACÁN wraps himself in the blanket. A moment later he pushes everything off the tomb in anger.*)

HURACÁN: Why is this happening to me?! Where are you, 'Amá?

[The small caterpillar remembers his past.
— *La oruga pequeña recuerda su pasado.*]

(*El valle—The valley appears. A barn sits on the edge of a green field and the valley is filled with blue sky. KIKA, Huracán's mother, enters, carrying a laundry basket.*)

KIKA: Huracán, you've got chores!

HURACÁN: But I'm hungry, 'Amá.

KIKA: There's plenty of time to eat later.

HURACÁN: I hate chores, 'Amá. Why can't we have a maid like in the movies?

KIKA: ¡Ándale!

(She takes the bread away and hands HURACÁN *a coffee can. He begins to feed the imaginary chickens.)*

HURACÁN: It's so hopeless. Things only get messy again.

KIKA: If everyone went around thinking like that nothing would ever get done. Laundry would never get washed. Rooms would never get cleaned. Your socks and *chones* would never get starched and ironed.

HURACÁN: It would be my kind of heaven.

KIKA: Well, heaven wouldn't be very clean now, would it? God would be very unhappy. Angels flying with filthy wings? *Imposible.*

(A train whistle is heard off in the distance.)

HURACÁN: The train's on time!

KIKA: I hate how it rumbles past our home. There's dust everywhere. My heaven is going to be a place without railroads and trains or specks of dirt anywhere. Your father promised he'd be back now. We live in the United States where everything's on time except for him. *(A little worried.)* Where can he be?

HURACÁN: Maybe he's buying something.

KIKA: He won't go into town. It isn't safe. People are being sent away. So, you stay near me.

HURACÁN: Do you know what's today, 'Amá?

KIKA: It's Tuesday.

HURACÁN: Yeah, but it's not just any Tuesday. There's something special about this Tuesday. Remember?

KIKA: No.

HURACÁN: 'Amá.

KIKA: Of course I remember! You're growing so quickly. You'll never be eleven again.

(She kisses him on the cheek.)

HURACÁN: So?

KIKA: So?

HURACÁN: So, is there anything I should open now, 'Amá?

KIKA: Ay, Huracán, can't you wait to celebrate tonight?

HURACÁN: No!

KIKA: You're just like your father. *Imposible. (She gives* HURACÁN *a small gift wrapped in burlap.)* Happy Birthday, Huracán!

(HURACÁN *immediately opens it. It is a glass jar with a monarch butterfly.*)

HURACÁN: It's a butterfly!

KIKA: It's not just any butterfly, Huracán, it's a *monarca*. A king butterfly.

HURACÁN: What am I supposed to do with it?

KIKA: Make a wish and then let it go.

HURACÁN: But I want to keep it.

KIKA: It isn't for you to keep.

HURACÁN: But what kind of gift is that, if I can't keep it?

KIKA: You're supposed to make a wish. Then let it go, and your wish will come true.

HURACÁN: Will my butterfly ever come back?

KIKA: No, but one of his children might. And when he returns, *Huracán*, there'll be thousands of monarchs with him, dancing like leaves in the wind. They'll stop here to rest their weary wings and quench their thirsty mouths. When they do we'll dampen the earth with fresh water.

HURACÁN: Why?

KIKA: So the flowers will be strong to feed these *mariposas* their sweet nectar. It's a glimpse at God's heart.

HURACÁN: God's heart?

KIKA: It's a blessing, *mijo*.

HURACÁN: How come you know so much about things?

KIKA: Not everything comes out of a book, Huracán. Who taught you to tell time by reading the sun?

HURACÁN: You did.

KIKA: Who taught you to eat cactus without pricking yourself?

HURACÁN: You.

KIKA: There are many ways to learn, and they don't all come from a book. The earth has secrets. If you watch and listen closely she'll share them with you.

HURACÁN (*closing his eyes*): Okay. Done. Time to go, *mariposa*. Fly!

(HURACÁN *opens the jar and releases the butterfly. The monarch butterfly flutters off into the blue sky. A siren is heard.* KIKA *sees something off in the distance.*)

HURACÁN: What is it, 'Amá?

KIKA: Oh, no, they're coming this way!

HURACÁN: Who is?

KIKA: Men with guns and badges!

HURACÁN: Why?

KIKA: There's no time to explain. We have to go!

HURACÁN: But my butterfly king. I've got to save him!

KIKA: No, *Huracán*, there isn't time!

HURACÁN: He won't make it by himself!

KIKA: *¡Huracán!*

(*A dust storm arrives. A moment later* HURACÁN *struggles to awaken from his nightmare.* DOÑA ELENA *enters, standing over him.*)

DOÑA ELENA: Wake up! Wake up, you!

HURACÁN: 'Amá?

DOÑA ELENA: How dare you call me your mother! I'm nobody's mother! You little thief, you've taken food from my dead husband!

(*She begins beating him with her cane.*)

HURACÁN: No! Stop hitting me!

DOÑA ELENA: I'll teach you never to steal from the dead! *¡Toma!*

(EL NEGRO *enters and crosses to* DOÑA ELENA, *taking away her cane.*)

EL NEGRO: Leave the boy alone!

DOÑA ELENA: How dare you interfere, *Negro!*

EL NEGRO: What's he done?

DOÑA ELENA: He's a thief!

HURACÁN: I was hungry.

DOÑA ELENA (*grabs* HURACÁN *by the ear*): Do you know what I do to horrible little children?

HURACÁN: Ouch!

EL NEGRO: Leave the boy alone!

DOÑA ELENA: Give me back my cane, *Negro!* (EL NEGRO *holds the cane up as if to strike her. She releases* HURACÁN.) How dare you try to strike me!

EL NEGRO: I ain't yet, but I might. Get up, boy.

DOÑA ELENA: I promise you'll pay for this insult!

EL NEGRO: Get in line.

DOÑA ELENA: Crazy old *gringo*, protector of the butterflies and now children too? Saint El *Negro*, is it?

EL NEGRO: This ain't got nothin' to do with saints.

DOÑA ELENA: That's right, *Negro*. How can I forget? There's unfinished business between you and me.

EL NEGRO: The boy's got nothin' to do with it.

DOÑA ELENA: I'll see you dead yet.

EL NEGRO: Them mountain spirits got powerful magic.

DOÑA ELENA: How frightening. But it's a matter of time. I have it and you don't.

EL NEGRO: You ain't won yet.

DOÑA ELENA: When I do I'll dance on your grave.

EL NEGRO: I ain't afraid of you. Everybody knows it. People laughin' at you 'cause you ain't got rid of me yet.

DOÑA ELENA (*to* EL NEGRO): Just wait! (EL NEGRO *lets out a loud howl. To* HURACÁN.) Your selfishness will cost you too, boy, mark my words! ¡Ay! ¿¡Oficial?! ¿¡Oficial?!

(*She exits.*)

EL NEGRO: You better go. She'll be back soon.

HURACÁN: Which way did my '*amá's* train go?

EL NEGRO: That old spider has no compassion in her.

HURACÁN: Will it come back?

EL NEGRO: ¡Ándale! Go!

(EL NEGRO *exits quickly.* HURACÁN *grabs as much bread as he can as the* POLICE OFFICIAL *races in. He is the same actor who plays* MOISÉS. *The* POLICE OFFICIAL *wears a mustache and a uniform. He holds a revolver in one hand and a lantern in the other.*)

POLICE OFFICIAL (*frightened*): ¿Negro? (*No answer.*) Oh, thank God. (HURACÁN *tries to exit.*) Who's there?

HURACÁN (*freezing*): . . .

POLICE OFFICIAL: Is that you, beggar boy? What have you done to Doña Elena? She's erupted like a volcano, spewing curses at everyone. No one will sleep tonight. Beggar boy?

HURACÁN: . . .

(HURACÁN *covers himself with the blanket. The* POLICE OFFICIAL *shines the light toward* HURACÁN.)

POLICE OFFICIAL: Oh, forgive me, *señora*. Or is it *señor*?

HURACÁN: . . .

POLICE OFFICIAL: ¡Ah, *señor*!

(HURACÁN *nods his head "yes." From beneath* HURACÁN's *blanket a piece of sweet bread falls to the ground. The* POLICE OFFICIAL *picks it up.*)

POLICE OFFICIAL (*suddenly*): What are you doing with Don Porfirio's sweet bread?! (HURACÁN *accidentally drops more bread onto the ground.*) ¡Ay! It can't be? Can it? ¿Don Porfirio? Is that you?

HURACÁN (*dropping his voice*): Sí.

POLICE OFFICIAL: ¡Sí! Of course it's you! It's the Day of the Dead. Are you well, Father?

HURACÁN (*dropping his voice*): No.

POLICE OFFICIAL (*to himself*): No! You fool, how can he be well? He's dead! (*To* HURACÁN.) I'm not used to talking to the dead, Father. Um, did you happen to see a beggar boy come this way?

HURACÁN (*dropping his voice*): No.

(HURACÁN *begins to walk away as the bread he collected keeps falling to the ground.*)

POLICE OFFICIAL: Wait! (HURACÁN *freezes.*) You dropped this, Father.

(*He hands* HURACÁN *all the sweet bread.*)

HURACÁN: Gracias.

POLICE OFFICIAL: No hay de qué. Forgive me for disturbing your meal, Father. I mean no harm.

HURACÁN: Boo!

POLICE OFFICIAL: ¡Ay!

(*The* POLICE OFFICIAL *exits quickly.* HURACÁN *exits the other way.*)

Scene 3

[Butterfly sanctuary. Deep within the forest, the caterpillar finds a home. —*Santuario de las mariposas. En medio del bosque, la oruga encuentra un hogar.*]

(EL NEGRO *sits by a fire. He opens his suitcase. It glows from within. He senses something wrong.* EL NEGRO *closes his suitcase and picks up a large stick.*)

EL NEGRO (*calling out*): Who's out there?

HURACÁN: . . .

EL NEGRO: ¿Doña Elena?

HURACÁN: No.

EL NEGRO: Is that you, boy?

HURACÁN: Yes.

EL NEGRO: How long you been there watchin'?

HURACÁN: Forever.

EL NEGRO: What's your business?

HURACÁN: I'm hungry. May I have something to eat?

EL NEGRO: I don't take freeloaders. What's you got to trade?

HURACÁN: I can work for my food.

EL NEGRO (*laughing*): You mean you gonna pull your own weight like a man? With them skinny arms?

HURACÁN: What's wrong with my arms?

EL NEGRO: They skinny!

(*EL NEGRO coughs.*)

HURACÁN: Stop laughing at me! I don't need your help, old man! I can do this all by myself!

EL NEGRO: Then go! No one stoppin' you!

HURACÁN: Okay, I'm goin'!

(*HURACÁN stops.*)

EL NEGRO: Well, I'm waitin'!

HURACÁN: I'm real hungry!

EL NEGRO (*throws HURACÁN some food*): Eat, boy. Then go! (*Singing.*)
O, sit down, servant, sit down;
O, sit down, servant . . .

HURACÁN: Why did that old woman beat me?

EL NEGRO: You probably had it comin'.

HURACÁN: I didn't do nothing to her.

EL NEGRO: 'Cept steal her food.

HURACÁN: I was hungry.

EL NEGRO: She's a nasty old crow. Dangerous too. Her name is Doña Elena. Wealthiest woman in town. Owns everything 'cept these woods and she wants them too.

HURACÁN: Why?

EL NEGRO: 'Cause she gotta possess everythin' there is. Take my soul if she could. Cut them trees down and sell it as lumber.

HURACÁN: She called you a crazy *gringo*. Are you?

EL NEGRO: I can howl at the moon and make it disappear.

HURACÁN: No, you can't. (EL NEGRO *howls. And the moon disappears.*) How'd you do that?

EL NEGRO: That's a secret.

HURACÁN: It's a stupid trick.

EL NEGRO: Ain't no trick. That's coyote talk. Where you from, boy?

HURACÁN: . . .

(HURACÁN *crosses his arms.*)

EL NEGRO: Oh, so now you ain't talkin'?

HURACÁN: . . .

EL NEGRO: I bet you must be from California.

HURACÁN: How do you know that?

EL NEGRO: 'Cause that attitude of yours is as big as that state. Gots to be California.

HURACÁN: So what if I am?

EL NEGRO: That means you and me from Gringoland. You a long ways from home.

HURACÁN: Me and my '*amá* got sent here.

(*A train is heard rolling through the night. A boxcar interior appears.* KIKA *enters.* HURACÁN *joins her.*)

KIKA: ¡Huracán!

HURACÁN: I'm right here, 'Amá.

KIKA: Stay where I can see you.

HURACÁN: Okay. Where's 'Apá?

KIKA: He must be on another boxcar.

(*She begins to cry softly.*)

HURACÁN: Are you crying, 'Amá?

KIKA: No, my eyes are just tired. Go to sleep.

(*Pause.*)

HURACÁN: Have you ever been on a train before, 'Amá?

KIKA: No.

HURACÁN: It's one of the most best things you can do. I mean, look out there.

KIKA: There's nothing to see.

HURACÁN: The moon's out, 'Amá. The earth has secrets. If you watch and listen she'll share them with you, remember? Look at the white clouds glow. You can see the shapes of family faces. See? There's *Nana Licha* . . .

KIKA: You're right.

HURACÁN: And *Tía Lupe*.

KIKA: And there's our *primo, Conejo*.

HURACÁN / KIKA (*placing their fingers on their head and making rabbit ears*): Rabbit cousin!

HURACÁN: Riding a train isn't so bad, is it, 'Amá?

KIKA: I guess not. Say a prayer to San Martín. (*Sadly.*) Happy twelfth birthday, Huracán.

(*The boxcar fades away.* HURACÁN *joins* EL NEGRO.)

EL NEGRO: You got "repatriated."

(*He hands* HURACÁN *some more food.*)

HURACÁN: What's that mean?

EL NEGRO: It means *los norte gringos* don't want you in their stinking country. That's why they sent you away.

HURACÁN: But why would they send me here? Mexico isn't my country.

EL NEGRO: They in a "Depression." Country's broke.

HURACÁN: I broke nothing.

EL NEGRO: Depression's made people crazy. Plenty of trains been comin' through Misas lately. Lots of folk. Steppin' outta them boxcars. Carryin' what they own. Old men, women, and children all lookin' like they come outta the Bible. Like them Israelites leavin' Egypt. Searchin' for the Promised Land. 'Cept this ain't Egypt and they ain't got Moses.

HURACÁN: Will you help me find my 'amá?

EL NEGRO: Ain't my business. You got to learn to help yourself. Understand? But you best wait 'til Doña Elena forgets about you 'fore you go into town.
(EL NEGRO *prepares to sleep near the fire. Sings.*)

O, sit down, servant, sit down;
Sit down and rest a little while.
You snore?

HURACÁN: No.

EL NEGRO: Good. You can sleep here tonight. But tomorrow you go.

(EL NEGRO *lies down to sleep. So does* HURACÁN.)

HURACÁN: ¿Señor?

EL NEGRO: What?

HURACÁN: Do you have anything else to eat?

Scene 4

[The caterpillar becomes a chrysalis, changing form and color.
— La oruga se transforma en una crisálida, cambiando de forma y color.]

(At the train station. Voices from EL NEGRO's haunting past are heard. EL NEGRO stands, holding his suitcase and a train ticket.)

EL NEGRO: I can't do it. I can't get on. (Pause.) Yeah. Made them indios a promise. Somebody's gotta look after them monarchs.

(He tears up the ticket. He coughs. The train departs. He exits as HURACÁN rushes in, picking up the torn pieces. A train is heard. KIKA appears as a memory.)

KIKA: ¡Huracán!

(She crosses to him.)

HURACÁN: ¿'Amá?

KIKA: Hold this.

(She places a handful of earth onto HURACÁN's palm.)

HURACÁN: What is it?

KIKA: Smell it!

HURACÁN: Why?

KIKA: Do as I say!

HURACÁN (smells it): It's just dirt.

KIKA: It's more than that! Taste it!

HURACÁN: No, 'Amá!

KIKA: Do as I tell you!

HURACÁN (tastes the earth): Aagghh . . .

KIKA: This soil is from the valley you come from. You mustn't ever forget.

HURACÁN: I won't.

(He cleans his mouth.)

KIKA: You've tasted it. It's in your body now. Our valley will always be your home. No matter what happens. Remember. Promise me.

HURACÁN: Okay, I promise. (KIKA *begins to back away.*) Where are you going, 'Amá?

KIKA: To look for your 'apá. Stay here.

HURACÁN: Can't I go with you?

KIKA: I'll be right back. Everything is going to be fine.

HURACÁN: How do you know?

KIKA: I just do.

(*Lights fade.*)

Scene 5

[Walking among the sleeping monarchs.
—*Caminando entre las mariposas monarcas dormidas.*]

(*The sun whispers in the night.* EL NEGRO *holds a dead butterfly in his palm.*)

EL NEGRO: Mariposa, you've traveled such a long way only to die. Was it worth it? (*He buries the butterfly. He hears something off in the distance. He picks up his stick.*) Who's out there?

HURACÁN: . . .

EL NEGRO: Boy?

HURACÁN: Yes.

(HURACÁN *enters.*)

EL NEGRO: Why do you keep followin' me?

HURACÁN: I don't like to be alone.

EL NEGRO: Come here. (HURACÁN *comes closer.*) Closer. (HURACÁN *crosses cautiously toward* EL NEGRO.) You don't spy on people 'cause they're gonna think you're a snake. And you know what happens to snakes?

HURACÁN: They get hit?

EL NEGRO: They ain't got friends.

(EL NEGRO *puts the stick down.*)

HURACÁN: Oh . . .

EL NEGRO: Sit down. (HURACÁN *sits on* EL NEGRO's *suitcase.*) Not there! That's my baggage!

HURACÁN: What's in it?

EL NEGRO: Ghosts! You wanna see?

HURACÁN (*afraid*): Uh-uh!!

EL NEGRO: Them cousins are afraid of it too. Got powerful magic. Doña Elena lookin' to take it from me. But she can't 'cause I won't let her. Nobody comes near it. Understand?

HURACÁN: I won't touch it.

EL NEGRO: Good. I suppose you want somethin' to eat?

HURACÁN: I'll work for it.

EL NEGRO: You gonna pull your own weight?

HURACÁN: I will.

EL NEGRO: There ain't gonna be no complainin'.

HURACÁN: Okay.

EL NEGRO: I like my peace.

(*They sit and eat.*)

HURACÁN: Why do you live here?

(EL NEGRO *shoots him a look. Pause. He hands* EL NEGRO *some sweet bread.*)

EL NEGRO: Where'd you get this?

HURACÁN: I stole it.

EL NEGRO: Ain't right for a boy to steal.

HURACÁN: Ain't right I'm in Mexico! Ain't right I've been beaten! Ain't right my 'amá's gone!

EL NEGRO: Now, hold on there. All I'm sayin' is, it ain't right. That's all. A man's gotta do what he's gotta do.

HURACÁN: Well, I'm doin' it!

EL NEGRO: You in a nasty mood. Man's gotta have himself a sense of humor. Be able to laugh at hisself. It helps cut the pain, boy. Understand? It's good bread. Hard, but good. (HURACÁN *shrugs his shoulders.*) Look up in them trees.

HURACÁN: What are they?

EL NEGRO: Them's monarchs.

HURACÁN: Monarch butterflies? What are they doing up there?

EL NEGRO: It's where they live. This here is the *Santuario de las Mariposas.*

HURACÁN: Is this where they come to?

EL NEGRO: Every year.

HURACÁN: I wonder which one is mine?

EL NEGRO: What?

HURACÁN: Why are they bunched together like that in the trees?

EL NEGRO: Maybe to keep warm. Maybe for protection.

HURACÁN: There must be millions of them.

EL NEGRO: Wait 'til the sun warms them. It's a beautiful sight when they dance in the air. The *indios* believe that the souls of the dead are carried up to heaven on the backs of butterflies. You think it's true? (HURACÁN *shrugs his shoulders.*) I want to believe. Believe in somethin'.

HURACÁN: I want to be eleven again.

EL NEGRO: Pretty soon their children will come out of them cocoons, dry their wings in the warm sun, and start flyin' home.

HURACÁN: I want to be in my home and my *'amá* waiting there for me. It's not fair! Why did this happen to me? I want everything back the way it was! I want to wake up in my bed . . .

EL NEGRO: Listen here, boy . . .

HURACÁN: I hate Mexico!

EL NEGRO: There once was a butterfly who wanted to be a caterpillar. Yeah. You see, them seasons started changin' and lots of them monarchs got to dyin'. So the butterfly asked the great Creator to change him back to a caterpillar. The great Creator told him he was gonna give the butterfly a gift but he had to stay a butterfly. "You gonna carry the souls of the dead humans up to heaven. And your children and your children's children too." "But I want to be a caterpillar again," said the monarch. "Let them other butterflies fly to heaven." Well, that butterfly got his wish and became a caterpillar once more. He was so happy he began dancin', 'cept he slipped off a leaf and landed right into a black spider's web. Bam! Never knew what hit him.

HURACÁN: Why are you telling me this?

EL NEGRO: You can never go back. Our lives are measured by moments. And them moments change your life forever. Sometimes you gotta grow up sooner than you want. Gotta move on. Fact of life.

HURACÁN: No! I don't want to be here!

EL NEGRO: This is all you got!

HURACÁN: I don't want to be like you!

EL NEGRO: All you got is me!

HURACÁN: No!

EL NEGRO: Your mama ain't comin' back!

HURACÁN: I did what she told me! I waited for her!

EL NEGRO: Get it through your head!

HURACÁN: Why didn't she come back for me?

EL NEGRO: Maybe she tried! Maybe the train never stopped! Maybe—

HURACÁN: Why didn't she come back?

(HURACÁN *cries.* EL NEGRO *reaches out to comfort the boy but stops himself.*)

EL NEGRO: You a cabezón! And lazy too!

HURACÁN: What are you talking about?

EL NEGRO: Where's my wood? Said you was gonna get me some. Man's gotta keep his word.

HURACÁN: I ain't a man!

EL NEGRO: Well, I'm treatin' you like one. (*Starts coughing.*) Get use to it.

HURACÁN: That's blood.

EL NEGRO: Ain't nothin'! Now go get me my wood!

Scene 6

[The Black Widow spider spins her web.
—*La Viuda Negra hila su telaraña.*]

(DOÑA ELENA *sits near her husband's tomb. She takes out a cigar.*)

DOÑA ELENA: From the grave you do me no good, Porfirio. Between all those cousins they can't capture one small boy and a howling old man. Why are they all so afraid of him? Stupid superstitious nincompoops. Magic spells, prayers, and potions are the poor's only answer to reality. I need someone with intelligence, discretion, and resourcefulness. Someone desperate. Someone with needs. Someone with a bad habit.

(THE ADDICT *appears. He lights* DOÑA ELENA's *cigar. He is the same actor who played the* POLICE OFFICIAL.)

THE ADDICT: You sent for me, Doña Elena.

DOÑA ELENA: I have work for you.

THE ADDICT: How wonderful it is to see you.

DOÑA ELENA: Be quiet. I want you to do a job for me. It must be done quickly and quietly.

THE ADDICT: What is it you ask?

DOÑA ELENA: Find a way to get El *Negro* and that boy off the mountain.

THE ADDICT: This will be very difficult. The land belongs to the *indios*. El *Negro* is their friend. Besides, he beats everyone who goes up there with a big stick.

DOÑA ELENA: I don't care how you do it! Just find a way. I won't be made a fool of. I hate that black man.

THE ADDICT: But you're black.

DOÑA ELENA: No, I'm not. I'm Spanish.

THE ADDICT: You're part black.

DOÑA ELENA: I'm Spanish, I tell you!

THE ADDICT: But you're . . .

DOÑA ELENA: Shut up, *idiota*! (*She hits* THE ADDICT *with her cane.*) Now, find a way to get El *Negro* off my mountain! I want that land and that suitcase. They should belong to me.

THE ADDICT: What's in it?

DOÑA ELENA: It's not your concern. Something valuable only to me. Just bring it.

THE ADDICT: Revenge does have its price, Doña.

DOÑA ELENA: I see you have your father's knack for business, and his addiction.

THE ADDICT: We all have our crosses to bear.

(DOÑA ELENA *hands* THE ADDICT *money. They exit.*)

Scene 7

[Within the chrysalis a metamorphosis begins.
—Dentro de la crisálida comienza una metamorfosis.]

(HURACÁN *and* EL NEGRO *sit by a campfire.* HURACÁN *has grown out of his old clothes. He eats quickly.*)

EL NEGRO: Slow down! You gonna get yourself sick!

HURACÁN: But I'm hungry.

EL NEGRO: You're like them monarch caterpillars. They eat everythin' in sight. They called *orugas*. That's what you are. An *oruga*!

HURACÁN: I ain't no *oruga*!

EL NEGRO: Well, you eat like one! You been growin' out of them clothes and eatin' everything in sight for the last few months. Pretty soon you gonna be growin' hair in places you never thought you could!

HURACÁN: No, I'm not!

EL NEGRO: Voice is gonna drop. Face gonna get bumpy and you gonna have thoughts about them females.

HURACÁN: Is that wrong?

EL NEGRO: Ain't nothin' wrong with it. It's nature's way of makin' you a man. Like them *orugas* becomin' monarchs.

HURACÁN: I'm startin' to forget things.

EL NEGRO: What things?

HURACÁN: My 'amá's voice. My 'amá's face.

EL NEGRO: Come spring them monarchs gonna leave. Under them milk-weed plants they're growin' big. Changin' form. Preparin' themselves for the trip home. You think it's true them monarchs carry the souls of them dead humans to heaven?

HURACÁN: I don't know. (*Two butterflies fall to the ground, fighting.*) Why do the monarchs fight like that?

EL NEGRO: You ever been in love?

HURACÁN: I love my mother.

EL NEGRO: That's not the same kind of love. See, that male monarch is courtin' the female. They catch each other in the air and fall to the ground. Now, he'll try to woo her. And if she wants him she'll close her wings and he'll carry her to the tops of them trees and . . .

(*The monarchs fly away.* EL NEGRO *begins laughing.*)

HURACÁN (*disgusted*): Ugghhh . . .

EL NEGRO: One day you gonna be just like this male. And hairy too!

HURACÁN (*embarrassed*): Ugghhh . . .

EL NEGRO: Fact of life.

HURACÁN: I wanna go home. Look for my 'amá and 'apá.

EL NEGRO: When I first come here, this was the only place I could stay. Now, it's the only place I wanna stay. This here is sacred land. Nature's church.

HURACÁN: Don't you got any family?

EL NEGRO: Them monarchs are my family now.

HURACÁN: There's no one?

EL NEGRO: No.

(*A train whistle is heard off in the distance.*)

HURACÁN: How come you always got that suitcase with you?

EL NEGRO: I told you. Me and that suitcase ain't your business.

HURACÁN: You walk to the station. I see you.

EL NEGRO: Why you gotta do that?

HURACÁN: Do what?

EL NEGRO: Get in my business?

HURACÁN: 'Cause you wanna leave without me.

EL NEGRO: I'm still here, ain't I?

HURACÁN: I see you standin' there, but you don't get on the train. What's stoppin' you?

EL NEGRO: Listen here, every man has got to have a code to guide him through life. A system of rules to live by. I call them my "Don'ts." "Don't let anybody know your business. Don't walk away from a fight. Don't borrow money if you can't pay it back. And don't mess with people, 'cause they might mess you up." These been my guiding principles through life. You best learn it!

HURACÁN: Then how do I get home?

EL NEGRO: Home?

HURACÁN: What'da I gotta do?

EL NEGRO: You got a train ticket?

HURACÁN: No!

EL NEGRO: You got any money?

HURACÁN: No!

EL NEGRO: Then you outta luck!

(EL NEGRO *coughs.*)

HURACÁN: You coughing up blood again.

EL NEGRO: 'Cause it's a curse.

HURACÁN: Was it Doña Elena?

EL NEGRO: It was long before her. Another lifetime. Things I wish I could change but can't. (*Singing.*)
Hush, hush,

Somebody's calling my name,
Hush, hush,
Somebody's calling my name.

HURACÁN: Did you do something bad?

EL NEGRO: Ain't no one gonna forgive what I done.

HURACÁN: You can't go back, can you?

EL NEGRO (*singing*):

O, my Lord,
O, my Lord,
What shall I do?

HURACÁN: Guardin' them monarchs is your penance, ain't it?

Scene 8

[The dreams of butterflies.
—*Los sueños de las mariposas.*]

(*Dawn. Voices from* EL NEGRO'*s past are heard once again.* HURACÁN *and* EL NEGRO *sleep by a smoldering fire.* THE ADDICT *sneaks in quietly. He opens his knife.*)

EL NEGRO (*in his sleep*): Snake eye starin' at me. Don't! Ain't gettin' onboard. No! Ain't afraid of no man. Beast. Night. Snake eye. No!

(THE ADDICT *picks up* EL NEGRO'*s suitcase and opens it with his knife. The suitcase glows. He smiles.* HURACÁN *awakens and sees* THE ADDICT.)

EL NEGRO (*in his sleep*): Ain't my time. No! Stay away.

THE ADDICT (*startled, mocking* EL NEGRO): El Diablo, huh! (*He crosses to finish* EL NEGRO *off.* HURACÁN *howls, throwing his blanket over* THE ADDICT. *Frightened.*) ¡El Diablo!

(THE ADDICT *drops the suitcase and runs off.*)

HURACÁN: Wake up, old man!

EL NEGRO: What is it?

HURACÁN: Are you all right?

EL NEGRO: What's goin' on?

HURACÁN: Somebody tried takin' your suitcase, but I scared him away. Just like you show me.

(HURACÁN *howls.*)

EL NEGRO: Was it one of them cousins?

HURACÁN: I think so.

EL NEGRO: That old crow is gettin' desperate. Ain't no tellin' what she'll do. You better be careful.

HURACÁN: They can't catch me. I'm too fast. I'm a coyote! (HURACÁN *howls. EL NEGRO starts to cough.*) You're coughin' up more blood.

EL NEGRO: I got consumption. Tuberculosis.

HURACÁN: Is it bad?

EL NEGRO: Ain't good.

HURACÁN: Are you gonna die?

EL NEGRO: Hell no!

HURACÁN: I'm just askin'.

EL NEGRO: I ain't dead yet. So don't you try buryin' me 'fore my time. I gots too much fight in me yet. (*He coughs again.*) Bring that blanket here! And put some more wood on that fire!

HURACÁN: Okay!

(*He picks up the blanket, and throws it at* EL NEGRO.)

Scene 9

[The spider captures her prey.
—*La araña atrapa a su víctima*]

(*The police station walls are filled with massive cracks as if a great weight rests on them.* HURACÁN's *hands are tied and he is dragged in by the* POLICE OFFICIAL. *The* POLICE OFFICIAL *is the same actor who plays* THE ADDICT. *He is eating some chocolate candy.*)

POLICE OFFICIAL: Come here, boy! You're one of those *deportados*, aren't you? Thousands have been coming through town. It hasn't been this busy since *Pancho Villa* and the entire revolution rode through!

(DOÑA ELENA *enters.*)

POLICE OFFICIAL: Doña Elena, good morning. I found the beggar boy! I found him wandering around looking at girls.

DOÑA ELENA: Shut up! You dishonor your father. Look at you. Stay out of the sun. And lose some weight.

POLICE OFFICIAL: Sí, Doña.

DOÑA ELENA: Beggar boy, stealing from the dead and assaulting me on a holy day has its consequences.

HURACÁN: That was a long time ago.

DOÑA ELENA: Eleven months. Twelve days. Six hours. Thirty-one seconds. I've burned you into my memory. One of my husband's sons is the town judge. He'll throw you in jail. I could see to it!

HURACÁN: I don't want to go to jail.

POLICE OFFICIAL: But you're already in jail!

DOÑA ELENA: Shut up! Turn around and cover your ears! This conversation doesn't concern you!

POLICE OFFICIAL: Sí, Doña Elena.

(The POLICE OFFICIAL turns around and covers his ears.)

DOÑA ELENA: Tell me, why does El Negro hate me?

HURACÁN: . . .

DOÑA ELENA: We used to be friends.

HURACÁN: . . .

DOÑA ELENA: You know, when El Negro came to Misas we offered him a job. He took our money and betrayed us. My poor husband went to his grave because he was so heartbroken. He left me all alone just like you.

HURACÁN: May I go now?

DOÑA ELENA: You poor boy. By yourself without a mother. How terrifying it must be.

HURACÁN: I can take care of myself.

DOÑA ELENA: Of course you can. If you were my child I would never have left you. I couldn't live with myself.

HURACÁN: Well, maybe my 'amá tried.

DOÑA ELENA: Maybe . . .

HURACÁN: And maybe she's still looking for me.

DOÑA ELENA: Maybe, but if she really loved you, don't you think she would have found you by now?

HURACÁN: . . .

DOÑA ELENA: But look how you've survived. You've triumphed over adversity. I admire that quality. It's sadly lacking in this town. You and I are very similar. We'll fight to survive.

HURACÁN: It's not easy.

DOÑA ELENA: No one can appreciate the sacrifice but us. (She caresses his face.) Would you like a piece of candy?

HURACÁN: Okay.

DOÑA ELENA: ¡Oficial! (*The* POLICE OFFICIAL *doesn't hear her.*) ¡¡Oficial!! (*He still doesn't hear her.*) ¡¡¡Oficial!!!

(DOÑA ELENA *strikes the* POLICE OFFICIAL. *He uncovers his ears and turns around.*)

POLICE OFFICIAL: Ouch!! ¿Sí, Doña Elena?

DOÑA ELENA: Why do these *tontos* all torment me?

POLICE OFFICIAL: I'm sorry, Doña.

DOÑA ELENA: Be quiet and give me a piece of *chocolate*.

POLICE OFFICIAL: But it's my last piece.

DOÑA ELENA: Give it to me! (*She reaches out and takes the candy from the* POLICE OFFICIAL. *To* HURACÁN.) Ay, pobrecito. (HURACÁN *begins eating the chocolate candy.*) Is it good?

HURACÁN: Ah huh.

DOÑA ELENA: Tell me, does El *Negro* ever talk about leaving?

HURACÁN: Sometimes. I tell him he should go back home with me, but then he talks about his ghosts.

POLICE OFFICIAL: Ghosts? What ghosts?

HURACÁN: They're in his suitcase. I'm not supposed to touch it.

DOÑA ELENA: His ghosts are a great burden. His soul is riddled with pain. You see, he has a very dark secret.

HURACÁN: What secret?

DOÑA ELENA: Hasn't he told you?

HURACÁN: No.

DOÑA ELENA: It's in his suitcase. He's never without it. Tell me, do you miss your home?

HURACÁN: Yes.

DOÑA ELENA: Your 'amá could be there waiting for you, do you think? I bet she would be so happy to see you. I could help you, you know?

HURACÁN: Help me?

DOÑA ELENA: Look what I've got for you.

(*She holds up a train pass.*)

HURACÁN: What is it?

DOÑA ELENA: A train ticket.

HURACÁN: For me?

DOÑA ELENA: Yes. Just think, you could be with your *'amá*. *El Negro* at peace with himself.

POLICE OFFICIAL: And you'll have the suitcase!

DOÑA ELENA: Shut up, *idiota!* (*The* POLICE OFFICIAL *covers his ears. To* HURACÁN.) All you have to do is bring El Negro's suitcase to me. Just pick it up and walk away. It's so simple. What do you say?

(HURACÁN *holds out his bound hands.* DOÑA ELENA *hits the* POLICE OFFICIAL.)

POLICE OFFICIAL: Ouch!

DOÑA ELENA: Untie him. (*The* POLICE OFFICIAL *unties* HURACÁN's *hands.*) Would you like another piece of candy?

(*She smiles.*)

Scene 10

[The monarch chooses.
— *La mariposa monarca toma su decision.*]

(*Santuario de las Mariposas. A coyote's howl is heard off in the distance.* HURACÁN *enters. The forest casts dark shadows.*)

HURACÁN: Old man? (*Pause.*) Are you here?

(HURACÁN *picks up the suitcase. A distant train is heard.* EL NEGRO *enters wrapped in a blanket and carrying some wood. He appears frail.* HURACÁN *doesn't see him.* EL NEGRO *watches as* HURACÁN *stands there deciding what to do.* HURACÁN *places the suitcase back.*)

HURACÁN: I can't do it. I can't.

EL NEGRO: She put you up to it?

HURACÁN: . . .

EL NEGRO: Why didn't you take it?

HURACÁN: What's in it?

EL NEGRO: My life. Doña Elena thinks I still got her money, but I don't. I give it away to them *indios* long ago, 'cause they was starvin'. I ruined her plans. Now, you too. She ain't gonna be too happy 'bout this.

HURACÁN: I won't go back into town.

EL NEGRO: Won't matter. She'll find you.

HURACÁN: I ain't afraid of her.

EL NEGRO: But you should be. There's no tellin' what she's gonna do now. It's time for you to go.

HURACÁN: Go where?

EL NEGRO: Anyplace but here.

HURACÁN: I can't leave you.

EL NEGRO: Don't you see? It ain't safe. I can't protect you no more.

HURACÁN: Then come back with me!

EL NEGRO: I can't.

HURACÁN: Why not?

EL NEGRO: I can't go back.

HURACÁN: I ain't leavin' you.

EL NEGRO: Pack your things and go!

HURACÁN: We's friends!

EL NEGRO: I ain't your friend! Don't wanna be your friend! Ain't never had a friend. You just in the way.

HURACÁN: No, I'm not!

EL NEGRO: And I'm through carrying you! So go!

HURACÁN (*crying*): But we's friends!

EL NEGRO: Get outta here! Get!

(*HURACÁN exits.*)

Scene 11

[The spider attacks.
—*La araña ataca.*]

(*DOÑA ELENA and the UNDERTAKER-BARBER enter. The UNDERTAKER-BARBER is played by the same actor who plays the POLICE OFFICIAL. He carries a shovel. They surprise EL NEGRO.*)

DOÑA ELENA: ¡Viejo Negro!

EL NEGRO: So the black widow spider's finally come?

DOÑA ELENA: Is that how you treat an old friend, Negro?

EL NEGRO: What do you want?

DOÑA ELENA: Perhaps the Undertaker-Barber could help you understand what I want? I finally found someone who isn't afraid of you. He even brought his own shovel!

UNDERTAKER-BARBER: Agghhh!

(*The* UNDERTAKER-BARBER *lunges at* EL NEGRO, *holding the shovel to his throat.* HURACÁN *runs in.*)

HURACÁN: Let him go!

DOÑA ELENA: You don't give orders here. I do!

(*She hits* HURACÁN *with her cane.*)

HURACÁN: Ouch!

DOÑA ELENA: We had a deal, *cucaracha*, and you betrayed me. You should've left while you had the chance. Now you'll never see your mother. (*She tears up the train ticket.*) She'll wander the earth like La Llorona crying and tearing out her hair! "¡Mijo! ¡Mijo!" (*To* EL NEGRO.) And you, *Negro*—we offered you a job, respect, wealth, and you refused!

EL NEGRO: You wanted me to burn this forest!

HURACÁN: He wouldn't do that!

DOÑA ELENA: He's done far worse!

EL NEGRO (*to* DOÑA ELENA): I ain't that man no more!

DOÑA ELENA: Tell him, *Negro*! Tell him the truth, why you can't go back to your own country. No matter how many times you've tried getting on board a train, you can't. Tell him why you're so afraid.

HURACÁN: He ain't afraid of nothin'!

DOÑA ELENA: Then let me enlighten you, *cucaracha*. Your patron saint of butterflies is a wanted man. A dead man. His ghosts are there waiting for him.

EL NEGRO: Don't you say nothin'!

DOÑA ELENA: He won't tell you his terrible dark secret.

HURACÁN: It don't matter!

DOÑA ELENA: But it does. He set a house on fire in your country.

EL NEGRO: Don't you believe her!

DOÑA ELENA (*mocking him*): He had been wronged. Mistreated. His pride demanded revenge so he burned it to the ground. But in that house children were sleeping.

HURACÁN: Children?

EL NEGRO: She ain't tellin' you everythin'!

DOÑA ELENA: Five little angels tucked away in their beds.

EL NEGRO: I was after the man who done me wrong!

DOÑA ELENA: He drenched the whole house with gasoline.

EL NEGRO: He stole my land. Burned my crops!

DOÑA ELENA: Lit a match and the whole house went up in flames. They couldn't get out. Only their cries got out. Calling for their mommy.

HURACÁN: Is it true?

DOÑA ELENA: Tell him!

EL NEGRO: They wasn't supposed to be there!

HURACÁN: How could you do that?

EL NEGRO: They wasn't supposed to be there!

DOÑA ELENA: Those little angels went to heaven and El *Diablo* ran away.

EL NEGRO: I ain't that man no more.

(*He coughs up blood.*)

DOÑA ELENA: Oh, how it breaks my heart to see you so disappointed, *cucaracha*. But revenge tastes sweetest when sprinkled with tears.

UNDERTAKER-BARBER: We're going to be rich!

DOÑA ELENA: Shut up! (*To* HURACÁN.) Get me that suitcase, boy!

HURACÁN: No!

EL NEGRO: Do as she says.

HURACÁN: It ain't right. It belongs to you.

EL NEGRO: I don't want it no more. Too many ghosts.

UNDERTAKER-BARBER (*to* DOÑA ELENA): Ghosts?

HURACÁN: Yeah, ghosts . . . (HURACÁN *crosses to pick up the suitcase.*) And devils too!

(*He suddenly throws the suitcase at the* UNDERTAKER-BARBER, *scaring him away.* HURACÁN *howls.*)

UNDERTAKER-BARBER: ¡Ay, qué susto! ¡El Diablo!

DOÑA ELENA: Come back, idiota!

(*The* UNDERTAKER-BARBER *runs off.* HURACÁN *chases after him.* DOÑA ELENA *picks up the shovel.*)

DOÑA ELENA: Coward! Just like your father! I should've done this myself long ago!

EL NEGRO: Whatcha doin'?

DOÑA ELENA: Taking what belongs to me! I'll have it all!

(She scoops up hot coals from the fire.)

EL NEGRO: No, you can't do that!

DOÑA ELENA: Watch me!

(She throws the hot coals onto the trees.)

EL NEGRO: You settin' the trees on fire!

DOÑA ELENA: No one cheats me!

EL NEGRO: The whole forest is gonna burn!

HURACÁN (entering): No!

(HURACÁN charges DOÑA ELENA, trying to stop her, but she holds the shovel threateningly.)

DOÑA ELENA: Not so fast, amiguito!

EL NEGRO (weakened): I gotta save them monarchs!

(He tries to stomp out the fire with a blanket.)

DOÑA ELENA: You selfish boy! You had your chance! (She picks up the suitcase, but HURACÁN grabs it at the same time. They fight for it.) Let go! It belongs to me!

HURACÁN: No, it don't!

DOÑA ELENA: Let go before we all die!

(A tree is heard exploding, startling DOÑA ELENA. She drops the suitcase.)

DOÑA ELENA (exiting): ¡Ay! Go ahead and burn, Negro. Burn like those children! I'll see you in hell!

(EL NEGRO howls.)

EL NEGRO: Wake up, mariposas!

(HURACÁN joins EL NEGRO, howling.)

HURACÁN: Fly, mariposas! Fly!

EL NEGRO: Get up and fly away! Fly!

(Another tree explodes.)

HURACÁN: We got to get out of here!

EL NEGRO: No, leave me!

HURACÁN: We gotta go! Now!

(He leads EL NEGRO out as the flames engulf the forest.)

Scene 12

[A chrysalis splits open and a new monarch emerges.
— *La crisálida se abre y surge una nueva mariposa monarca.*]

(*La frontera*—somewhere near the American border. A full moon. Two shadows appear.)

HURACÁN (*singing*):

Couldn't hear nobody pray
Couldn't hear nobody pray . . .

EL NEGRO: Come on, old man!

HURACÁN/EL NEGRO (*singing*):

Oh, I'm just a way down yonder by myself
And I couldn't hear nobody pray.

(EL NEGRO *falls to his knees. His breathing is labored.*)

EL NEGRO: We in the states now. We through walkin'.

HURACÁN: I thought there'd be fences, walls, men with guns and badges.

EL NEGRO: Not when we walk across. Gonna travel first class.

HURACÁN (*proudly*): I still got your suitcase.

EL NEGRO: I was hopin' you'd leave it. (*A train whistle is heard.*) There's our ride.

HURACÁN: We ain't got no tickets.

EL NEGRO: Don't need none. We gonna ride hobo style. Now listen here, we got to be careful of them yard bulls.

HURACÁN: Yard bulls?

EL NEGRO: They don't take to freeloaders on their trains. If they come chasin' after you, you run like hell. Them yard bulls carry guns and sticks. They ain't gonna ask questions.

HURACÁN: When do we go?

EL NEGRO: What's you in such a hurry for?

HURACÁN: I wanna get home. Find my 'amá and my 'apá.

EL NEGRO: We ain't goin' nowhere 'til that train moves. Hoboin' is about waitin'. Waitin' for the right moment. When that highball signals that's when we go. Gonna have to run fast and hard. Somewhere between the hog and crummy we gotta find ourselves an empty car.

HURACÁN: Hog and crummy?

EL NEGRO: Hog's the locomotive. Crummy's the caboose. Highball is the whistle signalin' the train's leavin'. Do I gotta tell you everythin'?

HURACÁN: Do you think them butterflies made it out?

EL NEGRO: Them monarchs got special magic. They fragile but they got a will to survive. They gonna be all right.

HURACÁN: Like us?

EL NEGRO: That's right.

HURACÁN: Them children . . .

EL NEGRO: What children? . . . Oh . . . I never meant to hurt them children but I did. I carry their cries wherever I go. And there ain't a day goes by that I don't wish it was me in that house instead of them. I'm sorry, boy. I'm sorry for all the bad I done.

HURACÁN: You think them children went to heaven?

EL NEGRO: I don't know.

HURACÁN: I bet they did.

EL NEGRO: How do you figure?

HURACÁN: Well, them monarch butterflies could've carried their souls up to heaven. And if they in heaven then their souls must be angels.

EL NEGRO: Angels?

HURACÁN: And if they's angels then they can forgive.

EL NEGRO: Why would they forgive me?

HURACÁN: 'Cause your butterflies carried them there.

EL NEGRO: You really believe that? (*A train whistle is heard.* EL NEGRO *coughs.*) It's time for you to go!

HURACÁN: Ain't you comin'?

EL NEGRO: I'll only hold you up. Go!

HURACÁN: I ain't leavin' without you!

EL NEGRO: You gonna miss your train!

HURACÁN: I ain't leavin' you!

EL NEGRO: Why you gotta argue with me?

HURACÁN: 'Cause you a *cabezón*!

EL NEGRO: ¿*Cabezón*?

HURACÁN: That's right!

EL NEGRO: Wait 'til I get my hands on you!

HURACÁN: Gotta catch me first, *cabezón! ¡Cabezón!*

(EL NEGRO *chases after* HURACÁN. *They exit.*)

Scene 13

[The monarchs search for home.
—*Las mariposas monarcas buscan su hogar.*]

(*Lights flicker as the train rumbles through the desert.* HURACÁN *and* EL NEGRO *are in a boxcar.* EL NEGRO *lies on the floor. His breathing is heavy.* HURACÁN *holds the suitcase.* EL NEGRO *inhales the night air.*)

HURACÁN: What are you doing, old man?

EL NEGRO: It smells sweet, don't it?

HURACÁN: What does?

EL NEGRO: Gringoland.

(*He coughs.* HURACÁN *inhales the air.*)

HURACÁN: We ridin' through the night, hobo style.

EL NEGRO: There ain't no borders for butterflies.

HURACÁN/EL NEGRO: We's butterflies.

HURACÁN: How much longer is it gonna take?

EL NEGRO: If we lucky, couple more days.

(*Something stirs in the boxcar.* HURACÁN *picks up a stick.*)

HURACÁN: Who's there?

EL NEGRO: Be careful.

(*Two* HOBOES *step out of the shadows. It is a husband and wife. They are the same actors who played* KIKA *and* MOISÉS.)

HUSBAND: Forgive us, *señores*, we mean you no harm. My wife and I are hungry. Do you have anything to eat?

HURACÁN: We got plenty. (EL NEGRO *starts to laugh.*) What's you laughing at, old man?

EL NEGRO: You a walkin' grocery store! You'll never go hungry.

HURACÁN: That's right, I've learned.

(*He gives the* HUSBAND *and* WIFE *some food.*)

WIFE: Thank you. (HURACÁN *stares at the* WIFE *for a moment.*) What is it?

HURACÁN: You remind me of someone.

WIFE: Who?

HURACÁN: Someone I once knew.

(EL NEGRO *coughs deeply. The* WIFE *touches* EL NEGRO's *face.*)

HUSBAND: El *señor* looks very ill.

HURACÁN: He's gonna be all right.

WIFE: He has a fever.

HURACÁN: No, he's just tired. That's all.

(*The* HUSBAND *takes his blanket and places it on* EL NEGRO.)

EL NEGRO: My lungs feel like they on fire. (*To the* HUSBAND.) Who are you?

HUSBAND: My name is Gabriel. This is my wife, *Esperanza.*

WIFE: *Hola.*

EL NEGRO (*to* HUSBAND): I seen you before. You from *Misas?*

HUSBAND: Oh, no, but I have lots of cousins there. We're heading north like you.

WIFE: Back to our home. We were sent away.

EL NEGRO: What's you got there?

HUSBAND: It's my *guitarra.* I can play something for you? Would *el señor* like to hear something?

EL NEGRO: Play me somethin' sweet.

(*The* HUSBAND *plays his guitar softly. A monarch butterfly gently floats into the boxcar and lands on* HURACÁN's *hand.*)

HURACÁN: Where did you come from, little fella? Lookin' for a free ride, huh? Hobo butterfly. You can rest here all you want. (EL NEGRO *coughs.*) We almost home.

Scene 14

[The monarch butterfly returns.
—*La mariposa monarca regresa.*]

(HURACÁN *enters, carrying* EL NEGRO.)

EL NEGRO: Gotta catch my breath.

HURACÁN (*singing*):

Roll, Jordan, roll
Roll, Jordan, roll—

EL NEGRO: Put me down.

HURACÁN (*singing*):

I want to go to heaven when I die,
To hear ole Jordan roll.

EL NEGRO: Please.

HURACÁN: All right. But just for a while.

(*He places* EL NEGRO *on the ground.*)

EL NEGRO: How come you in such a hurry?

HURACÁN: I just am.

EL NEGRO: What's so special about today?

HURACÁN: It's my birthday. I'll never be twelve again.

(*El valle—the valley. A barn sitting on the edge of a green field appears.*)

HURACÁN (*discovering*): We're here. Home. (*He searches.*) ¿'Amá? ¿'Apá? ¿'Amá?

EL NEGRO: They ain't here?

HURACÁN: ¿'Amá? ¿'Apá?

EL NEGRO: I'm sorry, boy.

HURACÁN: Maybe they waitin' somewhere else for me.

EL NEGRO: Maybe . . .

HURACÁN: Maybe I gotta just keep lookin'.

EL NEGRO: Maybe.

(*He coughs deeply.*)

HURACÁN (*panicked*): I can't do this alone. You gotta help me!

EL NEGRO: You gonna be fine, boy.

HURACÁN: How do you know?

EL NEGRO: 'Cause I just do.

HURACÁN: That's what my 'amá once said and she never came back. (EL NEGRO *coughs deeply.*) Don't you quit on me, old man!

EL NEGRO (*proudly*): My name's Benjamin Price.

(HURACÁN *opens* EL NEGRO's *hand and places some dirt in it.*)

HURACÁN: This is dirt, Benjamin Price. You hold it tight. This is gonna be our home.

EL NEGRO: Home.

(*Coughs deeply.*)

HURACÁN: Promise me you ain't gonna give up?

EL NEGRO: Do you see them?

HURACÁN: See what?

EL NEGRO: Them monarchs!

HURACÁN (looks around, but there are no monarchs): I don't see anythin'.

EL NEGRO: Sure you do.

HURACÁN: Where are they?

EL NEGRO: They all around you. Do you think they comin' for me?

HURACÁN: "Don't walk away from a fight!" Remember your code!

EL NEGRO: So this is where they come to?

HURACÁN: "Man's gotta pull his own weight!"

EL NEGRO: Look at them, circlin' all around me!

HURACÁN: Get angry and fight!

EL NEGRO: There must be thousands of 'em.

HURACÁN: Fight.

EL NEGRO: Ain't that a beautiful sight?

HURACÁN: Please don't leave me!

EL NEGRO: Don't you see 'em? Don't you see 'em, son?

(Coughs deeply.)

HURACÁN: Yeah, I see 'em. Maybe we gotta feed them hungry butterflies, huh?

EL NEGRO: I can feel them lifting me up!

HURACÁN: Dampen the earth with fresh water so the flowers will be strong.

EL NEGRO: They carryin' me up over the trees.

HURACÁN: Feed them mariposas sweet nectar.

EL NEGRO: Up mountains. Past clouds.

HURACÁN: A glimpse at God's heart.

EL NEGRO: To the highest heaven.

HURACÁN: Fly, Benjamin Price. Fly!

EL NEGRO (laughs): It tickles . . .

(He dies.)

HURACÁN: Benjamin Price?

(*The Negro spiritual heard at the opening of the play is introduced once again.* HURA-CÁN *covers* EL NEGRO *with a blanket. He crosses to* EL NEGRO'*s suitcase and opens it. It glows brightly. He smiles as hundreds of monarch butterflies emerge from it, fluttering everywhere.* HURACÁN *closes the suitcase. He picks it up and looks off into the horizon.*)

HURACÁN: I can do it. I can do it.

[The journey begins. — *El viaje venturoso comienza.*]

CURTAIN

Sit Down Servant, Sit Down

Arranged by Darrell Louis Morgan
As sung by Lucille M. Oliver

moderate to bright tempo

possible hand clap
rhythm for gospel
holy ghost feel

Hush, Somebody's Callin' My Name

As sung by Lucille M. Oliver
Arranged by Darrell Louis Morgan

medium tempo-church like

Couldn't Hear Nobody Pray

As sung by Lucille M. Oliver
Arranged by Darrell Louis Morgan

Roll Jordan Roll

Arranged by Darrell Louis Morgan

Glossary of Spanish Words and Phrases

ándale: go on!

'amá: mom

amiguito: little friend

'apá: dad

¡Ay, qué susto!: oh, what a fright!

cabezón: knucklehead; hardheaded

chocolate: chocolate candy

cucaracha: cockroach

conejo: rabbit

Día de los Muertos: Day of the Dead; a holiday that blends the pre-Hispanic Aztec beliefs honoring the dead with the Catholic Church's All Saints' and All Souls' Days (November 1 and 2)

deportados: those who are deported

El Diablo: the Devil

gringo: a United States citizen

guitarra: guitar

idiota: idiot

imposible: impossible

indio: Indian

La Llorona: the Weeping Woman; a legend has this ghostly woman wandering along canals and rivers, crying for her missing children; her story is told to frighten children into behaving.

mariposa: butterfly

mijo: my son

monarca: monarch butterfly

muchacho: boy

nana: grandma

no hay de qué: you're welcome; don't mention it

oruga: caterpillar

pobrecito: poor little one

primo: cousin

querido: my love

Santuario de las Mariposas: Butterfly Sanctuary

señor: gentleman, sir

señora: lady, ma'am

sí: yes

tía: aunt

toma: take that!

tontos: dummies

Viejo Negro: Old Black Man

Designer's Response

For *The Highest Heaven*, I initially looked at Mexican *lotería* cards, a game that uses highly symbolic images from Mexican culture. From there I studied photographs of the observance of El Día de los Muertos and others of monarch butterflies, which figure prominently as the allegorical symbol of the central character. Just as I was leaving that particular floor of the library, I noticed a display about paper cutting and discovered that one of the books was about the craft of Mexican paper cutting (*papel picado*). I had found my inspiration for the set design.

As is the case for many of José's plays, *The Highest Heaven* moves swiftly between many locales without major breaks. The question then becomes, how best to support the action of the script without interrupting its natural flow and momentum? González suggests that titles may be used to inform the audience of the allegorical meaning of the action in each scene. I decided to combine the textual passages, as projections or super-titles over the proscenium arch, with the design element of paper cutting. Plates B and C illustrate how these elements are unified for two specific scenes. In plate B, the paper cutting forms the leaves of trees; in plate C the cutting is a backdrop. The frame for the super-titles is in place over the proscenium. Plate A shows sketches for various scenes of the play with tree trunks and drops flown in or out as necessary for each.

Resources

Internet images
Trenchard, Kathleen. *Mexican Paper Cutting*. Asheville: Lark Books, 1998.

Plate A: Sketches of the setting.

Far from home a small caterpillar searches for food. —
Lejos de su casa una pequena oruga busca comida.

Plate B: Scene 2.

A chrysalis splits open and a new monarch emerges. —
La crisálida se abre y brota una nueva mariposa monarca.

Plate C: Scene 12.